# CAPTURED SHADOWS

*Ask the former generation
and find out what their ancestors learned,
for we were born only yesterday and know nothing,
and our days on earth are but a shadow.*

Job 8,8-9

# CAPTURED SHADOWS

## The German Goldschmidts of the 17th and 18th Century

*Dagmar Nick*

Translation: Carl Studt

VALLENTINE MITCHELL
LONDON • CHICAGO, IL

First published in 2019 by *Vallentine Mitchell*

Catalyst House,  814 N. Franklin Street
720 Centennial Court,  Chicago, Illinois
Centennial Park, Elstree WD6 3SY, UK  IL 60610, USA

www.vmbooks.com

Copyright © 2018 Dagmar Nick,
translation © 2018 Carl Studt

British Library Cataloguing in Publication Data:
An entry can be found on request

ISBN 978 1 910383 93 3 (Paper)
ISBN 978 1 910383 94 0 (Ebook)

Library of Congress Cataloging in Publication Data:
An entry can be found on request

*All rights reserved. No part of this publication may be reproduced in any form or by any means, electronic, mechanical, photocopying, reading or otherwise, without the prior permission of Vallentine Mitchell & Co. Ltd.*

Printed by IPG, Chicago IL, USA

# Contents

| | |
|---|---|
| *Prologue* | vii |
| Intrada | 1 |
| The Spaniers | 4 |
| The Fürst Family | 8 |
| Good Connections | 13 |
| The Goldschmidt Family | 20 |
| An Incident | 26 |
| Crazy for Luxury and Empty Pockets | 28 |
| Bendix Goldschmidt's Patron | 42 |
| Stirring Times | 46 |
| Departure | 62 |
| Marriages | 65 |
| Signs of the Time | 68 |
| The Heirs | 75 |
| Last Chance | 80 |
| The End. Flight | 84 |
| Arrested | 93 |
| Torture | 98 |
| An Epilogue | 114 |
| The Danish Protectorate | 116 |
| The Recruits' Treasury | 120 |

| | |
|---|---|
| Who is Leib Levin? | 124 |
| Ziporra | 131 |
| Porcelain | 135 |
| 1786 | 138 |
| A New Home | 141 |
| A Gentleman called Bauer | 149 |
| Following the Trail | 153 |
| Albert Bauer | 158 |
| Breslau | 161 |
| Epilogue | 165 |
| *Appendix* | 174 |
| *Acknowledgements* | 174 |
| *Curriculum Vitae: Sigismund Asch* | 175 |
| *Curriculum Vitae: Lina Morgenstern* | 177 |
| *Family Trees* | 179 |
| *Supporting Literature* | 183 |

# Prologue

Where do I come from? Where did Moses Spanier come from? He was the oldest of my ancestors to be documented, born in Hamburg around 1550 – a Jew from Spain, a Sephardic Jew? Whose predecessors had once effortlessly debated in three languages with Arabic doctors, astronomers and mathematicians in Toledo or Cordoba? Honing translations out of old Greek texts, securing the knowledge of the ancient world? Who were they, who served the Caliphs and later the Spanish kings as financial consultants and state officials? And were ever and again driven out. And how many persecutions did they survive over the centuries protected only by their devout beliefs and solidarity?

I wanted to know. I wanted to discover these Sephardic Jews who had grown up in an elite spiritual and artistic culture and who had mixed with the Ashkenazi Jews and mainstream Germans. I wanted to recognise the possible differences, legible on the old gravestones in the Jewish cemeteries of Altona and Hannover. And then the archives were opened: a catalogue of voices, pleadings, letters of protection, permits to travel were revealed. Privileges mercifully given by the authorities, for money, of course.

How was it possible, that refugees, driven from their homes – but not from their roots! – were able to assert themselves against all the prejudice in foreign lands? Excluded from schools, academies, guilds and official positions, humiliated and thus obliged to earn their livelihoods in the role given them, because Christians were prohibited from usurious money lending, as lenders of money for interest. What sacrifices were demanded, how much energy was required for them to rise within a few generations, from hawkers with self-made buttons, lace bobbins and candles to self-sufficient traders, to wholesalers, suddenly welcomed in the princely courts as suppliers to the military, appointed as court jewellers? In the end they financed their rulers. Active but invisibly involved in many decisive historical events, and prepared to undertake almost any personal risk to serve the lands which offered them asylum.

Escorted by their voices which I wanted to hear, I have followed them through 300 years until they were given civil rights and allowed to go to university. Then the representation of Jews as money tycoons was toppled: the sons of the court Jews and bankers became scientists, lawyers and doctors. One of their grandchildren – our grandmothers were sisters – became a historian: Fritz Stern, who today lives in New York. This retrospective of the early days of our family is dedicated to him.

D.N.

# Intrada

On the 31 March 1492 the Edict of Expulsion that ordered the eviction of Jews from Spain was issued in the Alhambra Palace by Isabella I of Castile and Ferdinand II of Aragon and Castile. These Spanish Jews, who called themselves Sephardic, fled to Portugal, but on 25 December 1496 they were ordered to leave Portugal within ten months. They fled to Genoa, Venice, Naples, Cairo, Alexandria, Salonika and Istanbul, where they were made welcome. Many moved on to Poland, where they joined German Jews who had settled there after being driven out of the Rhineland.

Only a few very rich Jews from Spain and Portugal, who owned trading ships or were able to pay for a place on a passenger boat, came directly to Hamburg. The earliest records of them are in 1570. They mobilised the economy with their import businesses bringing goods from the lands and colonies that had expelled them. Their fellow believers, who had been forced to convert and were forbidden to emigrate, gave them outstanding assistance. With their help they imported desirable spices, especially pepper but also tobacco, olive oil, cork, ivory, pearls and gemstones, even porcelain from China. Because of their business connections they were popular with the municipal authorities in Hamburg, but not with the small traders and citizens, who were often able to demand that Jews should pay higher excise duties. Whereupon the Jewish merchants could think of no other way to defend themselves than one day to declare that they would be glad to leave Hamburg in the direction of Amsterdam or Emden. Such a threat was alarming: one could see that the importance of the merchant city was endangered and immediately the first protection privileges for the Jews who were indispensable for foreign commerce were issued. They were without exception described as 'Portuguese', although the majority originated without any doubt in Spain. Among themselves they spoke Judaeo-Spanish; with the Hamburg citizens, the expected Low German. What they most lacked was at first, less a Synagogue than their own cemetery: they had to bear their dead to Altona to bury them.

The first German Jews in Hamburg appear in 1600, the so-called Ashkenazim, who were mostly refugees from Poland and Lithuania where they had been persecuted again and again. They spoke high German, and

Yiddish between themselves. And because of their poverty they threatened to just be a burden and thus found little sympathy among their 'Portuguese' fellow believers who were anxious to protect their wealth. So they moved on to Altona.

Altona seemed a kind of paradise, a rare place under the protection of the Count of Holstein-Schaumburg who guaranteed complete religious freedom to all faiths. In contrast to Hamburg at that time, where Jews were only allowed to practise their religion within their own four walls and not as a community, the German Jews were able to create their first congregation in Altona in 1627. Here they made a cemetery for their dead, after Count Ernst III of Holstein-Schaumburg had sold them a plot of land, 'ufen Heuberge', 'irrevocably and in perpetuity' for 100 Reichstaler in 1611. A certificate guaranteed every protection so that they would be able to bury their dead according to their 'own traditional ceremonies...but without music or singing...without being hindered by our subjects or in any way being abused, taunted, interrogated or molested by them'.

Hamburg, which was fortified, was spared in the Thirty Years' Wars that raged from 1618 to 1648. Altona, which belonged to Vogtei Ottensen, fell to the Danish Crown in 1640 and directly afterwards the Jews in Altona (Pinneberg, Stade and Wandsbeck) received Letters of Protection from the Danish King Christian IV (1588-1648) who was also Duke von Holstein and a German Prince.

But when Altona was besieged by Swedish soldiers in 1644, the Jews crossed to Hamburg for safety. There, however, Jews who had not been resident for at least 22 years were not permitted to stay. But for 900 Marks they could buy a Letter of Protection from the city treasurer. The City elders made no objection – after all, the windfall money filled the treasury but the citizens of Hamburg had no personal advantage and so in the end, on 7 January 1648, supported by anti-Jewish clergy who preached hatred in the churches, they demanded the expulsion of all German Jews. The municipal authorities, unable to withstand their demands, gave in and ordained that they must leave Hamburg by Easter, which was also the Jewish Passover, 1649. The 'Portuguese' who had organised themselves Letters of Protection were allowed to remain.

Of course a few Jews who had found friends among the Sephardic Jews remained in Hamburg, disguised as 'servants of the Portuguese Nation'. By their industriousness and skill they soon gained a certain prosperity, so that by August 1650 they too were permitted to settle. Poorer Jews such as hawkers and peddlers from whom no money could be squeezed did not receive permits to settle and for them another solution was found: they lived outside the city, mostly in Altona or Ottensen. But for one Gulden they could acquire a pass permit that allowed them to stay in Hamburg for three nights. With a three-day pass, they were often able to stay in the city for many weeks, without the councillors noticing or wanting to interfere.

Minutes kept by the Portuguese congregation in the year 1654 record which *'Tudesquos'* lived as 'servants of the Portuguese Nation'. The Mayor was given their names so that they could be correctly recorded in the register. Among these German Jews, who were by no means servants, we find the names of the brothers Leb and Felix Bour. Names that could be spelt Bauer or Pauer, according to which language one had learnt to write.

In the cemetery is grave No. 1094, a Frau Reichel, spouse of Salomo Pauer, who died aged 25 on 25 April 1660. The couple had a son, Feibelmann, which in Yiddish may mean someone who was knowledgeable about the scriptures. A 'fibel' is a reading primer, a first book for pupils. It was a given name that was often Germanised as Felix. This Feibelmann Bauer died on 7 *Schewat* (January/February) 1701 and was buried in Ottensen – not as one might expect next to his mother Reichel in Altona. Obviously it had in the meantime become so over-crowded there, that in 1663, the German Jewish community were forced to buy a plot of land for a cemetery in the district of Ottensen which was first consecrated in 1666.

It is with Feibelmann's brother Leb (officially Levin) Bauer, who was born in Hamburg in 1620 and died there in 1690, that the Bauer family come to our attention. We know very little about this Levin Bauer; only that on 13 March 1694, he was buried in grave No. 153 next to his wife Cornelia, nicknamed Kela but of unknown family name, who was also born in 1620. Their son, who had the popular given name Hirsch (Hebrew, Zwi) has left no other trace; but at least we know that his wife Frummet died in 1776 and left several sons. Among them was Juda Levin Hirsch Bauer, who died on 19 May 1766 in Hamburg: his mother found her eternal peace one day later in grave 895 in Ottensen. He was one of the patriarchs of our widely-branched family who although unable to boast any Portuguese ship-owners are able to document the Spanier family in our family tree. We have besides the Ashkenazi ancestors, to whom the Bauers belong, also Sephardic ancestors: Nathan Spanier, not an unknown name for those who have read the memoirs of Glückel von Hameln (1646-1724).

# The Spaniers

Nathan Spanier's father Moses, who was probably born in Hamburg in 1550 but who we know was a merchant there, married the daughter of a businessman from Stadthagen where he later settled and died in 1617. At that time, a few Sephardic families lived happily in the old Residence and Merchant city under the protection of the tolerant Count von Schaumburg but certainly less prosperously than their relatives in the noble Hamburg. However, Stadthagen was no sleepy backwater; there had been a Latin school there since 1565 and later a university. We do not know what Moses Spanier dealt in but he must have met with some success and been useful to the local nobility in some way because on 22 June 1586 he received a letter of protection from Count Adolf XIV zu Holstein und Schaumburg and was thus able to organise a similar letter of protection for his son as soon as he became legally of age at 16 in 1591.

Nathan had also been born in Hamburg. Because he was given this document, we know that Moses Spanier, before he moved to Stadthagen in 1586, had lived in Obernkirch a few kilometres away and later, temporarily in Wunstorf.

It appears as if Moses wanted to clear the way for his son Nathan to enjoy a remunerative life. Nathan not only became an outstanding businessman but also a worthy member of the Jewish community. The proof of this was that he took care of poor high German refugees who had fled from Poland and Lithuania but who had not been welcomed by the Sephardic fellow-believers. Nathan Spanier made no distinction between Ashkenazim and Sephardic Jews however different their origins, morals and some rituals in their religion might be.

We discover that Nathan was not an only child and had at least two sisters from a letter of protection and safe-conduct that was issued on 12 October 1601 that was also valid for his brother-in-laws, for Jakob zu Obernkirchen and Jobst zu Rodenburg – the place names tell us that people liked to live close to the family in the same community. Nathan owned his own house in Stadthagen, Krumme Strasse 35. He married Zippora, the daughter of a businessman in Stadthagen in 1598. A year later she bore him a daughter called Freude. Five other children followed: Isaak, Mosche, Chajim, Abraham and Esther, but none of them had such a glittering marriage as the first born, 'our little Freude', of whom we shall learn more later.

Whether all the children whose names have been passed down to us came from Zippora is not known, she died on 5 April 1632 and Nathan, as is expected of devout Jews, soon remarried – a girl by the name of Reize, daughter of Isaak. But she too had died by 1640, probably a victim of the then prevalent pest epidemic, and so it was that Nathan married a third time, this time with Hadassa, the daughter of Schmuel from Hildesheim.

The first letter of protection that was issued to Nathan Spanier in 1591 cost 6 Reichtaler per annum payable on St Michael's Day. It was valid for 10 years and in 1601 the next letter of protection and safe-conduct which included his two brothers-in law seems to have been valid for a further ten years too.

Nathan was well respected and perhaps indispensable to his masters, for in 1612 he received a further letter of protection which he needed because he often travelled to Altona where he assisted the Askenazi refugees, the so-called 'beggar-jews' who were unable to get a pass and thus had no residence permit. But Nathan aided by his contact to Count Ernst III von Holstein-Schaumburg organised these for them with his own money. How generously he was supported is demonstrated by the order, dated 4 May 1612, given by the Count to the 'bailiff and magistrate in Pinneberg' which permitted an unnamed Jew, presented by Nathan, to join Altona's protected Jews. So it is no surprise that later, certainly after 1632, Nathan was officially active as Court Jew in the Court at Schaumburg. That means he was given responsibility to supply certain goods which were primarily available in Hamburg such as spice and other precious goods from overseas. For these transactions one needed the excellent commercial affiliations that were without doubt tightly controlled by the Sephardic merchants.

Nathan was the leader and elder of the 'Landjudenschaft' of Schaumburg, a self-governing institution that enabled the Jews to regulate their affairs with the local administration. Despite this and the fact that he was able to buy privileges from his noble benefactors, he was not permitted to build a Synagogue in Stadthagen. He would certainly have preferred to have presided over the marriage of his first-born Freudchen in 1619 from there. Neither was his future son-in-law, the rich Josef (Jobst) Goldschmidt from Hameln, who owned Krumme Strasse 15 in Stadthagen, as well as several other houses, able to achieve anything despite his money. All the same, he was allowed to furnish a prayer room in that house so that the Jewish community were able to hold their services there – but please, without loud singing! The Christian neighbours knew and often complained that particularly the immigrant Jews from the east had such powerful baritone voices, that one could imagine a 40-strong male choir was in the smallest of prayer rooms.

The Thirty Years' War was still raging, not everywhere of course, but the roads were unsafe and travelling in a bumping covered wagon was no fun. Nathan, who, as a merchant was continually in transit between Stadthagen and Altona, decided after the death of his wife Zippora to transfer his main residence to Altona, where he perhaps married his second wife Reize who died so soon afterwards. When Nathan's patron Count Otto von Schaumburg also died in 1640, things seemed temporarily threatening for Nathan because of his need to renew his letter of protection. However, this vitally important document was promptly confirmed and extended by Christian IV of Denmark who was the ruler by then.

In the meantime Nathan was 65 years old and had risen to Parnas, Elder of the community. He had no need to worry about his children, three of his sons appear in his letter of protection with him. We have no information about his fourth son, Chajim, who perhaps had died of the pest. People did not care to talk about these victims, even their gravestones were set 'upside-down' in order to ward off any further misfortune.

His daughter, Esther, married Löb Jehuda ben Mosche from Hildesheim. He was not rich but very upright and honest and so Nathan soon brought him to Altona so that he could better support him. Esther was also a practical business woman – once a year in January, when not much business was being done, she travelled to Kiel to the Fair to sell her husband's wares. We do not know what they dealt in. Maybe this son-in-law introduced the widower Nathan to his third wife, whom he found in Hildesheim.

A year after her marriage to Josef Goldschmidt from Hameln, a 'shabby unamusing place', Freudchen, Nathan's eldest, moved to Hannover where she gave birth to her ninth and last child, Chajim, in 1640. This tells us that her brother Chajim was no longer alive: children were often named after the latest uncle or aunt to have passed on. Nathan did not need to worry about Freudchen and her Josef. He was usually called Jobst Hameln and his family belonged to the oldest Goldschmidt family, who were actually goldsmiths in Stuttgart and Frankfurt. Jobst traded in grain in a big way. In Stadthagen and Hameln people said that he forced all the small traders into ruin with his wholesale-prices. He also worked as a gemstone dealer, apparently as a jeweller and of course as a money-changer and lender.

How else was a Jew to earn his living in a world where Christian neighbourly love did not reach out as far as those whose ancestors had prayed beside Mary and Joseph on Temple Mount? What else could one do except that which was permitted: trading with a pannier on your back or a hawker's tray around your neck, naturally only from house to house, not even in an 'open arcade'. However, one was allowed to do things that were forbidden for the Christians, who thus claimed an apparent ethical superiority and looked down on the Jewish 'usurers': lending money at interest and the very risky pawn-broking. How often a silver goblet was foisted on one and never redeemed, and which later, long after the debtor had vanished, was declared as completely worthless or even stolen when the lender tried to sell it after the statutory year that it had to be kept. Then the pawn-broker might be stigmatised as a thief or fence, a dealer in stolen goods. A Jewish pawn-broker needed to understand not only the value of the offered pledges but also human nature, otherwise he was soon lost.

Of course Nathan would have vetted his children's future spouses very carefully before they were allowed to marry into the Spanier family, and he probably also would have taken the same interest in the marriage partners of his grandchildren insofar as he saw them into a marriageable age. In small places, where everyone was known to one another, a match-maker was not needed so much as a quick decision so that a suitable candidate would not be snatched away by another. Long engagements such as we understand them were not usual, but in every case a nuptial agreement needed to be negotiated by the relatives of the bridal pair to set the marriage settlement or dowry, which was expected not only for daughters but also for sons. The size of the 'Knass' (Hebrew for penalty) which would be payable if one of the parties withdrew and the marriage were not to take place was set. And naturally one would look at the chosen family's background, as their financial reserves were as important as breeding, education and vocational qualifications.

Jewish children at that time were not allowed to visit schools and so were taught by their grandfathers and uncles and sometimes by private tutors, but that had to remain under cover because officially Jewish teachers as well as rabbis had no permit to work. At the age of four they started with the Hebrew alphabet. The letters were painted on a slate with honey and the children were allowed to lick them off so that they would know the joy of being able to read books and learn quickly. Daughters had to be able to cook, sew and make lace, while sons needed to be perfect in reading the Torah, have full command of the German language, and of course be competent in arithmetic. Jews were not allowed to be apprenticed and learn a craft and so only trading remained. More prosperous Jews in the towns were able to be money-changers and trade in gemstones, pearls, silver cutlery, cloth and silk. Jews in the country had to be more modest. They bought and sold horsehair, pig bristles, feathers and tallow for making candles, while those who understood something about horses and cattle became livestock traders and a few worked as butchers. They could not sell meat of course as they had no shops.

It is not possible to ascertain exactly how many of his grandchildren Nathan knew as a septuagenarian. Freudchen alone had nine children, six sons, only one of whom did not survive his grandfather: a tragic end, on the way to his wedding, escorted by his servants and a rabbi and of course burdened with presents and a dowry for his bride, he was fallen on by robbers just outside Bremerfürde and so badly injured that he died two days later. The robbers fled with their booty and were never caught (this story is passed on to us by Glückel von Hameln in her memoirs).

When Nathan Spanier died in 1646 he had provided well for his children; three of them – Abraham, Isaak and Esther with her husband Löb Jehuda – lived with him in Altona, Mosche lived with his wife in Wunstorf and Freudchen, happily pregnant every two years, lived with her husband Jobst Josef Goldschmidt in Hannover. When Nathan was buried in grave 854 on the 12 November 1646 in Altona, it must have been a grand funeral because it was usual for all the relations who were not ill or too frail to gather together from all over for such sad occasions. Among them of course were friends and Chajim Fürst, the Elder of the Jewish community in Altona with whom Nathan had worked for a great many years. At that time no-one could have suspected that one day two of Nathan's great-grandchildren would marry great-grandchildren of Chajim Fürst.

# The Fürst Family

In those days one used a given name together with one's father's given name and it was neither usual nor a legal requirement to use a family name. It was sufficient to add one's job, goldsmith or peddler, and sometimes one's birthplace in order to prevent confusion. Above all, if someone was well-known because of their professional success, as Joseph Baruch Goldschmidt was, then one also knew him as Jobst or Jost (already adjusted to Low German). Everyone in his circle of acquaintances knew that this was the Joseph from the Goldschmidts of Stuttgart who had had to leave the anti-Semitic Württemburg as early as 1521. His father, Baruch Daniel Samuel Stuckart had long been the Eldest of the Hessen Jewish Community. Many Sephardic Jews were glad to demonstrate which highly-civilised country they came from by their choice of family name: Moses and Nathan Spanier were among them. Others, especially the Portuguese, arrived with feudal aristocratic sounding names, such as Gomez, Benveniste, de Castro and the incalculably rich Diego Teixeira who was simply known as Abraham Senior. Some later gave up their Hispanic identity, as did the Duques family who preferred to present themselves under the Germanised noble name of Fürst: Chajim Fürst.

Chajim Fürst belonged to those Portuguese Jews who because of their money and foreign connections were able to direct the fates of their fellow believers in a way that was satisfactory to them. All Jews were well used to all kinds of penalty payments. A particular sum was payable at every circumcision ceremony of their sons, a change of abode, employing new servants, at all weddings and funerals. If one had afforded safe-custody passes in order to visit the neighbouring town, then at the town boundary or state border, Jews had to pay a yet another custom duty. But when in 1612 the Senate found themselves driven to double the 'tolerance money' payable for a residence permit by their Christian citizens' hatred of Jews, the Jewish community declared its determination to emigrate and thus forced the Senate, who were afraid of losing their best source of income, to think up an incredibly refined chess-move: in order to appease the angry citizens, the Senate called on the evangelical faculty of theology in Frankfurt/Oder to give their expert opinion that *'from a theological stand-point Jews were to be tolerated'*, but only if they did not practise their religion in congregations. And so at first they continued to hold their services in secret in private houses as they had long done. It was important to avoid having more than five people standing at the entrance at one time. Also the price of a residence permit that was valid for five years, was payable. The cost of 1,000 Marks per annum remained unchanged. Chajim Fürst, who was one of Hamburg's richest merchants, was able to pay but he preferred to live in his house in Altona where he was safe under the patronage of the Counts of Schaumburg, later the Danish Kings, and where he enjoyed much respect as Parnas. In the end he was responsible for persuading the Ashkenzic Jews to allow the few Sephardic Jews in Altona to use their Synagogue in Muehlenstrasse.

A Parnas (Hebrew for *provider*), the leader of the community, did not need to have a theological education but he did need to be a diplomat because he was their liaison to the authorities with whom he was constantly in negotiation. Beyond that he had to arbitrate all arguments within the Jewish community and indeed had the right to issue fines for certain offences. If he had money on top of these virtues, that was all the more welcome.

Chajim Fürst had all these qualities. His home must have resembled that of Nathan Spanier. The children that Sara – her father was an otherwise unknown Abraham – gave him, were even more numerous and because they belonged to a theological as well as business elite, their details and some of their stations in life have been recorded. One son, Jeremia became a rabbi, another, Nathaniel inherited his father's position as Parnas.

Only one of Chajim Fürst's sons, probably Moses, the eldest, died before his father in 1640. We know little about him, there is no gravestone but we know the name of his wife, Bella Betty, who survived him by 25 years and we know the fascinating life story of his son, Israel Fürst whose children and their issue have been linked by marriage to the Spaniers and Goldschmidt families many times right up till the twenty-first century.

Chajim Fürst's last two years alive were overshadowed by further chicanery by the Senate. In 1650, under pressure by the Church, they extended the regulation of Jews, by which not only their 'religious delusions' but also above all their ostentatious wealth were pilloried. The sumptuous robes the Portuguese wore in the town were criticised; they should stick to the town dress code and they were no longer allowed to live in the city centre but only beyond the gates in the 'new town'. Chajim immediately purchased an appropriate house in Altona in Breitestrasse. The entry in the cadrastral register was recorded on 2 January 1651. In a certain way the new regulations were advantageous to the community because now Hamburg, Altona and

Wandsbeck coalesced into a 'triple-community'. However, before all the participants were in agreement as to the future Parnas there must have been so many unworthy arguments in the governing body that Glückel von Hameln regarded the outbreak of a rampant illness in Hamburg in March 1653 which caused the death of very many members of the community as a punishment from heaven. Chajim Fürst was one of them. He was buried in Altona on 28 March 1653. Two days later, his son Salomo who was treasurer and almoner and thus responsible for the welfare of the poorest members of the community, followed him. Salomo left a very young son called Ruben whom we will meet again later in the Court of Schwerin where he supplied the local coinage mint with precious metals.

Undoubtedly many wealthy Portuguese who had the required privileges were able to remain in Hamburg because by 1663, 120 Sephardic and 200 Ashkenazi families were recorded. Many of them in the 'protected community' worked in their tobacco factories or sugar-beet refineries. So that they would not be ridiculed for their visible poverty they were given a monthly stipend by their employers.

Although the high German Jews were able to build a modest Synagogue in Steinweg 75, the Shepardic Jews were refused a permit. Probably the unostentatious citizens of Hamburg were anxious about the Portuguese pomp. Only in 1673 did the Senate suddenly give way and granted the Jews a plot 'Auf dem Dreckwall'. (The name suggests a very grubby corner, today it has been renamed Altewallstrasse.) Here they immediately started to erect a 'decently large' Synagogue. And at once the pastors protested. In order to pre-empt a Christian uprising the Senate had no choice: they ordered the demolition of the half-finished Synagogue.

Everything remained more or less unchanged for the next 25 years. But as the Senate increasingly got into financial difficulties and decided to raise the general taxes, the outraged citizens demanded that first the Jews should pay a special levy of 20,000 Marks and on top of that an annual payment of 6,000 Marks for the residence permit.

That was too much: the first rich Portuguese began to leave Hamburg and re-settled in the competitor city of Amsterdam. Ineffectually, the Senate tried to persuade the citizens of the importance of the Portuguese merchants to the 'Hispanic trade' in order not to let Hamburg fall into irrelevance – but it was too late, the emigration of the Portuguese was relentless. Those who did not dare to move to Amsterdam, went to Altona, Ottensen or Wandsbeck, some to the ambitious Emden or Stade.

It took another ten years before the city councillors of Hamburg recognised the loss, which was like a 'golden blood-letting', and reacted: on 7 September 1710 a new *Regulation of the Jewish Community* was passed. It ordained the *'Citizens Relationships'* for Jews for the next century. From then on they could work together with Christians as brokers, notaries, merchants, factory-owners, doctors, teachers and even as junior civil servants.

# Good Connections

Life was full of events as the children of Chajim Fürst and Nathan Spanier grew older. They journeyed to weddings and sadly also to funerals and to family gatherings at every feast day, they enjoyed a growing crowd of grandchildren and thought about legacies and testaments.

Freudchen and her husband Jobst Hameln were able to arrange good marriages for their daughters and saw to it that those sons who were not destined to be businessmen were educated to become rabbis. For this a basic schooling which was not available in mercantile Hannover was necessary. And so the sons, Abraham, Samuel and Isaak, equipped with sufficient money for their keep and education were sent to Posen, far in the east, from where, after a few years of intensive Talmud study they returned without money but instead with pretty Ashkenazi wives at their sides. They probably did not have to learn Polish, it was unnecessary for a graduate of theology, but they soon learnt to speak Yiddish with their new friends and wives. Yiddish was similar enough to German to pose no problems. It would have seemed quite normal that their father Jobst should support them until they established themselves as rabbis or teachers.

Freudchen was in the final weeks of her last pregnancy as the wedding of her first daughter was being organised. Just before she became eighteen, Jette (sometimes called Jente) married Salomon Gans from Minden in 1641. His family was one of the oldest in the region near Hameln; they could trace it back to the 14th century and the family emblem, a goose, can be seen on some gravestones in Hannover. Apart from the fact that he had six children with Jette in 13 years we know no more about Salomon Gans. He died unexpectedly in 1654 and his widow and six young children came to Hannover where her mother could help them. During the two year mourning, Jobst was on the lookout for a new son-in-law. And he hooked the biggest goldfish available on the marriage market: Leffmann Behrens. The fact that he was eleven years younger than Jette must have given rise to some gossip. But no more than that.

Leffmann Behrens was as ambitious as he was educated and skilled. He seems to have been a promising social climber with every noble virtue and cleverness despite not having a rich family. Jobst Hameln anticipated him ascending over the Goldschmidt family with his courage and diplomacy. In just a few years Leffmann Behrens became the most important Court Jew of Duke Ernst August von Hannover, one might say his closest advisor. Not only did he understand financial matters, he also was able to organise everything that a Court needed, starting with jewellery and brocade for the ladies, from silk wall-hangings to supplying the army with horses and weapons. The most significant source of revenue were the subsidies that were contractually payable by associated towns in exchange for supporting troops in time of need. Leffmann knew his way around every difficulty and was wise enough to hold his tongue when a duke had special wishes. Indeed it was he who procured the longed for status of Elector for Duke Ernst August in 1692. This was only possible by the payment of an extravagantly large sum of money which the royal treasury was unable to secure. An amount of 1,100,000 Taler was spoken of. A few years later in 1701 he provided a similar sum for Frederick III, Prince-elector of Brandenburg so that he could attain the King's crown. In between he had assisted the court banker Behrend Lehmann to arrange sufficient monies for August the Strong of Saxony to become King of Poland in 1697.

In order to match the demands of his duke, Leffmann had to engage many agents to purchase the desired wares from abroad while he himself undertook diplomatic duties in the courts of Amsterdam, Brussels, Vienna, London and several smaller principalities in Germany. Despite all this activity he still found time to set up rooms in his house for learned academics and provided finance for an edition of new works in the area of Talmud research.

Three years after Jette married Leffmann there was another wedding in the Hameln-Goldschmidt family. Jette's brother Chajim took Glückel Pinkerle as his bride. At the time she was just 15, later she would record her life in her famous diary. Although Jobst had started to train his son Chajim in the skills of trading in gold, pearls and gemstones from an early age, the inexperienced Chajim found it hard to earn a living at first. The farmers in Hameln were not good customers for his business. Soon the young couple moved to Hamburg hoping that it would be easier there and indeed for the next two years they lived with her parents while Chajim sounded out the terrain. He discovered that the Gentiles in unostentatious Hamburg were not keen to wear jewellery. Glückel wrote

> *...the fashion at that time was to wear pure gold chains and if one wanted to make a gift, then gold was chosen. Although one could not earn so much as with jewels it was my husband's first business to go from door to door buying old gold which he then sold on to a goldsmith.*

In the end Chajim became relatively prosperous and was able to feed his ever increasing family.

It is Freudchen's daughter Esther, who interests us most as she was one of our direct ancestors. For her, Jobst found a husband who was as rich as he was educated, Lewin Bendix. He belonged to another branch of the Goldschmidt family but there was no blood-line. He was generally better known as Löb Hannover. Esther must have been in delicate health and she gave him only three daughters and a son. She passed on before his brilliant promotion to treasury agent at the Danish Court. She died hardly forty years old, on 31 March 1675, before her aged parents, and one can imagine the grief of Jobst and Freudchen when their daughter Zippora was carried to the grave six months later (graves 113 and 115). Glückel von Hameln describes the ancient Jobst with his waist long white beard as an imposing figure as if he were an angel of God. When he died two years after his daughter Esther on 30 January 1677 at the age of eighty, it was as one expects of a wise man, 'gently in his sleep'.

The community 'memorbuch' in Hannover, a record of all the deceased members and their lives, has an especially complete obituary that should be included here.

> ...the devout, modest, highly venerable old man, the leader of his time, who devoted himself to the study of the laws, serving God and the welfare of others, was one of the greatest benefactors known to us; his house was open to academics, teachers and pupils, rich or poor, he presided over his children's worship; he gave generously to bridal trousseaux, and every year he sent charitable gifts to the Holy Land and encouraged his children to follow his example. It is impossible to portray the magnificent virtues that he demonstrated from his youth until his eightieth year.

'De mortuis nil nisi bene', one should say nothing but good about the dead – but nevertheless one small crazy chapter that dominated Jobst's family for a while has to be squeezed in here: Sabbatai Zwi.

We do not want to deprecate Jobst Hameln's virtues and talents, nor cast doubts on his intelligence but once, when he was already an old man, he did indeed temporarily act stupidly.

Among the kabbalists, who by referring to various Biblical apocrypha and hidden meanings of characters and numbers created their own philosophy which they had been developing since the sixth century, was the Spanish Jew Sabbatai Zwi. He had no Talmud learning but was drawn by mystical things. He had been born in Smyrna in 1626, an ascetic of his own special kind, divorced by not only his first but also his second wife because he refused to consummate the marriages, surrounded by youths who gradually became convinced that he was the Messiah for whom the Jews had so longingly waited. Together with his youths, whom he allowed to occasionally flog him, he travelled to the kabbalistic masters in Constantinople and Saloniki where he staged a mystic wedding ceremony with the Torah, the five books of Moses, whereupon the rabbis chased him out of town. After the same thing occurred in Cairo he fled to Jerusalem and counted the days till his hoped for coronation as the saviour of the sinful world.

Not only the Kabbalists but the Christians too, who studied the visions of the 'epiphany of John' gave a magic meaning to the year 1666, the date when the depraved world would come to an end or be renewed. This date was also important in Hameln and of course one knew about Sabbatai Zwi who would at last fetch the Jews out of the Diaspora and return them to Jerusalem. Everybody could see that the time for the wonderful change was coming. The Thirty Years' War had left nothing but misery and wounds; from Poland laid waste by the cossacks came refugees with harrowing stories of the massacre in which thousands of Jews had lost their lives. The pest was rife in Hamburg in 1664. Every week there were another 150 victims and whole families had been obliterated – but exhilarating news from Jerusalem was delivered to the Portuguese merchants in Hamburg. Letters that were read aloud in the Synagogue told of the wonder-worker, Sabbatai Zwi, who had already entranced the few Jews that still lived there. Now the congregation in Hamburg, indeed in all of Europe were infected. Only a few Rabbis were suspicious, there had often been cases of suddenly celebrated Messiahs, who later turned out to be charlatans.

But Jobst Hameln began to prepare a journey to Jerusalem with an ardent zeal. Two barrels were filled with linen, beans, lentils, dried meats and fruits and were sent to his son Chajim in Hamburg. From there they could quickly be loaded onto a ship which would take them all away under full sail and songs of praise.

For a year or more the barrels stood in Chajim and Glückel's house in Hamburg until, worried that the dried meats might go mouldy and damage the linen underneath, the barrels were opened and the provisions consumed, for in the meantime the year with the magical number, 1666, had passed, Sabbatai Zwi had been imprisoned in Turkey and the dream of a return to the Promised Land had died.

Freudchen survived Jobst by two years before she was buried in Hannover at the age of 82. Her pointed gravestone (No. 119) with the date 25 September 1679 is still there.

Freudchen's youngest brother was now the last remaining child of Nathan Spanier. He must have been a son from the marriage with Nathan's last wife, Hadassa. Moses (Mosche) Spanier from Wunstorf.

He must have still been small when his father Nathan died in Altona in 1646. It seems that it was not possible for his mother to have him trained for a particular trade, at any rate, she died just ten years after her husband on 26 November 1656 in Altona. Moses was still under-age. We can imagine that he grew up with his relatives in Stadthagen because we meet him again in nearby Wunstorf. We know that at first he was trained as a butcher, that he soon gave that up so that he could trade in nettle-cloth and other fabric and hair. Nettle-cloth was used by poorer country people, hair was used in the manufacture of *allongeperücke*, which had become fashionable at the court of the Duke Johann Friedrich von Braunschwieg-Lüneburg. The Residence was not far from Wunstorf near Hannover. If we look at the pictures of the time, such as that of the Duke together with Leibniz, who had been summonsed to his court in 1676, we see that all the men in those elevated circles wore those extended curly wigs that hung over their shoulders. Black was the favoured colour and we can just imagine how many beautiful plaits from Jewish girls were twisted and braided into them!

In Wunstorf there would have been no periwig-maker and we must assume that Moses Spanier with his plaits and textiles, which included silk, went directly to his ruler in Hannover and was made welcome. On 23 November 1676 he was given a Letter of Protection by Duke Friedrich that was valid for ten years and cost 8 Taler per annum. Besides many other details on the duties and rights of Moses Spanier recorded in it, there is also the exceptional exemption from the normal Jew taxes for him and his family on journeys within the Principality. At the end of the Letter is the command

> *...to each and every one of our servants and subjects and their kinsmen to undertake nothing against this Letter given by us nor any certified copy thereof but to obey the same and to allow the Jew and his household to enjoy the merciful concessions unhindered, also by reason of their office to provide them protection.*

Duke Johann Friedrich was not only a patron of the arts and science, he also understood the value and benefit that certain wealthy Jews afforded and thus offered them the chance to settle in the new town, that is outside the city gate. At the age of twenty-six the Duke had converted to the Catholic faith and knew the prejudice that the Jews suffered from the Protestant bigots. Accordingly he not only ordered tolerance of other faiths in his principality but when necessary, protected them as well. When Leffmann Behrens learned that blasphemers had repeatedly carted sand away from the cemetery despite signs prohibiting it and that in some cases corpses had been uncovered, he demanded the threat of the strictest punishment of those who disturbed the peace of the dead. The announcement was published on 26 August 1673.

Moses Spanier received two permits with his first Letter of Protection. Firstly permission to slaughter animals for his own consumption and that he might sell whatever he could not use himself on the market where he lived, but only at a lower price than the Christian butchers. And secondly he was granted the right to work as a money-changer and pawnbroker. He must have been very good because when his daughter Brendle married he gave her a dowry of 3,000 Reichtaler (a Taler may be worth as much as 80€ in 2015, so 240,000 €) in Danish Krone. Because we have data on Mordechai, his son-in-law – a son of Glückel and Chajim Hameln-Goldschmidt – we can guess that the marriage took place around 1694 when Mordechai was twenty, the normal age for young people to marry. By this time the first Letter of Protection must have expired. The reference to Danish Krone which we have from Glueckel of Hameln, suggests that Moses was well established as a money-changer and knew the going rates of exchange exactly. Probably he had help from Leffmann Behrens, the son-in-law of his sister Freudchen. In any case there was close contact between the two because Moses Spanier, who only rented his house in Wunstorf, had given Leffmann his valuable Letter of Protection for safekeeping. We know this from an impatient official demand to the privy chancery in Hannover dated 19 August 1702 to hand over a copy of the Letter. Perhaps Leffmann was on diplomatic business elsewhere so that the copy could not be produced, Moses gave this as the reason in order to explain the delay. Moses may also have received other assistance from Leffmann as he seems to have managed very well without a new Letter of Protection. His first wife Gelle, with whom he had four children, died on 19 April 1683, later he married Michle, who then died on 30 June 1708, by which time he must have been an old man, supported by his son-in-law Levin Jacob and his grandson Bendix Abraham. Both names are to be seen as a footnote under a second significantly more comprehensive Letter of Protection which was given to Moses Spanier in Wunstorf by the new Head of State Georg Ludwig Elector of Hannover in 1712. We read that all three men, who belonged to the same family, only had to pay four Taler a year for it, an astonishingly modest amount.

Moses Spanier died 'at a ripe old age' in Wunstorf on 13 June 1718 as the last of his generation. Indeed he had out-lived his second wife and nearly all his nieces and nephews, the children of his half-siblings and his son-in-law Mordechai. His sons and grandsons did not pass on details of his spiritual virtues, nor whether he really met the genius Leibniz on the steps of the princely palace while clutching an armful of silks. Certainly neither Leibniz nor Leffmann were expected to use the tradesmen's back-stairs.

Moses is the last Spanier in our documentation, and with him the imaginary separation between Sephardic and Ashkenazi Jews also vanishes. In starchy Hamburg, some snobbish Portuguese Jews, proud of their wealth, may have felt their connections with their relations-in-law, who might have come, not from the elite of Mainz and Worms but rather from Posen or Lemburg, to be impossible. The simpler Spanish Jews, some of whom had come on foot from Navarra, over the Pyrennies to France and then onward to southern Germany were less formal. The differences between Sephardic and Ashkenazi Jews were mostly visible in the ceremonies in the Synagogues and were becoming unimportant. By the time the Goldschmidts from Stuttgart, Frankfurt, Hannover and Hamburg married their gifted sons with the families Spanier and Fürst the dividing rituals were less significant than their professional interests. Cliques or networks that functioned well were necessary and often enough life-saving in a country where all Jews, from hawkers to Court Jews at the prince's household, were treated without respect, humiliated and extorted by their Christian neighbours.

# The Goldschmidt Family

The pest wiped out whole streets in Hamburg in summer 1664. The Senate closed the city gates. Those who had been able to slip out to relations in the country in time, like Glückel and Chajim Hameln-Goldschmidt seemed to have saved themselves, but lived in constant terror that they might have already become infected and they were well aware of how their worries increased the nervousness of their hosts. But families held together. It was the time of the Sukkot or Feast of Tabernacles which one gladly celebrated among relatives in Hameln or even better with those in Hannover. For there, Levin Bendix Goldschmidt, also known as Löb Hannover, who was connected by marriage, had a very roomy house. The house even had a prayer room for the community which was used because there was still no Synagogue.

On the first of the seven days of celebration, family and friends crushed together for the Sukkot. Leffmann Behrens and his wife were there, Glückel Hameln's four year old daughter was running happily about – but oh God! What was that suspicious mark in her armpit? A small boil? Perhaps a pest bubo? Panic in the house. Perhaps it was nothing. But in any case, send for the barber surgeon as quickly as possible. He had dressings for everything. But it was the Sabbath of all things! On that day, no Jew was permitted to handle money. Consultation with the men in the prayer room. Should one buy medication on the Sabbath? One could. If it is about saving lives, all Mosaic Law may be put aside. No delay: put the healing dressing quickly on the suspicious spot and send the little daughter with a maid from the house to an unsuspecting farmer where maid and child could be accommodated under some threadbare excuse but for good money until one knew for sure whether the child had really been infected. Each day the family sent meals to the farmer's garden and daily the heart-breaking ceremony where one waved and cried at a suitable distance and then withdrew. Leffmann Behrens, and he should know, had decreed that no-one was allowed to touch the child! What might happen if the Duke were to discover that the Goldschmidt family had brought the pest to Hannover – a catastrophe! Ten days of perverse retreat, after that it was clear that the child was in sound health and one could take it at last into one's arms and kiss and cuddle it as was normal in Jewish homes.

Löb Hannover had prayed. A devout man, who would step in whenever a prayer leader was lacking at a service, who attended to the cemetery, to which he would have to send his delicate wife Esther and shortly thereafter his daughter, Zippora, sought permission once more to build a Synagogue. But the time was apparently not yet come, perhaps his brother-in-law, Leffmann Behrens, who could manage anything, had not yet been able to raise the subject with his Duke. But it would come.

After Esther's early death, Löb looked for another wife as was the custom. He found Merle, already twenty-nine, daughter of Rabbi Jakob, (no other name is known) and she gave him three more children. Only two of their names are known: Ruben and Uri Phöbus, who would, like many of his ancestors, live to be very old; the date on his gravestone in Hannover is 3 September 1771.

Little that is spectacular was recorded about Löb other than that he succeeded in building Hannover's first Synagogue on his plot of land. It was however too small and a few years later Leffmann Behrens had it extended or even maybe rebuilt. But it was this modest Löb who is the reason our family tree became so interesting. From this time on there are no more unwritten pages.

Because it was Löb, usually more formally addressed as Levin Bendix Goldschmidt, who joined the Hannover Goldschmidt family with that of the honourable Fürst family from Hamburg.

Of course they knew one-another. Grandfather Nathan Spanier and Chajim Fürst were respectful friends but there was no business connection. Children, however, were suitable for making family connections. Löb/Levin Goldschmidt had an unmarried daughter, and also a son, Bendix, still unmarried at twenty. His intelligence, education and mercantile skill offered all the virtues required for a brilliant mercantile career. If a Goldschmidt from Hannover could add Leffmann Behrens as a brother-in-law to all this, then the doors of Israel Fürst in Hamburg, the current senior of the house, must have opened by themselves. And behind these, two Fürst children were both waiting for a spouse to be found. Marriages were arranged by the parents as a matter of principle because they knew what was important: the Goldschmidt's devout daughter, whose name has not been passed down to us, seemed to be the ideal wife for the already prosperous jewel dealer and 'rabbinatassesor', thus a high ranking person in the community, Jeremia Fürst; and his sister Henriette, known as Jette, could have wished for no better husband than the very promising Bendix Goldschmidt.

While Löb's second wife, Merle was still carrying their first child, he was able to marry off his two adult children into the Fürst family. Dream marriages that took place in March 1676, probably in the Altona Synagogue, to which Israel Fürst together with other community members had donated a metre high brass Hanukkah menorah, the candelabrum with nine branches. It must have been a gigantic wedding.

For Bendix Levin Goldschmidt, (his father's first name became his second name) the serious matter of a successful and exciting life was just beginning. And Israel Fürst was his mentor.

Bendix Goldschmidt, only son of his newly widowed father, grew up with just three pretty sisters and now was suddenly part of a large family with brothers, cousins, brother-in-laws and uncles.

Israel Fürst and his (probably eldest) son, Jeremias, took Bendix under their wing, that is, they taught him. His father-in-law was a quiet, solid advisor, Jeremias Fürst on the other hand was very active in many areas. He was the owner of a Permit to Trade 'with the right to trade in jewellery in Pomerania'. This was granted in 1663 by the Brandenburg Principality to 'the Portuguese Jews in Hamburg'. He was often at the Court in Schwerin. Duke Christian Louis was favourably disposed towards him, a ruler who wanted very much to copy the Sun King Louis XIV. His palace at Schwerin was spruced up accordingly, regardless of cost. But the ducal purse was quite exhausted, not only was money lacking but the precious metal for the Schwerin coinage too. An uncle of Jeremias, Ruben Fürst, who worked there, knew all the difficulties. Occasionally the Duke appeared in Hamburg with a splendid equipage to seek out the Jews, particularly the Fürsts, who thanks to their foreign contacts, were able to furnish everything that his heart desired and from which he could enrich himself, such as tobacco imports on which the highest excise duty could be levied.

Jeremias Fürst arranged not only precious metal supplies and jewels for the ladies at the court in Schwerin but also founded a tobacco consortium with two colleagues, Elias Ries and Michel Hinrichsen, a Portuguese Jew whose proper name was Henriques. They needed to hurry because although the Hamburg competition were more cautious, they could not be allowed to be quicker. Poor quality tobacco had been grown in Germany for a while but had been prohibited as a crop in almost all the principalities. So people were dependent on supplies from overseas and the most important point of import was Hamburg.

Bendix had to move. Hannover was a good place to live and most of his Goldschmidt relations stayed there but Bendix needed to visit the Bourse in Hamburg in order to keep in touch with the some of the posh Portuguese and to be readily available whenever a cargo sailing ship arrived. Of course German Jews like Bendix had no residence permit in Hamburg – but trade was allowed. Thus Bendix moved to Altona. There he was not dependent on the Senate's mercy; there, one was protected by Danish law. Naturally a fee of 6 Reichtalers was payable as protection money; poor Jews paid only half that. But the right to establish a business, so-called 'entrance fee' cost more. Bendix, we are told paid nineteen and a half Reichtalers.

Thereafter he had little time for a private life. Jeremias Fürst accompanied his brother-in-law to Schwerin where he was shown the possibilities that existed there. His uncle Ruben Fürst showed him the poor state of the coinage in the dukedom. Duke Christian Louis often travelled to Paris with his French wife to let themselves be inspired by the Court of the Sun King which then led to heavy expenses. Bendix was already indispensable for the board of the tobacco consortium, now the next endeavour awaited him: the silver consortium that Jeremias had started with Elias Ries in Hamburg needed him.

Bendix was to supply silver. But rather differently to the way his ancestors had hawked from door to door seeking out half-forgotten or carefully buried silver-goblets, necklaces, jewellery that was no longer really wanted and old coins that were no longer legal tender. Following disastrous harvests or having soldiers billeted in their houses or after Danish and Swedish troops had devastated the fields, people needed every taler to buy new seed-corn and to replace stolen cattle.

Bendix organised several hawkers from the Jews living in the country neighbourhood. They would work for him to earn a bit of money, and above all, as a money-changer and lender he was able to withdraw 'bad' coinage from circulation, replacing them with new coins which at the ruler's command contained significantly less precious metal. As the demand at the princely courts for baroque luxuries grew by leaps and bounds in recent years, the mints produced ever smaller, so-called 'Heckenmünzen' (hedge coins). These coins were stamped out with much less valuable metal than even the imperial minting ordinance demanded and were used to buy better quality Taler. This practice was one of the most degrading that the Christian potentates thought out for their Jewish dependants. Unlike Christians, who would only try to earn money in this way in cases of the utmost need, Jews, who were prohibited from many professions and all official and university posts, were often enough persuaded by their dukes to engage in this trade in order to survive and were later criticised for it and discriminated against. Branded as 'coinage Jews' or as coin-clippers, they were considered by their Christian neighbours as the sole cause of the coinage debasement and the resulting inflation.

As far as the Court at Schwerin was concerned, in 1678 everything was fine. Jeremias Fürst and his father Israel now had passes as 'Mecklenburger Court Jews', a title that Bendix had to wait some years for. Israel Fuerst must have had a good relationship to Duke Christian Ludwig; he, after all had a

Danish pass and the right to settle and trade in Copenhagen. That could only be of benefit to those in Schwerin.

Being named as a Court Jew was an honour because the local ruler needed first to be persuaded that one was an upstanding and discreet person and that one had sufficient money to occasionally be able to fill any holes in the Prince's purse. A talent for languages and negotiating skills were also required. A Court Jew – more often called 'Hoffaktor' or court banker, which was religiously neutral – was expected to furnish every luxury that a princely court might desire for a more or less trivial annual remuneration. Chinese silks and porcelain, south-sea pearls, jewellery with rare gemstones, ostrich and birds of paradise plumage for the latest fashions, and for daily consumption sufficient wine and hundreds of white candles, (not the honey-coloured ones!) music instruments, well-sprung carriages, draught horses, material for uniforms, everything that a well-turned out prince's guard could need, so weapons of every size, rafts to convey cannon, stallions and troops and naturally forage. For this service the prince would provide a carriage and servant for the Hoffaktor who was continually travelling. The money required for all the purchases, which swallowed huge sums, would be advanced by the Jew. It might be years before this credit was repaid to the lowest of all subjects but in favourable cases a few extra percent interest was taken. However, if the prince was unable or unwilling to service the debt after his orgy of wastefulness, there was a well-tried remedy: the Jew could be ousted on a trumped-up charge of 'fraud', or one waited till he died hoping all the while that one's debts would go to the grave with the Jew. But some defaulting rulers were caught out: if the heirs of the duped Court Jew, who were otherwise penniless, finally took action in the German law courts against the princes they were astonishingly almost always successful!

A Court Jew might also be expected to be a chess partner and to teach the prince the game. The relationship to his prince was thus very confidential. They would meet with the court chamberlain to receive the daily commands and one was responsible for the preparations for journeys. On his travels, Christian Louis was sometimes accompanied by his court orchestra, which included 14 string instruments alone.

Whenever possible Israel Fürst managed everything from Hamburg or his home in Altona so that his life was not quite so hectic as that of his son, Jeremias, who could hardly change horses quickly enough because he was always on his way somewhere else on business. Bendix Goldschmidt on the other hand seems to have been focussed on the acquisition of precious metals and concentrated more and more on the Court at Gottorf where Duke Christian Albrecht von Schleswig-Holstein lived in a pomp that resembled that of Christian Louis in Schwerin. But in Gottorf there was different intellectual climate because the Duke liked to be surrounded by muses of all the fine arts and strove to emulate the music scene of Hamburg where in 1678, the curtain was raised for the first time in the new opera-house.

# An Incident

For Israel Fürst, 1679 started badly. He, the blameless Leader of the Jewish community in Altona was under suspicion that not only included him but also some other members of the governing committee who were noticeably the wealthiest in the community. The Town council had noticed that obviously more Jews lived in Altona than were registered there, and that these could not all therefore be Jews protected by Danish law because they had not paid the authorities the required 6 Reichstaler per annum. Was it possible that their protection money was being retained in the community treasury that was responsible for the payment of all their taxes? The matter needed to be investigated.

On 8 February 1679 a commission was set up to audit the community account books. Three members of the community had to act as translators because the books were written up in Hebrew. One of them was Israel Fürst's uncle Samuel who was also one of the Elders.

The books were impeccable. But the board were covering-up for the irregular Jews who lived and were undoubtedly trading in Altona and this was – as the commission formulated it – a breach of faith against the Danish King and had to be punished.

An indictment was raised on 15 March 1679 against six board members, Israel Fürst at their head, demanding that the community pay a fine of 5000 Reichstaler within four weeks, in cash.

Israel Fürst answered that they were prepared to pay the fine but the demand was much more than the community's finances would allow more especially as the Synagogue and the rabbi's and teaching staff's accommodation was tumbling down and in urgent need of repair...

Thereupon the Danish King's residence in Glueckstadt sent an order to the president of the Altona German chancellery, Roland, commanding the arrest of the accused. And so on the 24 March 1679 (I have toned down the original convoluted old German text)

> ...on which day the Jews frequent their Synagogue for their so-called Easter ceremony, by the use of those soldiers such as are present in Altona at the time – to occupy the named Synagogue and to evict the above

> *mentioned Jews including the servant of the Elders, Meyer Max, commonly known as Schielmeyer by name, and bring them each separately to a secure place, at the same time have the Rabbi announce that the Jews concerned have been arrested for important reasons and that the other Jews under Our Protection be unaffected by this action, but rather that they should continue to enjoy their privileges so long as they behave appropriately...'*

The president hoped that the last appeasing clause would avoid possible over-excitement in the Synagogue.

The Rabbi was now expected to act as a bailiff giving information on the assets of each accused individual, which of course he knew very well. The objective was naturally not punishment nor imprisonment which was of no benefit to anyone. The authorities wanted money and with this information they would know how much each could afford.

The commission calculated and the amounts attributed to those affected was enormous – between 14,000 and 3,000 Reichstaler; Israel Fürst was assessed at 6,000 Reichstaler – and the dry comment 'if each of the accused pays the amounts stated readily then there will be no further consequences' sounded rather like extortion.

Did the city want to ruin the successful merchants, drive them into bankruptcy?

No, not that.

Thus a few days later: If the fines had been assessed too high, one could discuss the matter and would be mercifully satisfied with a lesser amount. And the moneys demanded would be shared by the exchequer and the Jewish alms fund. That sounded much more reasonable.

In fact the fines demanded from the accused while they waited in prison were quickly reduced by 10,000 to 2,000 Reichstaler. Israel Fürst paid an exceptionally small 400 Reichstaler.

Two weeks after the start of the spectacle, Israel Fürst was released by a royal writ of 7 April 1679, but because in the mean time one of the co-accused seemed to have gone away without giving any explanation, and 'another' was 'travelling', only against bail of 12,000 Reichstaler until all the other Jews had paid up.

Whether because of Israel Fürst's good personal relationship to the Danish Court or his outraged complaint against the nature of his arrest, in the end no fine was demanded, some files disappeared and the whole matter ran into Danish sand.

# Crazy for Luxury and Empty Pockets

After the tension of the past weeks that the Fürsts of Hamburg had suffered under, there was a hardly believable relaxation and as soon as Israel Fürst found himself no longer under the shadow of a prison sentence, and furthermore, realised that his reputation was unstained the relief was enormous and he returned at once to his business, procurement of jewels and silver. He was acknowledged as Court Jew at Gottorf and Schwerin and while the courtiers' craze to satisfy every desire for luxury, which had emptied the treasury at Hannover, continued, he was soon to become indispensable. Of course his astute sons, his son-in-law Bendix and Leffmann Behrens as part of the Goldschmidt family, all worked even more diligently. The younger generation had to chase every possibility to establish themselves. That meant: keep moving. Travelling. Often they sat for days and nights in shaky carriages on rutted roads, where the wheels would be sucked into the mud after every fall of rain – the princes had no interest in spending money on good roads when it was much more pleasurable to squander it in the palaces on grand celebrations. Ballet had become very popular.

Until recently Duke Johann Friedrich's court orchestra in Hannover had consisted of just eight trumpeters and four other musicians, now it had to be more opulent. Leffmann Behrens had amazing contacts in Antwerp where not only strings of pearls were threaded and gemstones cut and polished; now he was commanded to obtain two silver trumpets at a cost of 726 Taler apiece and at the same time wallpaper for 400 Taler and rings for 1,000 Taler. He paid for everything himself, only later would he be recompensed with premiums and interest by the Treasury.

The princesses demanded dress-jewelery and above all a trousseau that one could be seen with. Anyone who wanted to attract sons-in-laws from the best princes' palaces (Brandenburg was not far) had to show off his wealth as well as his lovely daughters. Some observers maintained that the Dukes in Hannover were wealthier than the Emperor in Vienna. A pretty rumour.

On 11 September 1671 the Duke Johann Friedrich borrowed one-thousand Taler from Leffmann Behrens, perhaps he needed more money for one of his journeys to Italy; he would not have wanted to miss the Carnival in Venice, and in any case the best musicians could be found there. In his Court choir he already had eight Italian singers, among them the highly paid tenor Borgiani. He was not stingy with fees for the fine arts, indeed for a converted Catholic duke, avarice would have been a mortal sin. He had a 'Commödienhaus', or theatre, built for his beloved opera in Herrenhausen in Hannover. The park still lacked a grotto. Leffmann Behrens was to procure stone from Holland and a Dutch sculptor to work it and to advance the money to pay for it.

Leffmann Behrens was by then used to having to advance money for everything he procured. Even when the Subsidies, which he had been organising since 1672, were sent from France, he had to pay out while waiting for the highly vulnerable bullion to be riskily transported. How he was able to raise the amounts, which depending on the political situation and contracts, were between 20,000 and 40,000 Taler every month, remains his secret: we must assume that the Goldschmidt and Fürst families supported him with their own resources because in such situations no-one left the others in the lurch. He never accompanied the bullion himself but he carried the responsibility to ensure that the silver ingots and coins which were packed into barrels in the Parisian bank's treasury arrived in Hannover without any loss. If at all possible such transport was made over waterways because they were safer than the roads where one had to anticipate being robbed at any time. In any case, the load needed to be as inconspicuous as possible: ordinary brown barrels under somewhat shabby canvas grey covers.

In 1678 the Duke's treasure chest was once again so empty that Johann Friedrich had to borrow 12,100 Taler from Leffmann Behrens. The royal household, which consisted of very many insignificant servants, cooks and coach-men as well as Leibniz, the librarian and counsellor, swallowed huge sums of money and still the revelry continued unabated. One can see that the Duke was a man of pleasure. His mother, Anna Eleonore von Hessen-Darmstadt said he was *'grotesquely fat and very short, much shorter than everybody else'*. But he had a taste for the good life and the journeys to Italy awakened an appetite for future acquisitions.

He travelled south with a great escort at the end of November 1679. But this time they did not reach Italy, for on 28 December 1679 his journey through life ended unexpectedly in Augsburg.

One might have thought that it was an accident, robbery or an unlucky fall were it not for Leibniz the chronicler who has passed on to us the end of the *'rather corpulent body'* of the Duke, very vividly portrayed in a gigantic biography. Although the description does not really belong in this family history it does however give an insight into that far off time so that I wish to include at least part of it, abbreviated and using today's spelling: How the

Duke was delayed on his arrival in Augsburg while waiting for permission to travel on to Venice because the mountain passes were closed due to an epidemic. He was *'quite happy and in splendid condition'* except that *'owing to certain cause was suffering from obstruction'*, or constipation, *'which could be treated with medication and good diet'*. But three days later a new *'blockage of his abdomen'* afflicted him. *'By application of the usual enema and internal medication'* it was relieved but the trouble soon made itself apparent again after more delectable banqueting.

He endured two weeks of pain in his arms and feet, dreadful thirst and *'dryness of the mouth and tongue.'* But *'his pulse was natural'* and there was *'not the least sign of any malignancy or danger to be seen'*. On the evening of 27 December, the Duke

> *...dined with quite a good appetite, settled tranquilly an hour later but in the same night became disturbed in a deep sleep, threw himself about, woke at midnight and hallucinated a bit but then came to himself again. Laid back to rest again and slept soundly until between 3 and 4 a.m., when he got up and complained that his arms were very heavy. Laid himself down again, fell asleep and as before respired with difficulty for a while until he eventually became quiet'...*

which after a time, his chamber servants found to be suspicious.

> *They approached with lights and discovered with great consternation that life and movement were gone and that His Highness had gently and blessedly departed this life in his fifty-fifth year without any words or signs between 6 and 7 o'clock. The next day his corpse was embalmed and a long thin piece of flesh, called 'polypus cordis' by his physician was extracted from the right chamber of his heart. The physician opined this had grown there and then been released and blocked the artery to the lung and thus the circulation of blood and movement of the heart with which life must end.'*

For the youngest brother of Duke Johann Friedrich, who had been with him for this last journey, the year 1680 began with a pompous funeral. He took over the Regency because Johann Friedrich had left only three daughters and no male heir.

For Leffmann Behrens the year began with a new principal: Duke Ernst August.

Fortunately for the Goldschmidt and Fürst families no-one at the Royal Courts in Schwerin or Hannover considered making economies and the

Court in Gottorf was not prepared to be less spendthrift. There the Duke Christian Albrecht wallowed in the pleasures of music-making and good cuisine; his drinking sprees were famous; the walk-in giant globe, which the genius mathematician Olearius had invented for his father Friedrich III, delighted his guests. If they crawled inside through a door in the *'Indian Ocean'* they could sit under a slowly rotating scene of heavenly stars. And Israel Fürst, who on occasion had presented the Duchess Sophie Amalie with jewelled trinkets, could ponder how long it would be before the ducal purse was once again empty.

Christian Albrecht, obviously less interested in politics than in the fine arts, nurtured his library, gathered learned heads to his Court who advised him on the foundation of a university in the port of Kiel, which belonged to Gottorf. He enlarged his Court orchestra with several well-known musicians and commissioned new musical compositions. Above all he was very taken by dramatic opera and was passionately supported in this by his mother Maria Elisabeth. The old lady, once a pupil of Heinrich Schütz, had already installed a refuge for musicians in her dowager's residence in Husum. She had her own court music ensemble – and let Israel Fürst flatter her with a beautiful ring which she could flaunt while playing the spinet. The bill would have been paid by the Court at Gottorf, some invoices can still be found in the archives.

I do not know the reason nor the excuse why on 10 July 1675, Duke Christian Albrecht was torn out of his musical dream and commanded to attend his brother-in-law, the Danish King Christian V, at his fortress Rendsburg in order to be told that he, who had till then been sovereign in his Schleswig lands, would from then on owe the King allegiance again, lose control of his castle and his mint. Did the Danish King fear that his brother-in-law could drag the country into the abyss by his spendthrift life?

Christian Albrecht no longer wanted to live in his Gottorf palace which was now sequestered and in which Danish troops were billeted. He dismissed all his court musicians except for three that he could not part from, packed up his silver and fled to Hamburg. Israel Fürst was a reliable and discreet helper there. The Duke needed money. All the income of the Court now flowed into the pockets of the Danish King The nobles of Holstein who had previously aided him with credit from time to time now politely withdrew themselves. And thus did Israel Fürst receive the commission to convert all the silver that had been rescued into cash. Thanks to Israel Fürst's trading privileges there, the objects were sold in Copenhagen.

At any rate the proceeds seem to have kept the Duke's head above water for a while. In dire straits there were besides Israel Fürst and Bendix Goldschmidt, always other even more financially capable sources of money such as the two Portuguese Jews Teixeira and Mussaphia to whom he could turn. The Duke was keen to finance the Hamburg opera house that was being built at the time. He felt that he owed that much to the Gottorf musical director, the composer Johann Theile whom he had taken with him into his exile. And in 1678 the Hamburg Opera was inaugurated by Theile's latest work *Der erschaffene, gefallene und aufgerichtete Mensch*. (The Created, Fallen, and Uprighted Man). The shorter name was a bit simpler: *Adam und Eva*.

And then a wonder! After the Peace of Lund in 1679, Christian Albrecht, who had fallen out of the Danish King's favour, was given back his rights and on 1 January 1680 returned to Gottorf with great pageantry. The life at the court which he so loved could start again and benefit everyone and not least our Israel Fürst. His first act was to deliver jewels to a worth of 330 Taler to the Dowager Duchess Maria Elisabeth of Husum and then to ascertain that the Mint in Tönning which was to be put back into operation lacked the prerequisite precious metal. It may be assumed that Bendix Goldschmidt and the Fürst sons who had been engaged in the silver consortium, would now become active.

But the financial situation at the Gottorf Court was disastrous and soon Christian Albrecht, out of consideration for his security, fled back to Hamburg. He had a premonition that he might once again suffer humiliation from his royal brother-in-law. In fact things were as bad as he had feared: in 1684 the Duke's property was once again annexed. So began for the next five years the so-called second sequestration of the Court and for Israel Fürst a series of mandates. Now he was to sell off the costly valuables and the Duke's complete silver service that once had been admired by so many guests while banqueting at his table. There is a marginal remark in the Duke's own hand: 'any excess over 6,000 Taler resulting from the proceeds of sale of the gemstones shall be allowed to Israel Fürst for his efforts in raising and collecting the moneys.'

Christian Albrecht, at last liquid again, was able to appear generously in his Hamburg exile, especially as patron on the Hamburg Opera House where in the meantime some of his musicians were working. His last but one musical director, Johann Philipp Förtsch (1652-1732) had already composed an oeuvre that would one day be premièred at Gottorf when his brother-in-law released the sequestrated property. *Das betrübte und erfreute Cimbria*, a homage to the Duke as well to Jutland where the Cimbria were once at home and where from 1689 Christian Albrecht was once again allowed to live. Before that, he ordered a ring for 600 Taler from Israel Fürst with the instruction to the court officials on 12 July 1687: *'Israel Fürst shall in time receive payment over the amount of the cost of the rings he bought for 600*

*Taler'*. From that it seems the proceeds of sale of the silver service were insufficient for all of the expenses. It is certain that Christian Albrecht must have often borrowed from Fürst because in 1690 Fürst received 18,972 Marks from the Court banker Mussaphia, who was once again in charge of the Mint at Tönning, and at the same time was advised of 'assignments on Husum, Trittau and Reinbeck'.

If the Duke did not want to borrow directly from Israel Fürst, he would let him lend money to his administrator Wedderkop or his chamberlain Freiherr v. Goertz. Both gentlemen however, preferred to borrow from Bendix Goldschmidt. For their personal requirements too, they approached Bendix who was by now very wealthy and was generous in his dealings and did not put pressure on them to repay. Should he need a financial boost, he could turn to his brother-in-law, Moses Fürst.

Bendix had been recognised as a court supplier since 1689, but after Christian Albrecht in Gottorf appointed him as court jeweller, a synonym for court banker, in 1691, Duke Friedrich Wilhelm von Mecklenburg

> *...gives notice and makes known that We have taken the Holsteiner Benedikt called Bendix Goldschmidt and Moses Israel Fürst to us as Court Jewellers and that they both provide Our Court with the required jewels and silverware and that they be allowed to serve our merciful needs for taxes and purchases.'*

When one looks at the documents from that time to be found in diverse town archives, one is shocked by the self-evident greed and at the same time serenity which dominated in relatively small royal courts. How, from the duke to the chamberlains, the available or frivolously borrowed money was squandered on private luxury. Louis XIV's Versailles was still the shining example for the baroque life-style. When one reads that in 1707, the Freiherr v. Goertz gave his brother-in-law, Reventlow, 75,000 Taler via Bendix Goldschmidt, one can imagine the hunter's celebrations after the haloo at the hare-hunting on the Lüneburg Heath – and also Goldschmidt's covert head-shaking, especially as he, as a Jew, could not enjoy the non-kosher roast hare. Indeed he would not have even been invited to the banquet!

As a court Jew one was expected to remain in the background but at the same time to be ever available to be useful for *'taxes and purchases'*. Christian tongues might now wag that the Jews made great profits from the excesses but it was not so much as one might imagine. The decisive factor was number of loans granted, that means the size of the customer base. Usury? By no means. Because the rate of interest was determined by the rulers and fluctuated between a half and four percent. Rarely was it more, it depended on the affection felt by the debtor for his 'court jeweller' upon whom he relied for discretion. Israel Fürst and Bendix Goldschmidt seem to have enjoyed a certain preference. Both the Jews were also popular with the 'lower ranks' such as the State councillor Breyer or the treasury councillor Fock in Schwerin. Only now and then, when the debtors dallied too long with their repayments, were the rates of interest pushed up to 6%, as for example when Goldschmidt and Fürst had to wait till 1693 for the 5,729 Taler for jewels delivered in 1691 and 1692.

The new ruler in Hannover was no stranger to Leffmann Behrens. Duke Ernst August, until then Prince-Bishop in Osnabrück, followed his brother Johann Friedrich who had left no sons. He was already 51 years old when he ascended the throne in 1680 and had often visited Herrenhausen which he now intended to make more musical and beautiful. Of course the two men knew each other and they would have socialised as equals – had not Leffmann been stigmatised as the Court Jew. However, he had significant merits, not least as a supplier of funds and the necessary discretion that went with that function but also as far as the finance business was concerned: he had imagination.

Leffmann, who had by then gained enormous experience, was able to look further beyond the silver platter of the princely court than any others. He knew how one could also earn money by making economies. He had ideas. He proffered, humbly, as was expected of him, proposals that were well aimed. Why should the Duke buy the material required for the 15,000 uniforms of his army and his court servants at the fairs, when it would be much more convenient to use wool from his own heaths in a cloth factory that he could set up in nearby Lüneburg? In that way the local economy would benefit. Not just the girls out of the orphanages who usually were occupied as seamstresses but also the countless housewives in the area who sewed the cut out uniform pieces in their own homes. Leffmann, who already ran a linen manufacture in Lüneburg could also weave cloth there, and if the Duke found his suggestion convenient and he was permitted to do so, he would of course take no commission on the goods. He was willing to make such a concession because as a manager he thought in other dimensions. If the material which he laid before the court for inspection was acceptable then the facility in Lüneburg would become a money spinner in the future. The court's wardrobe was constantly on the Duke's wish-list, even the trumpeters needed new livery every two years with appropriate silver buttons, braids and ribbons. The court quickly accepted the estimates, was satisfied with the strictly inspected material samples and gave its blessing.

Leffmann's proposal was soon put into action. And we may be sure that he kept his family in mind: His son Herz Behrens, educated in business just as much as in the Talmud and who already at the age of twenty had been sent to Paris to organise the money transfers, was named as manager of the enterprise. Soon after a nephew, Isaak Behrens, joined him and also Leffmann's youngest son Jakob, who wanted to set up his own business as well as taking care of his father's cloth production. As he could show no Letter of Protection from the Duke, he needed a residence permit. As a consequence the Lüneburg Councillors were in uproar. Should they betray their own principles and give a Jew such a permit? For centuries that would have been unthinkable! They gave the permit. But with the proviso that his business must restrict itself to *'precious metals and manufactured goods'*. Thus Jakob Behrens was the first Jew since 1530 to be allowed to settle in the officially anti-Semitic city. Alone the name of Leffmann Behrens had made it possible.

Who was responsible for the troops' provisioning? Why were supplies of cereals and flour delayed again and again, even when the harvests were good? Why were there problems providing for soldiers who might well be marching off to God knows where the next morning in order to make war for a neighbouring state against payment of Subsidy moneys that benefited the Duke alone? Everyone at Court was aware of the soldiers' complaints about too little and often stale or improperly baked bread. Leffmann Behrens, the born organiser, was called to close the gaps in provisioning; more bakers in the area were asked to deliver more army bread so that every soldier could be given at least five or six days' rations in the event of any military exercise. Leffmann asked for prior information if troop movements were anticipated so that he could organise extra supplies, carts, draught horses, oats and hay. As a Jew he knew where to find horses: perhaps the only advantage that Jews had over Christians was that they were spared the billeting of soldiers on them but even so, as *'country Jews'*, they were obliged to keep horses ready for the use of the princes. By now Leffmann had an office in his house in Hannover-Neustadt, Langestrasse 8. A clerk, book-keeper and a cashier were busy there, also two junior dealers who accompanied him on his travels. The loans that he chose to grant, especially when the Subsidy-moneys were late and enormous sums had to be advanced, were well-known. His connections with his brothers-in-law Goldschmidt and Fürst were not so well-known.

The financial support that he received from both sides in the case of emergency remained inconspicuously 'en famille'. And this family had been extended in a satisfactory manner by the marriage of Leffmann's son Herz Behrens, for his brother-in-law was no less a person than Samson Wertheimer, creditor to the Emperor in Vienna. Also the banker Samuel Oppenheimer who had arranged the moneys for the Emperor to fight the Turkish War and thus rescue Vienna from the Ottomans, belonged to 'us' after Leffmann's daughter Genendel married the nephew of the banker David Oppenheimer. We shall learn more about him.

Rulers do not ask where their creditors get their money from. But they do know that one can obtain almost anything one desires with money. They just need the right financiers and advisors.

Duke Ernst August knew who would stand by him to fulfil his greatest wants. And they both knew, just as did the Court in Hannover and all the princes between Schleswig and Vienna, that some wishes were simply impossible in the Holy Roman Empire of German Nations: There were eight Electors. A ninth was not permitted.

But this was exactly the prize that Ernst August von Hannover-Braunschweig-Lüneburg had before his eyes. If it were possible to influence certain Princes – the most intransigent was the Prince-Elector August the Strong – by means of money or the opportunity to acquire property to acquiesce to the granting of a ninth Electorate then all that was required was the necessary money. Disregarding the bribes that were referred to as 'extraordinary' and the expenses of diplomatic receptions at home and on journeys to other royal courts, that is, manageable sums, if it were possible to transfer 1,100,000 Reichstaler to the Royal Treasury in Vienna, then Emperor Leopold I would declare himself agreeable to a 9th Electoral Prince.

The preparations took almost a complete year. One may read in the State Archive in Hannover how the eight Prince-Electors, among whom were spiritual dignitaries, were lured into agreement with presents valued at between 2,000 and 4,000 Taler. Of course Leffmann Behrens served only as an inconspicuous money provider in the background during these transactions. No-one wanted to see him entangled in an embarrassing situation. One needed him, and over the years it was evermore apparent, one liked him. For us it is breath-taking to discover that he, who possessed only a Letter of Protection for which he paid 20 Taler each year and until now had not been appointed as Senior Court Factor nor even Chamber Agent, responsible for buying-in, was suddenly included in the ranks of diplomats in the mission to obtain an Elector's crown. In January 1692, he accompanied them to August the Strong in order to negotiate the neutrality alliance between Hannover and Saxony and to persuade the strong August and his advisors, with the aid of a pleasing sum of money, of the possible importance of Ernst August as the ninth ruler in the Council of Prince-Electors. Finally it may be that the Court Jew and Banker, Behrend Lehmann helped with a nod of his head and possibly a wink to Leffmann. They both had known each other in business over many years and only a few years later they were personally connected: Lehmann's daughter Lea married the grandson of Leffmann, Isaak Behrens; what else could one expect?

In December 1692 all the hurdles on the way to an Elector's crown were cleared, the barrels of bullion had been organised and the journey to Vienna could begin. Once again, Leffmann Behrens was allowed to accompany the Hanoverian diplomats to witness the coronation of the Duke to Elector. A court Official, the secretary Rat Grote received the crown, which looked more like a winter hat of dark crimson velvet with a white ermine edging, as deputy because the journey to Vienna, days of exertion in rumbling coaches, was too arduous for the 63 year old Duke Ernst August. It may be imagined that for Leffmann there was also a happy family re-union in Vienna before or after the celebrations, for there he could meet the related Wertheimers and even perhaps his daughter, Genendel, now married with an Oppenheimer and who lived in Prague.

It took nearly five years before Leffmann Behrens received repayment of the moneys advanced in individual tranches from the Prince-Elector's Treasury and it was only possible for him to continue to lend because he had a comprehensive base of clients who were addicted to luxury. The next large loan that Duke Ernst August demanded – apart from the 12,078 Taler for a particularly urgent service (tableware) and 27,800 Taler for his private needs – was a sum that was at first undefined, for the purchase of the small State of Lauenburg from Saxony. Hannover was prepared to offer 400,000 Taler but August the Strong demanded 1,100,000 Gulden. Despite the fact that the Court Councillors found the figure (equivalent to 733,000 Taler) wildly overpriced, the newly crowned Elector was determined to pay it. With Leffmann Behrens' help.

If the Court's purse were tipped out to the last penny and the Welfen brother Georg Wilhelm von Celle added 200,000 Taler, then Leffmann Behrens would only need to conjure up 300,000 Taler. For several months until 1697, Leffmann was active in the diplomatic negotiations. But after the contract had been finalised with the Saxon mediators and the wine barrels packed with bullion were ready, he asked his Prince for the dispensation to send his son Herz to accompany them from Hannover to Dresden because he, Leffmann was in mourning. On 19 January 1697 his younger son, Jakob had died at the age of 35 during the Fair in Leipzig. It was the second calamity within three years for on 5 July 1695 he had lost his beloved wife Jente.

Just how convenient the sale of the State of Lauenburg was for August the Strong showed itself during the negotiations. The Polish Throne had been vacant since the death of King Sobieski in June 1696 and there were enough pretenders to the enticing title of King of Poland. The question was, however, which of the Polish magnates was able to pay the 1,100,000 Gulden demanded for the title. August could, because he anticipated receiving exactly this amount from Hannover and so he was the first to eagerly propose himself. Now he had the money – but for Poland the wrong religion. No problem. He immediately converted to Catholicism. Now nothing stood in his way and everything could go ahead quickly.

The transfer of the gigantic amount of money was not solely in the hands of Leffmann's son Herz who, under dramatic circumstances, was to accompany the barrels of money from Hannover to Breslau in order to deliver the money to the Saxon Court Officials and those Polish Magnates who had travelled there from Cracow. The difficulty, which no-one had considered, was that the sum would be demanded in coin. Even Leffmann did not have so much cash available because most business was done by exchange. He chased messengers off to his relative Behrend Lehmann in Halberstadt and to his colleagues in Dresden and Breslau so that they could pack up the cash that was lacking in barrels and send it on without delay. The Order from Hannover dated 1 July 1697 stipulated as follows: The journey with change of horses at each post station by day and night should progress at such a speed that the transport would arrive in Breslau in just twelve days. It was financially as well as strategically a master stroke without parallel, for none of the Jewish money lenders knew when they would ever receive repayment of the loans. No particular thanks were given by August the Strong who had achieved what he wanted – except for the immediate request to borrow 300,000 Taler from the Prince-Elector Ernst August for certain expenses which were now necessary for his coronation. The Treasury in Hannover was empty. Even for the sake of his Prince-Elector, Leffmann Behrens was only able to raise the 200,000 Taler with the greatest of difficulty. This time, instead of 6%, he demanded 12% interest.

In contrast to the newly appointed Polish King, who called himself August II, the Welfen Court, represented by Duke Georg Wilhelm in Celle showed its thanks to Leffmann and Herz Behrens by a Certificate appointing both to Court and Treasury Agents.

I take the liberty to make the certificate, wonderfully handwritten by a chancery clerk, digestible for impatient readers by presenting it here in current spelling although many words remain in the old-fashioned form that is typical of the time.

> *We, Georg Wilhelm, by God's grace, Duke of Braunschweig and Lüneburg, announce and make known that the Court and Protected Jews Leffmann Behrens and his son Herz Behrens who have most humbly given good and useful service to our Elector and Princely House in various ways and particularly recently with his Royal Majesty of Poland as Elector to Saxony in the settlement of the Lauenburg State will further be able and willing to serve as our Court and Chamber*

*Agents and also remain faithful and true to us and our descendants at the Elector and Princely Government as they have been until now and continue to procure and solicit, and with their industriousness keep malice, damage and disadvantage from us and to the best of their ability warn, protect and deflect especially that which with the appropriate industriousness, care and discretion, as is suitable and expected from Court and Chamber Agents, is their commitment as assigned Court and Chamber Agents. For this service we wish our Court and Chamber Agents to annually render invoice at the usual time to our Princely Payments chamber for one-hundred and fifty Reichstaler with the first year at Easter 1697 and to make their services available to the same.*

*Certificated under our Princely hand-mark and Secret Chamber seal. Given out at our Residence Zelle 10 February 1698.'*
*Georg Wilhelm.*

Significantly, this announcement was made three weeks after the death of the Elector Ernst August on 23 January 1698 and almost immediately after his son Georg Ludwig ascended to the throne in Hannover – almost as if here a failing which had had no relevance under Ernst August had to be corrected. Anyhow, Leffmann Behrens had worked for this Court at every level for 30 years, starting as cereal supplier and money-lender and rising to delegate in diplomatic service and possibly it was a personal gesture of sympathy and respect by Ernst August to spare the Protected Jew Behrens from a future denigration and thus to overlook his Jewishness. The Duke's 74 year old brother Georg Wilhelm, who was responsible for certificates and contracts may have regarded it differently; it is beyond any doubt that Leffmann's appointment as senior Agent of *'Bleie und Glätte'*, the precious metals mine that was exploited in the region of the Welfen von Braunschweig-Wolfenbüttel, in 1683 was stored together with all other documents in safe-keeping in Celle. Be that as it may, Leffmann's sudden appointment as Chamber Agent was not necessarily occasioned by the new Regent in Hannover.

Georg Ludwig was, as were all the children of Ernst August, liberal and open-minded. His mother Sophie had helped: an extremely clever and eloquent lady who had a close spiritual contact to Leibniz – and a secret financial one to Leffmann Behrens. She often had to borrow large sums from him to cover the gaming and drinking debts of her sons Karl Philipp and Maximillian Wilhelm. Bills that were mostly more than 10,000 Taler and which her Elector spouse should remain unaware of. Ernst August took care of, admittedly less secretly, the welfare of his mistress with whom he had two children and also, besides beautifying Herrenhausen, he looked after the future of his daughter Sophie Charlotte who was at the time curtseying before the great Elector at the Prussian Court in order that she might later marry his son Friedrich III von Brandenburg. In that way the desire of the Duke to bind the Houses of Welfen and Hohenzollern would be fulfilled. When the Prussian son-in-law ascended as Ruler in 1688, a far greater desire which his daughter Sophie Charlotte energetically supported, was to be fulfilled. She understood that in case of need, Leffmann Behrens would have to help because the matter would prove expensive. Friedrich III had only one aim: to attain a King's dignity. Just as Duke Ernst August had been able to gain the 9th Electorate by the payment of a considerable sum of money, he, the Elector of Brandenburg wanted to set a King's Crown on his head by making a similar contribution.

No, it was unthinkable. 'Not under my Sceptre!', shouted the Emperor and then perhaps supposed that, bled white financially as he was by two wars against the Turks: How many ducats could Potsdam send to the Viennese treasury if one could find an irrefutable way to negotiate such a crown? Leopold I found a way: Look abroad. A King of Brandenburg in the Holy Roman Empire was not a possibility but beyond the frontier where the Emperor's omnipotence did not extend lay the solution to all those ideas: there, in the distant north-east lay the Duchy of Prussia which belonged to Brandenburg! If the Elector of Brandenburg chose to set a King's crown on his head in Königsberg and thereafter call himself not King *'of'* Prussia but rather King Friedrich I *'in'* Prussia, then everyone would be agreeable, despite the anticipated objections of the Pope. Everyone did agree, especially as there were rewards. The Emperor was able to demand two million ducats for himself for this chess-move. The German clergy requested 600,000 ducats and for their persuasive arguments the Jesuits took 20,000 Reichstaler. And naturally in Vienna one expected that the Emperor would be able to call upon Prussian troops at any time.

How much Leffmann Behrens advanced toward these enormous sums is unknown. But it is certain that he helped his colleagues in Potsdam to raise the moneys. After all, he was related to the Senior Court Factor there.

Duke Ernst August did not live to see his son-in-law crowned, nor the gigantic procession of knights that set off on a cold day on 13 December 1700 from Potsdam to Königsberg in order to reach their goal on 18 January 1701: Friedrich III did in fact set his crown on his head himself before crowning his spouse Sophie Charlotte and letting himself be anointed by two Protestant bishops.

Georg Ludwig, the ruling Duke of Hannover who was not present at the coronation of his sister, was meanwhile considering when the next ceremony between the Welfen and Hohenzollern families could take place. His daughter Sophie Dorothea was almost of marriageable age and one had already set one's sights on a suitable Prussian Prince for her. How satisfying that Leffmann Behrens would assume responsibility for the preparation of this celebration, so long awaited by the family.

Naturally in splendid Herrenhausen.

# Bendix Goldschmidt's Patron

The Duke of Schwerin was satisfied. The tobacco monopoly under the control of Bendix Goldschmidt and Israel Fürst brought in goods to the value of 100 Taler annually and because the pair of them were also responsible for the lights at the court and delivered torches and candles and procured horses and wine, not to mention jewellery, Duke Friedrich Wilhelm showed his gratitude toward them and their partner, the Court Jew Hinrichsen, alias Henriques, in an unusual document. They received a privilege (which was repeatedly confirmed) which assured them of the freedom to deal in all kinds of merchandise and in any amount and beyond that an exemption from all taxes and duties as well as permission to buy land *'Auf der Schelffe'* in Schwerin. They were allowed to let, to build and certainly to live there. Their religious ceremonies were permitted and they could bury their dead in *'a convenient place'*.

However, probably neither Bendix Goldschmidt nor the old Fürst settled themselves there because they had their offices in Hamburg where the Exchanges were and where they were able to oversee the unloading of their precious cargoes from faraway countries in the harbour. And so they agreed that their colleague Hinrichsen should remain in Schwerin and undertake everything that needed doing there and that Bendix would visit once a quarter to check on everything in a quick visit.

The duke could understand that. Bendix Goldschmidt was reliable in his care for all the money transactions that benefited the Court. He even set up a wax bleaching works so that the Duke could enjoy pure white candles. And in return, so that the dear bankers should not freeze in cold Hamburg, he commanded his Head Hunts-master (on 3 May 1701) *'that Secretary Krull deliver 30 Faden'* (about 30 cubic meters) of fire-wood each year to the Court Jew Bendix Goldschmidt.

The Duke used his influence for his Court Jews in legal matters as well. In disputes it was the Ducal Court and not the city council that was relevant. Apparently the Duke knew his Christian subjects well enough to realise that they would have dual standards when a Jew appeared before them as plaintiff. In Mecklenburg justice would be done: on 23 April 1697 Bendix Goldschmidt complained to Friedrich Wilhelm in writing that the shopkeepers were breaking the tobacco monopoly again by secretly selling tobacco under the counter in packages that had not been assessed for duty and that it was principally the Duke's interest that was being damaged. Four weeks later the Duke commanded 'all Officials, Mayors, Clerks, Courts and Councils' to protect the privileges of Hinrichsen and Goldschmidt.

The wax bleaching operation that Bendix ran as entrepreneur was particularly successful. At the end of 1705 he concluded a contract to deliver white and yellow wax lights to the Court for the next four years. When the contract was extended for a further six years in January 1709, Goldschmidt suggested extending the wax bleaching works so that *'in time trade could be widened to the Mecklenburg Land and so that the Excise could benefit'*.

Friedrich Wilhelm was always willing to extend his interests and he listened gladly to Goldschmidt's ideas, objections or requests. Thus, years earlier, he had acted on Goldschmidt's observations. So that the Court Jews could widen their trading over a greater area without having to pay a duty on their own bodies as if it was an object, as was usual for Jews whenever they passed through the city gates, the Duke had summarily cancelled the body or head tax as being a humiliation.

> *By God's Grace Friedrich Wilhelm etc. announces and makes known that we for special merciful reasons exempt our Court Jews and Jewellers Bendix Goldschmidt and Michel Hinrichs from the poll-tax as long as they live and order all and every of our Excise Administrators, especially in Dömitz and Boizenburg that they respect this ruling and that they will not demand the poll-tax from Bendix Goldschmidt or Michel Henrichs nor each and every Jew passing through, whether they be poor or rich but to record the names of the travelling Jews in their registers and to only demand duty on the goods which are subject to duty and which they have with them. This is Our merciful Will and Opinion.*
>
> *Certified by Our Princely Hand-mark and Seal.*
>     *Effected at Our Residence and Fortress in Schwerin 17 July 1701. (signed) Friedrich Wilhelm.'*

This innovative Certificate was extended for a further 30 years after Hinrichs' death in 1715 and was soon recognised in many small German States. The poll-tax on Jews was only finally abolished by the Emancipation Edict in 1812.

Bendix Goldschmidt was not somebody who was just satisfied with his own achievements. He could never be sure just how long his patron would live nor how long he, as a Jew, would continue to be welcome at the Court.

In Schwerin he was regarded as the most important Court Banker. He managed the Dutch Subsidies, he made short-term advances in case of need out of his own pocket, he took care of the money transfers to the Mecklenburg diplomats and to the troops stationed in the field and, at the same time, he was a gladly welcomed guest at the Duke's relations in Güstrow and Strelitz. At Christmas 1709 he delivered five diamonds to a value of 45,000 Reichstaler to the Duchess Christiana Amalia Antonia, the widow of the Duke Adolf Friedrich von Mecklenburg-Strelitz. However, he only received payment for a third of this on 28 December 1709, for the rest he had to wait *'most respectfully'*. In such matters, Bendix was patient but never for longer than one year, then he made an approach to at least obtain payment of a partial amount.

At the same time he worked at the Court in Gottorf, which had just allied itself with the Swedes against Russia in the Northern War and which, after the Duke Friedrich IV lost his life in the Battle of Klissow (19 July 1702), found itself in financial difficulties. The Duke's inheritor was his three-year old son Karl Friedrich, for whom his uncle officially acted as Regent, but unofficially the Minister Weddekop and Treasurer Freiherr von Görtz took over. Both gentlemen had long been good clients of Bendix Goldschmidt and now they could demonstrate their affiliation because in Kiel the Dowager Duchess Sophie Amalia had died (1704) and Bendix together with Israel Fürst was allowed to buy gold and silver from the Estate in the Palace at Kiel for 9,000 Taler out of the jewellery that had once been delivered there by Israel Fürst. On this occasion the old Fürst received '2 Marks and 2 Lots silver from the foot of a small table as a mark of gratitude for his nine years of discretion'.

Probably this noble gesture at the cost of the Court at Gottorf did not originate from the parsimonious Minister Wedderkop but rather from the Freiherr von Görtz. This spendthrift was continually seeking new sources of money and the families of Goldschmidt and Fürst, to whom the famous Leffmann Behrens belonged, could help as money-lenders. Israel Fürst, who was mainly occupied with the sale of valuables, was hardly in a position to give a large loan but Bendix Goldschmidt could. He was to fill the 'Savings Treasury' that the Freiherr von Görtz had set up so that the ducal treasury could help itself – however, 6% interest and 2% commission was to be handed over to the Freiherr. The Freiherr gladly played the generous patron for these extra earnings: he appointed Goldschmidt as provisions administrator to the Gottorf Court, gave him the salt monopoly for Schleswig and apart from new trading partners in Copenhagen, gave him the *'concession of the Lombards'* in Friedrichsstadt. Naturally the Freiherr and his friends helped themselves generously to the contents of the 'Savings Treasury'. Sums of money that were missing were not declared and when in the summer of 1708 it became apparent that Görtz had also taken credit of no less than 83,000 Taler in the name of the Court from Leffmann Behrens, the fraud was in the open. The Duchess Hedwig Sophie, mother of the under-age Karl Friedrich, drummed the Court together and demanded an explanation. The negotiations took time. By the time the Duchess died in December of the same year the whole matter seems to have been forgotten at the Court.

But for Goldschmidt, the business that might have brought him discredit was over. He remained provisions administrator for a time but then he turned his back on Gottorf. For a long time he had had had other ambitions. Firstly, he had enough to do in Schwerin and at the Courts of Ratzeburg and Mecklenburg-Strelitz, business was calmer there and from that distance he could watch the progress of his former patron the Freiherr von Görtz: The Freiherr must have departed Gottorf in very obvious haste; he served the Swedish King as advisor and on 28 February 1719 was beheaded in Stockholm for dubious political and financial tricks.

# Stirring Times

We do not know about the private life of Bendix Goldschmidt, only that in the meantime two sons grew up under the care of their mother Henriette. Although Jewish women, unlike their Christian neighbours, could almost always read and write, there has been no second Glückel von Hameln. She portrayed half a century with her 'Memories'. The women were at least bilingual (as well as the Hebrew they used in religious services) and they understood arithmetic astonishingly well, for they looked after the household accounts. Many of them continued to run the businesses left them by their deceased husbands very professionally, especially when it was a matter of pearls and gemstones which they could import cheaply from their relatives abroad and then sell on. The transport of such goods required no special precautions and also no protective masculine accompaniment. The men would have needed an escort's safe-pass for which they would have had to apply to the city-council, an unnecessary bit of bureaucracy for which they might wait months without knowing whether it would be mercifully agreed. Pearls and gemstones were easily sewn into the seam of a skirt and carried from principality to principality without bother from the excise-men. The baroque style of Court was indeed still unchanged 'en vogue'.

In some cases it seemed as if the death of the head of the family released enormous energy in the often young widows, at least until they remarried, as was proper, and once again cared exclusively for the family household. They were responsible for the children and the servants too. Christian servants were forbidden to Jews by the authorities. Perhaps they would have learnt something about the other religion which for Christians had led the way from the rhythm of the feast-days to the last ecclesiastical benediction. Or even worse, they might discover the truth about the rumours that had been spread with a shudder since the middle-ages: Jews were reputed to have caught small Christian children only to slaughter them and drink their blood. One of the most notorious malignments that Catholic priests dreamt up to vilify their Jewish fellow citizens.

These scary atrocity myths had not been completely expunged from the heads of the gullible. In 1700, two volumes by a professor of the University of Heidelburg appeared. Johann Andreas Eisenmenger's (1654-1704) *Judaism*

*Unmasked. About the greatest falsities of the Jewish religion and theology, written for all true-hearted Christians.* In these one could find everything that most of his contemporaries had already forgotten: the bubonic plague, the black death, all the fault of the Jews who had poisoned wells but of course they themselves were unaffected thanks to their bloody ritual killings.

Already in 1236, this sort of nonsense which Emperor Friedrich II heard in Mainz, seemed so incredible that at a commission of high priests in Fulda he asked whether the Jews really used Christian blood on Good Friday. The question was decisively and unanimously denied. Ideas that had been rejected from the world of superstition in the thirteenth century were rekindled by the author Eisenmenger at the start of the eighteenth.

The Jews of Frankfurt who were the first to hold copies of the book in their hands immediately sent a written protest to the Emperor's Court Jew Samson Wertheimer with the request that he present himself to the Court at Vienna to prevent the further distribution of the work if at all possible, for they were concerned that it could incite the rabble and that the consequences could be momentous. And they were not wrong. Even as Samson Wertheimer, '*in the name of all Jews*', was laying his petition to confiscate the book, or at least prevent its sale in the streets, before the Emperor on 12 July 1700, the house of the imperial banker Salomon Oppenheimer was stormed and plundered by the mob. Leopold I, shocked by what had happened to his highly valued financier, caused the work to be impounded. Thus the 2,000 copies that remained unsold were put under lock and key for the next fifty years. But that was insufficient for the Frankfurt Jews who knew how many books were in circulation. They demanded that the work be destroyed and were prepared to pay Eisenmenger 12,000 Gulden. He, however, demanded more than double, 30,000 Gulden, an amount that the Jewish community were unable to scratch together.

A copy of Wertheimer's petition to the Emperor remained in the Hannover town archive. It was from Samson Wertheimer and was directed to Leffmann Behrens.

One can imagine that Leffmann Behrens discovered just how busily Eisenmenger set about getting his book printed in contravention of the Emperor's prohibition. Otherwise Leffmann would not have decided to hand over a copy of Wertheimer's letter to his Duke Georg Ludwig and to plead in an attached letter that he address the Emperor once again about the Jews' worries over the secret distribution of the book. The fact that this letter was given, not at one of the usual audiences which mainly dealt with business and policy but in a completely private courtesy visit on Christmas Eve at the Palace Herrenhausen is proof of the intimacy, despite the respectful deference, that existed between the Jewish Chamberlain and his Ruler. Duke

Georg Ludwig had long appreciated the worth of the man behind the fundraiser Behrens, who took devoted care of his needy fellow believers and who requested letters of protection for them that he then paid for himself. The Duke had often enough debated with his Secretary Leibniz on theological questions, about tolerance of other faiths, so it was no wonder that just two days later, on 27th December 1700, the Duke instructed his emissary at the Viennese Court, von Oberg, to inform the Emperor of the justified fears of the Jews of an inflammation of anti-Jewish violence. The Emperor immediately took action to see that his imperial vicar, Elector-Prince Johann Wilhelm supervise the implementation of the Emperor's commands as was the duty of such an imperial administrator.

Leffmann Behrens was clever enough not to give a penny toward the amount that the Jews in Frankfurt were prepared to pay the author Eisenmenger for the destruction of his book. In his eyes that would have been bribery. The Emperor's veto ended the Eisenmenger case for him. From other people we know that true church-going Christians were ready to give credence to Eisenmenger's medieval fairy tales. One of them was the Prince-Elector Friedrich III von Brandenburg, who with his spouse Sophie Charlotte, the sister of Duke Georg Ludwig, was on the way Königsberg to crown themselves, just at that time. The fact that the Duke of Hannover did not accompany his brother-in-law on this journey – which, because the route was normally through many soggy sumps and marshes, took place in the coldest winter month may seem strange. But he would not have been keen to travel for weeks on a sledge just to take part in a peculiar coronation in the far east when the War of Spanish Succession was brewing.

All possible diplomatic help was now required and troops were recruited for a possible struggle on distant battlefields. Leffmann Behrens had to look after the Hannovarian war chest and chase a throng of debtors so that he could grant the court more credit. The list of cases in which his Duke supported him, by Writs of Intercession, to gather in the debts of small but spendthrift courts such as Gotha, Weissenfels, Eisenach or Goslar is long. Also the Dean's Residences of Eichstätt, Paderborn and Münster who had spent astonishing sums on the purchase of jewels, knew how to stretch out the repayment of their debts, which is understandable when alone, one invoice for jewels given to the Bishop of Eichstätt was for 270,000 Gulden. If a cathedral chapter did not react to repeated reminders from Leffmann and – as for instance Hildesheim in 1700 – and wanted to avoid litigation so as not to annoy the Archbishop, then only an appearance before the Imperial High Court remained. There, the judges who were answerable only to the Emperor, did not cower before the appearance of a dean or count, there, one had to remain impartial even to a Jewish plaintiff.

Georg Ludwig von Hannover was truly a pleasure loving baroque prince who did not hide his mistresses, celebrated pompously in Herrenhausen and – enthusiastic about music as was his sister, Sophie Charlotte, who gave and conducted harpsichord recitals in Berlin, – he engaged the young Georg Friedrich Händel as his Court musical director for a salary of 1,200 Taler per annum. Despite this, the budget of his Principality did not go adrift thanks to the trouble that Leffmann Behrens took. Not even in 1703, when the threat of bankruptcy hovered over the portals of the Hofburg of the Emperor in Vienna. Or more precisely over the bank of Samuel Oppenheimer, the financial genius on whom the Emperor Leopold I was dependent.

Since the beginning of the War of Spanish Succession in 1701, Oppenheimer had advanced the Emperor a total of 8 million Gulden, which was to be repaid out of taxation. But the tax revenue was sufficient to repay only 3 million. The outstanding 5 million could be regarded as lost. And when Oppenheimer died on 3 May 1703 his bank broke under the weight of state debts. Because the Oppenheimers, through two married sons, belonged to the family in which everyone supported the others with interest-free loans, the débâcle was manageable. Also the Goldschmidt family and the banker Behrend Lehmann, whose daughter Lea had married Leffmann's grandson Isaak, helped.

Posterity is fortunate that Samuel Oppenheimer's gigantic library, which his friend Prince Eugen, a collector of distinguished and also Hebrew literature had presented him, had already been bequeathed to his nephew David Oppenheimer. He was the chief rabbi in Prague and husband of Leffmann's daughter, Genendel. When Leffmann learned that this costly library – 6,000 books and almost 1,000 manuscripts – was kept unprotected in Prague, he tried everything possible to bring it to Hannover, so as to know that it would be safe. Without doubt he spoke to his Duke about it because on 25 July 1703, the Duke sent him a Declaration which I give here, abbreviated and in modern words:

> *By the Grace of God, Georg Ludwig Duke of Braunschweig and Lüneburg etc. After Our dear and true Court and Chamber Agents Leffmann Behrens and his son humbly pleaded to Us, We wish that Our Cousin Duke Friedrich, equally loved by the Grace of Our Lord's mercy, impart a written concession to the Chief Rabbi David Oppenheimer so that when he, his wife or any of his children should come to Our Land, to live with their possessions in Our Neustadt, they be permitted to take pleasure from the same Freedoms and Privileges that Our Court and Chamber Agents and other Protected Jews enjoy.*

> *Therefore We declare by the Grace of God, that when he, the Chief Rabbi David Oppenheimer, his present wife or any of his children take up residence here in Our Neustadt for a long or short time, and when they apply appropriately, they should receive the same Letters of Protection and Safe-escort as Our Court and Chamber Agents and other local Protected Jews.*
>
> *Hannover, dated 25 July 1703. Georg Ludwig.*

This generous gesture by a Christian prince to a Jew who was unknown to him personally may be unique and stems exclusively from Georg Ludwig's personal relationship to Leffmann Behrens. Certainly the prospect of giving a roof to such an already famous library in his own Residence must have played a role. What else could the Duke do for the benefit of his *'beloved faithful servant'*? Give him permission to erect a new Synagogue to replace the crumbling old one. Herz Behrens, Leffmann's son wanted to take on the building costs, he could afford it. As his father's companion he had long been as well anchored in the business of money as he was with all the commandments of the Jewish faith. A man who more and more frequently represented his father on diplomatic journeys but who refused to deal with money or even to touch it on the holy Sabbath even if it meant that a transaction or a diplomatic mission failed. His wife Sara, usually referred to as '*Serchen*' in all documents, had been selected for him by his father, Leffmann. She was the sister of Samson Wertheimer who as Court Factor in Vienna had been involved in the confiscation of the deplorable Eisenmenger book and now, after the death of Samuel Oppenheimer, had been appointed by the Emperor as sole credit-giver of the government, equipped with far-reaching privileges that should rescue the desolate finances. Whether the Oppenheimer-heirs ever regained the 5 million Gulden blown in the War of Spanish Succession is not known. We only know from the Hannovarian State archives that Leffmann Behrens also forfeited at least 300,000 gulden through his support of the Oppenheimer Bank and that Georg Ludwig wrote to the Emperor on 29 November 1703 with the request that everything possible be done so that his Chamber Agent would recover his money. The concern of the Duke was not entirely selfless: if Leffmann was not 'liquid' the Court of Hannover, too, could slip into pecuniary difficulties. Who else was there to spring to their aid if the Subsidy moneys from Vienna were in default as was now expected?

Apparently by the spring of 1704 there had been no reaction from Vienna, so that Georg Ludwig wrote to the Emperor about the debt problem a second time on 15 April 1704. Probably at the same time Leffmann sent his son Herz Behrens to Bohemia where he presumably not only ventilated the subject of the library with his brother-in-law, the Senior Rabbi David Oppenheimer in Prague but also passed on Leffmann's instruction to travel to the Oppenheimer heirs in Vienna to discover whether a repayment of the debts was even thinkable.

Georg Ludwig helped his *'beloved faithful servant'* in the mission too: Herz Behrens, by now almost as important as his father at the Court in Hannover, took not just his own accountant on the journey but also a lawyer from Hildesheim as legal advisor at his side. But what the three gentlemen found at Vienna was an empty State coffer, a bankrupt Oppenheimer clan and many promises of 'later'. Prince Eugen, the friend and patron of the family, would hardly have met Herz Behrens and his brother-in-law David Oppenheimer in Vienna: the Field-marshall commanded the Emperor's troops and developed the strategy for the imminent battle of Höchstadt on the Danube. 1704 was a significant year.

In Hannover-Neustadt plans and options for the future were made: Leffmann was ready at any time to accommodate his daughter Genendel and her spouse the senior Rabbi David Oppenheimer; everything was prepared for the arrival of the valuable library for which the cornerstone had been laid by Prince Eugen himself. In a few weeks he would be at the head of an army to which mercenaries from the Principality of Hannover belonged and that would determine the fate of the Holy Roman Empire.

Of course a Senior Rabbi could not simply leave his congregation, and so in Prague, thousands of books and manuscripts were packed and impressed with the Prince-Elector's seal and freighted to Hannover. One may imagine just how many escort-certificates and excise declarations for the diverse State boundaries were needed. It was not unlikely that a lightly armed escort from Hannover accompanied the transport, the contents were of incalculable worth and the unsafe country roads were feared. (To complete the story the library did arrive safely and is now, to the continuing regret of the Jews of Prague, in Oxford.)

At the Court in Hannover not only the Subsidy Moneys and politics were discussed. The propositions of the Court Librarian Leibniz had long sparked over to the princely family: his pursuit of harmony; his conviction that all rash splits could be reconciled and unity reconstituted, and thus religious wars avoided; his respect for the dissimilarities of neighbours whose opinion one must learn in order to recognise that even apparently irrevocable differences come from the same sources. *'It is as if'* he wrote to Georg Ludwig's sister Sophie Charlotte on 8 May 1704 *'God created the universe so variously as there are souls or as if he has created so many worlds in miniature which at the deepest level are in agreement but appear to be different. That is my whole philosophy in a few words'*.

Leibniz had set his stamp on the Court with his philosophy, universal education and open-minded way of thinking for 28 years. Whether any of the Prince's children who were growing up at the time had the least benefit from his differential calculus or monadology is anyone's guess. Certainly he was always available for discussions with Prince Georg Ludwig and his Chamber Agent Behrens, especially concerning knowledge of different religions and the bridging of their contrary ideas. He had already made the suggestion to hold a symposium at which a Catholic Bishop should represent the Protestant view while he, Leibniz as a Lutherian, would take the side of the Catholic faith. This seemed much too curious and was rejected as was a prayer that he had drafted and could be used by all confessions refused on the grounds that it referred only to the Father but not the Son.

Leffmann Behrens may have talked to Georg Ludwig and his well-educated mother Sophie about the idea of a discussion about religions including Judaism, particularly as a Jew who had converted to Christianity had appeared in the Jewish community as a sort of wandering preacher. He wanted to convert obdurate Jewish souls to a belief in the Trinity – which for Jews was as unreasonable as it was superfluous, because God, the Only One is indivisible; all of us are his children and we have direct access to Him, no intermediary is required.

How often the convert, regarded by Jews as merely an apostate, was rebuffed by the Jewish community can be seen in this complaint: the congregation offered him money if he left them alone. He had of course always refused money. But in 1704 he was hurrying around the region between Hildesheim, Hameln, Stadthagen and Celle. When he appeared in Hannover and the Parnas of the Jewish community, who would rather have thrown money at him than listen to him, Leffman Behrens said that this man could not be silenced with money! He was to have his performance. At the Court. Duke Georg Ludwig had commanded.

Surprisingly quick decisions by rulers are not unusual. If something was thus achievable, then immediately, please. Or the day after tomorrow at the latest.

Messengers on horses rushed to Celle and Loccum, the eighty-year old Duke Georg Wilhelm von Braunschweig-Lüneburg-Celle had to be fetched; from Loccum came the abbot Gerhard Wolter Molanus, professor of Protestant (Lutheran) Theology at the University of Rinteln and a long-time friend of Leibniz. The Rabbi of Hannover-Neustadt, Aron Alterode had already been told of the date and that he should bring a pile of books with him from which the apostate would quote to prove the validity of the Christian religion; the apostate was counting on the books that he had listed being available in Hannover. What he perhaps had not expected was that the famous Rabbi Joseph Samson could be brought from Stadthagen so quickly. A religious dispute between practised intellectuals who would not be so easily matched by an ever-so convinced convert. Rabbi Joseph had to be there.

It is clear that Leffmann took control of matters here. How he managed to remain in the background is explained by his personalty, his wisdom and diplomacy. There was no time to lose. He chased messengers in his private carriage to Rabbi Joseph in Stadthagen with the demand, or rather a command to come to Hannover at once. Tomorrow at three-thirty there was to be a unique discussion in front of the Prince-Elector and collected Court in which he, Rabbi Joseph was indispensable. The apostate who had been travelling about was going to defend his knowledge as a baptised Jew, with the aid of passages from the Bible if needed. Certain books that were lacking should come too.

Immediately? What was that supposed to mean? He had just returned home from Evening prayer in the Synagogue, surely he could have his breakfast in the morning first?

No, at once please. The messenger knew what that meant: the miserable road! And Herr Behrens expected his guest before midday tomorrow at the latest, then there would be time for a snack. The coach of the Chamber Agent was very comfortable, the nags were supplied with oats. One was awaited.

How quickly the news spread. The neighbours were already gesticulating (who is unaware of the Jewish temperament!) in front of the Rabbi's house, where the books were being hastily gathered together and stowed in the coach. But it was midnight before they were ready to travel.

The carriage reached Hannover at eleven the next morning. Lange Strasse 8, Leffmann's house. Three hours later a lackey appeared requesting the presence of Rabbi Joseph in the name of the Prince-Elector to an audience in the city palace, of course accompanied by the Chamber Agent and Rabbi Aron. Both Rabbis had been precisely instructed by Behrens on how to appear before the dukes, such disputes were held standing, leaning was disobedient. One should be ready for surprises regarding the discussion. The apostate might produce new polemic written material that was possibly unknown to them. If the Rabbi Joseph needed time to consider a response then Rabbi Aron should leaf through the books which were lying on the table in the middle of the room as if he were seeking something particular. Otherwise they should communicate by glances.

It is a Monday in the middle of July 1704, according to the Jewish calendar 19 *Tammus*.

The mother of the Prince-Elector had made her private chamber available. In the ante-chamber where the discussion will take place, the Court

Councillors and all the officials are all standing together, stiff with respect, Leibniz among them. The abbot and the apostate are not visible; they are chatting with the Princes behind a door which a lackey is now opening so that the gentlemen may enter. Leffmann Behrens first, behind him Rabbi Joseph and then Rabbi Aron with a servant to carry the books. Some papers are already on the table set out for that purpose, mostly in Hebrew. Only then do the Courtiers arrange themselves in the background; they are not going to contribute. Only the Princes and the abbot Molanus, the highest spiritual authority, have the right to ask questions, perhaps also the Prince's mother Sophie who is sitting comfortably in an armchair a little way from the table with the old Duke from Celle.

Rabbi Joseph seems not to have noticed that the hostess Sophie has offered her hand after the Princes have said a word of welcome. A glance from Leffmann is enough and the Rabbi bows deeply and dares to touch the extended fingertips of the offered hand,

'Where is he from? And where does he live?'

The questions are obviously asked in French as is normal in educated circles; perhaps the Princess wishes to test the education of the Rabbi. 'I understand French' he answers 'I was born and grew up in Metz and now I live in Stadthagen'

Meanwhile the abbot observes the rabbis and then asked Leffmann for the name of the man that he seems to recognise. Ah, Joseph Samson! And suddenly he remembers that forty years before he had a public argument with him and other learned men and priests at the university in Rinteln. So they know one-another. Rabbi Joseph is noticeably relieved.

Whether the arrangement of the debaters next to the long book table followed a plan or co-incidence is not known. The Prince-Elector positioned himself in the middle of a long side of the table, to his left his younger brother, Prince Ernst August, to his right Rabbi Joseph. Opposite, vis-à-vis the Princes, Leffmann Behrens between the abbot and the Convert, who immediately starts to proclaim with baroque circumlocution his fortunate conversion to Christianity by reason of various passages he has unearthed in the Holy Scriptures, and that he now will...Rabbi Joseph throws a glance over the list of quotations, written in Hebrew, that the apostate has in his hand and is appalled: This could take all day.

It does. And the speaker has not even found his theme yet. Finally the Rabbi Joseph lets his energetic 'Now!' be heard, which in no way stems the Convert's flow of words. A second 'Now!', this time in a louder voice to signify that the other should get to the point.

It could not have been more Jewish. Now the Convert turns directly to the Princes: '*Your Majesties have typical Jews before them! Always interrupting!*

*Never letting others finish!'* And then, turning to Rabbi Joseph, *'who requested your presence here? I asked for Rabbi Aron, because of the books. What do you want here?'*

Rabbi Joseph had anticipated the question and had his answer, prepared with Leffmann, ready: *'It was my intention the travel to Hildesheim, there Herr Leffmann asked me to come to the conference to hear how a lapsed Jew talks about our Holy Books and desires responses from us. Thus am I here. But should Your Majesty the Prince-Elector so command, I will humbly withdraw.'* with these words he stepped (as had been previously arranged) back a little.

The Prince-Elector, dry and short: *'He stays!'*

So Rabbi Joseph had something more to say: *'Your Majesty the Prince-Elector! I interrupted the speaker not only because he is beating about the bush, but with my intrusion I wish him to finally come to the beginning of his actual speech.'*

Abbot Molanus agreed and the Prince-Elector bid the apostate to keep it brief. Whereupon he folded together the large document that he had spread before him and jumped to the middle of his actual speech. To Jesus as the unique medium between God and humanity and he quoted from the tract that the long deceased Rabbi Saul Mortiera had written, a passage that he hoped would be unknown to the listeners. But he was wrong. For Rabbi Joseph did know the text and advised the speaker that this quote was unfortunately not serviceable because it referred to Moses as intermediary (Book of Deuteronomy, Chapter 5, Verse 5) in which Moses carried the Ten Commandments down from the mountain Horeb to his people.

A shocked sobering up. But the apostate immediately presented a second quote, again from a largely unknown work of an Isaak Arama in the sixteenth century. The book was not on the table, the apostate had only an excerpt which the Rabbi Joseph would now kindly read for himself, it was on the theme of circumcision, an action that since the time of the Messiah had been unnecessary. The slightly overwhelmed Prince-Elector threw a couple of questions and Rabbi Joseph explained to him that even if the Christian faith belief allowed that eternal peace had reigned since the time of the Messiah 1,700 years ago, non-Jews who wished to take the Jewish faith would continue to be circumcised; it was not just a form of commonalty...*'it does no harm'* said the Abbot so as to close the point, *'even our Saviour was circumcised according to the law after his birth'.*

Now, of all things, the convert seized on the Book of Zohar, a kabbalistic wonder-book full of symbolism and number mysticism. However, he found himself among Jewish theologians who, as non-kabbalists were very sceptical of this type of irrational mysticism and his thoughts were thus rather out of place. At this point Rabbi Joseph was easily able to flatten the arguments of the apostate almost before he began to speak, while at the same moment the abbot seemed to be whispering an explanation to the Elector.

At once the came a command from the Elector: this book will not be discussed! Next topic. For both Christians and Jews, the inexhaustible Isaiah, in which, according to the apostate, everything the Christian Church was based on could be found.

He particularly wanted to refer to Chapter 60 – which prompted the Rabbi Joseph to ask the Elector for permission to make a remark on the first three verses.

The Elector gave permission.

But the remarks which were supposedly intended only to clarify some misunderstandings of interpretation, developed into one of the most profound digressions over the appearance of light at the creation of the world as recorded in Isaiah and the meaning of and change of light, yesterday, today and in the messianic future. After this equally poetic and philosophical addition, the discussion took an odd turn because the apostate put forward the theory that after the Messiah appears, all peoples who believe in God might call themselves Israelites. It is written: *"all they gather themselves together, they come to thee"*.

The Elector, probably already thinking beyond this said *"Does that mean that every nation, from whichever direction shall come?"*

*"Exactly"*

And again the Elector, almost to the point *"Then the Jews need not let themselves be baptised!"*

A princely answer that appealed to the rabbis but which the apostate evaded so as to get to his next idea as quickly as he could: the various names of the Messiah, who at first was a Spirit but who, after He took on the form of man, as written in Ezekiel 1, verse 26 was named Adam because he had become the new Adam.

The Rabbi asked the convert if he would translate the word 'adam'. But Rabbi!" the Abbot Molanus interrupted: *"we know that Adam means 'man' in German!"*

"My Lord Abbot," responded the Rabbi now:

> *He who instructed me as to the proper German meaning of 'Adam', is He who created Heaven and Earth. Thus, it is written in the story of the creation: "Male and female created he them; and blessed them, and called their name Adam". Thus the Holy Scriptures tell us that only male and female together were called 'Adam'. It is therefore impossible to give your Messiah the name Adam because he was alone, he never had a*

*spouse. And by the way, the Verse in Ezekiel, where the appearance of the Spirit is described, belongs to the study of the Kabbalah!*

At this point the Dowager Duchess called: *"Herr Rabbi, come and explain that to me!"*

The listeners, thankful for the lively interruption, relaxed a little, they had all been standing for some time, the gentlemen, except for the ecclesiastics, in heavy chest-length wigs, Leffmann Behrens of course without a wig, just a dark beret over his platinum curls. We see them in an oil-painting by the court portrait artist, Andreas Scheits. Leffman is now around seventy, Abbot Molanus somewhat older. Discipline and patience were virtues that one required at that time. After the Dowager had her explanation she no doubt checked with the abbot whether is was truly so written in the Scriptures, which he could confirm.

The audience mumbled their astonishment.

The apostate, a bit off his stride then accused the Jews of obstinacy. The Patriach Gamaliel had already complained of that at the time of Christ.

*"I know the text"* said Rabbi Joseph, *"perhaps the braggart can tell us where it is to be found?"*

But the apostate remained silent. Even when asked three times, he knew no answer.

*"Well! Do you know then, Rabbi Joseph?"* asked the Elector.

*"Naturally. It is in the Gospel."*

*"You read the Gospel?"*

*"Yes, Your Majesty, I hope I do no wrong."*

*"Certainly not"* replied the Elector. And then turning to the apostate: he should not spout so much Latin, *"Speak German! So that the people can answer you!"*

Just who he meant by 'people' remains unclear. But the Rabbi Joseph thanked him at once and added: *"Until now I have understood everything."*

*"Good"* nodded the Elector.

Two hours might have passed, some of the audience discreetly signalled to the Elector that the Rabbi, rather tired from standing so long was leaning on the edge of the table rather more often. He should take a seat called the Elector to him. The Rabbi obeyed at once, and then soon sprang up again.

At last the apostate moved decisively to the offensive and requested the Elector to command the Rabbi to swear which religion he held to be the right one, the Jewish or the Christian. The Rabbi was unable to hold back; he invoked all the biblical references, which tested the ability of the audience to stay standing but which we will not pass on to the reader in their fullness.

His first phrase in a loud voice seemed more like a ritual prayer:

*In God's name and with His help, what should I say! Your Royal Majesty! Humbly do I acknowledge that I have often taken part in religious debates but never other than defensively, that is to refute something, never in the offensive, never to persuade believers of other faiths. And so have I conducted myself today, defensively as is seemly. However, if anyone here should take what I have said so far as being evangelical then I must protest! I am not accustomed to speaking ambivalently.*

Short aside by the Elector: *"He speaks well enough."*

*Your Royal Majesty! It seems as if my opponent wishes to reach into my soul because he is trying to damn our Jewish nation. It is written in the Gospel that anyone who does not believe and is not baptised is not blessed. But we Jews do not condemn anyone who believes in God as the Creator of Heaven and Earth. In our Scriptures (Exodus 19,5) it is written: then ye shall be a peculiar treasure unto me above all people, but not that others are damned. It is also written "thou shalt not abhor an Egyptian; because thou wast a stranger in his land." He has indeed done us ill but he let us live in his land. How much greater is our obligation to meet the high authority with awe for we live under your protection and seek our sustinence in your land. It is written in Jeremiah "And seek the peace of the city whither I have caused you to be carried away captives, and pray unto the LORD for it.." Thus it is our holy duty to pray to the Almighty for our ruler, which we do and will continue to do. May God exalt our Elector-Prince, watch over him, shelter him and protect him and bless all his enterprises. Amen.*

Just in the moment when the rabbi allowed himself a pause in his momentum, the Abbot Molanus took the opportunity to invite the Rabbi Joseph to his house for the next day, an invitation that was gratefully accepted.

But could he ask another question of him as representative of the Jews: whether he knew the reason for their exile? One knew that the Jews were driven out of their land for their transgressions – the three sins of incest, worship of false gods and blood-letting and that they were taken into Babylonian captivity and that their Temples were destroyed but these reasons were not given for the second expulsion and the destruction of the second Temple. *"At that time, the time of the Roman Government, were you not guilty of the same three sins?"*

Rabbi Joseph contemplatively: *"Who knows God's will? He has indeed scattered us over every land but we must remain united in the acknowledgement of the one true God".*

The answer was perhaps not comprehensive enough. And so the rabbi decided to name the current sins of his fellow believers with an unmerciful honesty. Indeed only two Jews were present to hear this, Rabbi Aron and Leffmann Behrens, who were truly the least culpable: *"Each of us seeks his own advantage and wants no competition from other Jews! No matter how many Christians live nearby, he will not tolerate a second Jew! That alone is the origin of the endurance of our exile!"*

The Rabbi knew his people, who, because the authorities demanded it, would chase the beggar Jews, who might bring shame on them, out of the town and allow no asylum-seekers among them and who were worried that their Letters of Protection might be forfeit if they contravened the rules and that they might in their turn be put on the streets and be chased out. How closely they were all lumped together!

But because this statement by the Rabbi Joseph was insufficient, he added a storm of quotations that came from all the books from Genesis to Jeremiah and demanded the last shred of self-discipline from the audience who had by now been standing for three and a half hours – until suddenly the Elector left the room without a word: the signal that the gentlemen councillors and officials were permitted to follow so as to at last relax their stiff legs in the ante-chamber. Leffmann Behrens went with them. Only the old Duke of Celle and the Dowager Duchess remained with the two rabbis and the apostate whom the Duchess waved over to her to set a further question. She lacked a proof for the correct validity for one or another religion. The gentlemen would please be seated.

Because they remained standing out of deep respect, the old Duke grumbled: *"She commands you to be seated!"*

The gentlemen obeyed and the apostate explained that he still had something to prove,

*"But as yet you have proven nothing!"* exclaimed the Duchess.

*"No!"* agreed Rabbi Aron *"he has proven nothing yet and he will be able to prove nothing."*

For Rabbi Joseph the last remark seemed to have brought the moment to make his departure from the Princess with a deep bow and many thanks. But she had the last word: *"I thank you! We all have the same true God".*

In the ante-chamber the other gentlemen were still in discussion together and when the Rabbi Joseph came out of the chamber with the Elector-Princess to join them they bowed before them with applause.

We should thank Rabbi Joseph of Stadthagen for the transcription that he later made of the debate. Certainly he only noted the parts that were important to him: A document of the only known public religious debate between Christians and Jews at that time. A copy in the Hebraic script, that was made for Gumprich ha-Levi of Göttingen in 1721 was found among the family treasures of Aron Hirsch of Halberstadt. At his request the script was translated out of Hebrew by Prof. Dr Abraham (Adolf) Berliner and in 1914 privately published in two languages by Louis Lamm.

During the whole debate, Leffmann Behrens had remained silent. He was indeed a devout man but no theologian and he clearly understood how easily a single remark that might be misinterpreted could damage the respect which he was given by the collected courtiers. He had his reasons for hurriedly fetching Rabbi Joseph who was experienced in such religious debates from Stadthagen. If the seventy-year-old Leffmann Behrens was able to stand for three and a half hours, it was because he felt himself responsible as the initiator of this debate and wanted to maintain his usual respectful attitude to the Elector-Prince until the end.

For the baptised Jew, who is nowhere given a name, the debate ended without any resulting success. He disappeared nameless into the history of the year 1704, while at the same time another, whose name one hoped not to hear again suddenly became a worrying topic once again: Eisenmenger, the author of the book that the Emperor had confiscated, *"Judaism Unmasked"* had died and his heirs were attempting with untiring energy to get the Emperor's edict reversed. But Leopold I was not open to persuasion. Also his successor Joseph I, who ascended the throne in Vienna in May 1705, stubbornly continued to forbid the book. Even when the heirs coaxed the Prussian King Friedrich I to persuade the Emperor they had no success. Only six years later did the Eisenmenger heirs achieve anything. After Friedrich I had been deeply impressed by the appearance before him of two converted Jews who were convinced that Christianity was the only true religion, did he allow the book to be reprinted in distant Königsberg where the Emperor's censure could not reach. Oddly by 1711, it was hardly taken notice of, at any rate the Jews were relieved to find that it caused no damage.

Actually, Rabbi Joseph wanted to return to Stadthagen directly after the religious debate but Leffmann Behrens held him in his house for a further eight days until the summer-fair had started and other guests were expected. Presumably the Goldschmidt relatives from Altona arrived, Bendix with his two sons Ruben and Aron. By now they were well established merchants thanks to the tobacco import business and gemstone dealing. Both were married to cousins of the Fürst line which makes our perspective of the weave of relations much more complicated. Leffmann's son Herz too, would have visited his father; he lived in the same Langestrasse, just a few doors away, which was ideal if there were any important things to be agreed quickly. As Leffmann increasingly started to feel his age, Herz must have taken on commissions as his deputy ever oftener, especially if inconvenient journeys were required. As Court Factor, Herz had long enjoyed the same recognition and trust as his father, one spoke of them as the Behrens Firm. A house without women? Certainly professionally. Leffmann lived as a widower surrounded by clerks and house servants almost exclusively in his counting house. Whether he yearned for a second marriage after the death of his beloved Jente, we do not know. It is certain that there was an 'Elke' whom he presented as his wife.

Nobody is able to tell us what Herz Behrens' family life was like. His wife Särchen (Sara) Wertheimer gave him four children: the first born died aged eleven and the other three were married to well chosen partners, and maybe his daughter Lea had made the best catch. A son of the banker Berend Lehmann had been selected. It was Berend who had been assisted by Leffmann in the financing of the Polish Crown for his employer the Saxon Elector-Prince. Herz's second daughter married Salomo Philipp, Chamber Agent of Mecklenburg-Strelitz who on occasion helped the Goldschmidt relatives when they were on their way to Denmark as often was the case.

The relatives would presumably not have travelled with their wives and children to the Annual Fair in 1704 because only two months later the important Jewish feast-days took place. The whole family would take part to celebrate Sukkot, the Feast of Tabernacles, to sing, to pray and finally to greet the New Year but not as elsewhere according to Roman tradition with fireworks and jumping jacks. The Jewish calendar counts the New Year from the time that the harvest is gathered from the fields and vineyards in autumn: Then can one reflect to oneself self critically what the year has brought. Humility is appropriate. No lamenting. In many places one visits the graves of relatives in the cemetery the evening before to *'pour out one's heart'*. One understands the thanks that are due the ancestors, the role-models. And on this earnest evening one remembers the centuries old verse from Job:

> *"Ask the former generation*
> *and find out what their ancestors learned,*
> *for we were born only yesterday and know nothing,*
> *and our days on earth are but a shadow"*

# Departures

The Prussian Royal Court laid no worth on self-pity and when the Queen Sophie Charlotte wanted to visit her aged mother Sophie in Hannover she did not cancel the journey despite a serious throat inflammation and despite the atrocious cold January 1705. She was the old Elector-Princess' only daughter, and one such as she, this delicate artistic Muse who had given birth to the crown-prince and undertaken the days long winter journey to Königsberg for the coronation, knew no pity for herself. Feverish, wrapped in furs she reached the palace where she had grown up with her brothers. But some days later, on 1 February 1705 she died there '*unexpectedly*'. At 37.

Sophie Charlotte, Queen of Prussia and sister of King George, in Schloss Charlottenburg.

How much she must have had to discuss with her Elector-Prince brother Georg Ludwig, whose daughter, her niece, Sophie Dorothea was to marry her son the Crown Prince Friedrich Wilhelm. At first in deep mourning, the nineteen-year old bride's dreams of wedding dresses had to be postponed. Special wishes such as silk brocade in the latest fashion could only be ordered from Paris. But at that moment mercantile relations with France were icy. But Leffmann Behrens, who still had his agents from earlier in Paris, would without doubt get everything delivered to gladden the heart of Sophie Dorothea, whom he had known since she was a child. Everything else that the bride's trousseau lacked could be bought in Hannover; furniture, beds and linen to a cost of 10,793 Taler. (The 'Hannover History Sheets' recorded in 1904.)

The suddenly widowed King Friedrich was determined to spare no expense to give his dead wife's remains a worthy homecoming to Berlin. It was not possible to organise overnight. Prussian protocol demanded an exact implementation and was gigantic. No-one could calculate how many weeks were needed for the preparations for the Memorial Service and the Sarcophagus to be made by Andreas Schlüter. So Sophie Charlotte's body was embalmed in Hannover and only on 9 March 1705 sent to Berlin. The cortège, accompanied by knights on horse, took thirteen days with many stations for the proscribed bell-ringing and gun-salutes in the garrisons before the old chapel of rest in the Cathedral in Berlin was reached. The coffin was laid there until the official burial in the Cathedral Crypt on 28 June 1705.

What a year for deaths. In May the death of the Emperor Leopold I was mourned in Vienna; on 28 August 1705 the very aged Duke Georg Wilhelm von Braunschweig-Celle died. He had given our family so many exceptionally accommodating Letters of Protection.

And at the start of the new year in Hannover the Goldschmidts were standing around the grave (No.108) of the head of the family, Levin Bendix Goldschmidt, called Löb Hannover who had died on 24 January 1706. Leffmann Behrens, his last living brother-in-law had organised the ceremony in the Synagogue that he and his son Herz had sponsored. The entry in the '*Memorbuch*' was read out to the congregation:

> *As eulogy we remember the honest and true Juda Löb, son of Baruch Bendit of the Levi tribe out of the Goldschmidt family and son-in-law of the well-known and highly respected Joseph Hameln. From the purity of his heart he practised charity his whole life long and showed his love far and wide. He was devout and prepared to make sacrifices. He built a Synagogue to praise God and caused the Duke to prevent the de-*

*consecration of the cemetery. In all his doings he was good and noble. He died on Saturday the 9th Shewat 5466 and was buried the next day.*

The death had been very unexpected and so his son Bendix and none of the family in Hamburg were able the attend the burial. But the Goldschmidts were all there. At their head were Rubin and Uri Phobus, sons of his second marriage to Frau Merle. And of course the family of Leffmann's son Jakob who had died early: his widow Süsse Gomperz and her six children whose education had been paid for by Grandfather Leffmann. His youngest grandchild had only just come into the world after Jakob died; three granddaughters were still in the family home while the two eldest, Isaak and Gumpert were already employed in Leffmann's counting house. Leffmann had arranged suitably rich wives for them both. Gumpert had finished a bank apprenticeship in Frankfurt and in 1705, had married *'the daughter of the rich Herr Kann'* who was called Sprinze, perhaps because of her Sephardic given name *'Esperanza'*. Isaak, regarded as the first-born and later to be the head of the Behrens Bank was married to Lea, a daughter of Behrend Lehmann whom we have already met as a trusted financial genius. And thus Isaak had the best opportunity to be welcomed as the financially sound Court Jew to the Prince-Elector Georg Ludwig in Hannover.

First however, under Leffmann's watchful eye, his son Herz handled the Prince's commissions. Now after the deaths and a black year of mourning were past completely new matters needed attention at the Courts in Hannover and Berlin.

# Marriages

The palace at Herrenhausen was refurbished. Whoever married his daughter to the Crown Prince in Prussia knew what to expect. Friedrich I was the last Prussian Ruler who understood something of boundless baroque extravagance and he made appropriate demands. There had been no paved way here since Roman times. When the Prussians with an expected cavalcade of 870 horses arrived to carry away the bride in a fabulous carriage from the wedding ceremony to the yoke of married life in Berlin, there was no need for a thousand hooves to raise the dust near Herrenhausen! Now at least the route between the Leineschloss in Hannover and Herrenhausen was surfaced.

The new relationship between two dynasties – of which the Brandenburg was not actually noble, if one looked closely – was first blessed in November 1706 but this was not because of the year of mourning. Instead it was necessary that the bridegroom should be 18 so as to marry. He attained the age of majority on 15 August 1706, high time for the bride, who at nineteen was already unusually old for a bride at that time.

The planning according to strict Prussian pattern was under way. At the Court in Hannover, the robes that Sophie Dorothea had desired had arrived from Paris, God knows how. Leffmann Behrens had advanced 19,946 Taler for them, also another 26,801 Taler for jewellery which the Prince-Elector had ordered Leffmann to get for his daughter.

In order to make the waiting time before the wedding pass more amusingly for Sophie Dorothea, Georg Ludwig drove them to Bad Pyrmont, a health spa in the summer. There they both enjoyed not just the spring waters and admired the new palace but also took lessons in Hebrew from a Herr Jablonski. They should at least be able to decipher the writing – perhaps the religious talks also woke a longer-lasting interest. While Leffmann Behrens served at this court there could be no mention of the anti-Jewish feeling that was common elsewhere. Rather a certain curiosity had arisen, especially from the Princess-Elector and her children, to understand these Jews, who despite all humiliations had achieved so much. Leibniz, from whom we learn about the visit to Bad Pyrmont, (Letter to Henrietta Ch. von Pöllnitz) had without doubt spurred the open-mindedness of the

Hannovarian Prince. In Berlin, where he often visited Queen Sophie Charlotte, he would hardly have had the same effect on the Calvinist Prussians.

There have been many spectacular reports about the pompous wedding ceremony between the daughter of the Welfen family and her cousin Friedrich Wilhelm of Brandenburg. He later became less spend-thrift in Berlin but what happened after Leffmann had done his best for the bride is not our story.

By now all of Leffmann's grandchildren had stood under the chuppa, the wedding canopy. New family names were Wertheimer, Oppenheimer, Lehmann and Gomperz, almost all were active in finance but there were also rabbis among them. These are mentioned less frequently however. Every wedding was celebrated in style but none so much as that of Genendel's son Joseph Oppenheimer with Tolze, a daughter of the Emperor's banker, Samson Wertheimer. He invited the complete congregation of the town where he had been born, Worms, to Vienna for the great occasion on 21 July 1706. Many granddaughters had moved to their husband's towns, to Halle, Dresden and Dessau. The few who had remained in Neustadt, Hannover were chiefly concerned with their own households and the care of their children. Who looked after the old Leffmann who had been a widower for twelve years, other than two maids, a foot-boy and a book-keeper? Elkele. The daughter of a Rabbi Jacob from the Gomperz side of the family. The nickname Elkele reminds one of the North-German name of Elke but actually she was probably really called Elischewa (Elisabeth). The assimilation into the Plattdeutsch dialect spoken near the coast was so normal that no-one was surprised when a Joseph became a Jobst or Chajim was called Hein.

If Elkele, whose age we cannot guess, visited the old man rather often, they could not give the impression of *'living in sin'*. Normally no widowed Jew remained unmarried for long, the done thing was to find a bride, preferably one who had been a near relative to the deceased wife. Age was unimportant. If she were younger, the family might hope for more children. Elkele cannot have belonged to these. Whatever the case, whether it was love or the need not to be alone in old age, in 1707 Leffmann and Elkele married and we may assume that the ceremony was modest, despite his wealth, and occurred quietly. Leffmann had never followed Court tradition as far as luxury was concerned. We have his oil-painting, where he observes the onlooker with all-seeing eyes full of wisdom, no courtier, a reserved gentleman with a dainty moustache and a thin rounded beard parted in the middle that touches his gold-coloured silk jabot or neck tie. A few years later the same court portraitist, Andreas Scheits, painted his grandson Isaak

Leffmann Behrens, oil by court painter Andreas Scheitz (Courtesy of the Fränkel family)

Behrens, whose grandmother's Sephardic ancestors are clearly apparent: the picture of an assimilated Jew, naturally with a curly chest length wig 'à la mode', a ruffled lace-jabot and – like no other Jew of his time – no beard. Between Leffmann and his grandson Isaak was just one generation but they were worlds apart. Indeed the grandson kept true to the religion that he grew up in. He kept the Sabbath and all the Jewish feast days but external appearances which would mark him as a Jew were avoidable. It was not a matter of assimilation at any price but rather more of emancipation. Times were changing noticeably, the tempo of life and work was accelerating. Leffmann Behrens still used a carriage and pair. His grandson Isaak required his own riding horse for his service at Court if the Prince's commission needed haste.

# Signs of the Time

In Vienna the financial position of the Emperor Joseph I looked as threatening as it had earlier and when in 1708 his banker Samuel Wertheimer, whose sister was wedded to Herz Behrens, no longer knew where he could raise credit to pay and arm the Emperor's troops who were battling against the French in the Spanish-Netherlands, only a call for assistance to the relations in Hannover could help – and at once Leffmann Behrens sprang into the breach with 200,000 Gulden.

Perhaps just at that moment his son Herz was on his way to Vienna or arranging the modification of his cloth factory in Lüneburg which he had extended to a cloth hall and dye-works. He was unavailable so that he could not relieve his father from a journey of many days to Brussels and Amsterdam that seemed very urgent. Oh, how urgent and with such a fidgeting impatience was this desire of the Duke Ernst August, that is the youngest brother of the Prince-Elector of Hannover, whom no-one could deny any daft wish. In this case: the acquisition of a conspicuously fine, uniquely expensive carriage that was only to be had in Brussels and that regardless of cost should be fetched either via Amsterdam and Rotterdam by sea to Bremen or by another absolutely safe transport that only the Chamber agent Leffmann was able to determine. Only he knew how to get around the various customs barriers. Naturally he should advance the costs for the splendid piece. It was all to be arranged by his agent in Amsterdam. And in the event that the youngest was unable to afford this idle wish to a value of 1,000 Taler, then certainly his princely brother Georg Ludwig would pay for it out of his private purse. The querulousness of the young duke (documented several times in letters) to become the owner of the carriage as soon as possible must have been so overpowering that Leffmann Behrens decided to undertake the onerous journey to Brussels himself despite his 73 years. Anyone who had been so closely linked to the Court in Hannover for decades and who had seen the small Ernst August grow up would not allow themselves any clemency. Nor fear. This journey would cross a war-zone. The English Field-Marshall Marlborough was in the process of conquering Lille with the help of Prince Eugen. Whether Leffmann travelled to Brussels is uncertain but in any case he stopped awhile in Amsterdam where he met many important business partners and a few Goldschmidt investors and meanwhile he let his son Herz in Hannover deal with all the Court commissions. There was no doubt that Herz Behrens managed everything to the satisfaction of his father and the Prince-Elector. The year before on 17 July 1707 he had received the merchant privilege that was supported by a ten years older privilege from the previous Ruler and extracts are given here in a somewhat simplified form.

> *By God's Grace, We Georg Ludwig, Duke of Braunschweig and Lüneburg, Prince-Elector and Treasurer of the Holy Roman Empire etc.*
>
> *Certify that we, for especial reasons, permit our Court and Chamber Agent and beloved true Herz Behrens, exactly the same privilige, which Our Father, may he rest in God's Mercy, granted on 7th April 1697, which We confirm under today's date for dealing with Our Court Chancellor and Military Service in this Old City, him, Herz Behrens, also for dealing with foreigners, or those coming from other lands or travelling through, who find themselves in this local Old City and who themselves have no fixed abode here but are only lodging here, without any difference may they be of whatever standard or condition, freely and considered...*

Things were rather different for the children of Leffmann's son Jakob: Gumpert and Isaak still had things to learn. Particularly Gumpert, the younger, who had just finished his bank apprenticeship in Frankfurt am Main, lacked the experience and foresight that he needed if he were to stand on his own feet as quickly as he wished. Naturally he was already lending money but he hoped to make much more profit with gemstone dealing in the Court that so yearned for flamboyancy but he had not sensed that the times had changed. Besides the fact that war-like clashes on all the frontiers were creating insecurity and that no-one could know if tomorrow their own region would be involved, many baroque princes were meanwhile sated with noble knick-knacks. The princes, most of whom were already in the field, were rather more interested in new weapons than the jewellery that their fathers had decorated themselves with. On top of this many gentlemen and higher clergy no longer sought to invest their income in precious things whose value did not fluctuate: In a few big cities there were already banks that were fire and burglary proof.

Gumpert, with his great uncle Bendix Goldschmidt's brilliant career before his eyes, was convinced that he could conquer the royal courts with fashionable jewellery in the same old way. Therefore he bought-in jewels for

102,000 Taler in Frankfurt, where there were many gemstone polishers – an amount that would have shocked his grandfather Leffmann Behrens. How did Gumpert imagine that he would divest himself of his wares in an increasingly falling capital market! If the gemstones had been purchased on tick, then he would soon be trapped in a web of debt that only Leffmann could extract him from. And it was intended that Gumpert should lead the planned Behrens Bank with his brother Isaak at a later date.

The only calming factor for Leffmann was that after his death, which for a seventy-four year old could not be too far away, the fate of the famous Behrens firm would lie at first in the careful hands of his son Herz. But fate, of whom we so gladly believe only good, decided things differently. One day before the jolly Feast of Purim, on 23 February 1709, Herz Behrens died at the age of 52. With him, Leffmann lost, twelve years after the early death of his son Jakob, the second of his three children, and with him his strongest, absolutely irreplaceable support. The cause of Herz's death is not known to us: only that he was buried in Hannover.

Beside his widow Särchen (Wertheimer) he left two married daughters and a son, Seligmann, whose battered gravestone (1744) credits him with being *'a Benefactor to the Poor'*, an expression that says little. But because there are no state documents that mention him, we may presume that he was not active in his father's business.

All the work which Herz Behrens had taken off him in recent years was now back on the old Leffmann's shoulders. As ever he carried the full responsibility for complete budget of the Hannovarian Court which involved closing contracts with foreigners and managing subsidy moneys in millions. His money-lending business with his other private clients was independent of this. Gathering in debts from tardy court officials and secretaries in outlying counties cost time and patience. He was powerless against some of the manipulations of those taking his credit; such as in 1708 when the Bishop of Münster rather than repaying the debt in the correct way to the Chamber-agent Behrens, instead assigned a payment of subsidy money from England, a sum of 149,997 English Pounds, which the diocese anticipated receiving from London. Only Parliament in England had never authorised it or simply never paid it. This time, he could not even get help from his Prince-Elector Georg Ludwig, who in such cases, at any rate when it was a matter of heavily indebted bishops and Imperial Princes that he was friends with, would often send a pleasantly worded reminder or even sometimes give a guarantee for these gentlemen so that his banker would not be left in the cold.

The void that the sudden death of Herz Behrens ripped open was barely closable. Who could continue to manage the cloth factory in Lüneburg, who could take over his tobacco manufacture with the brand name 'Wilder

Mann'? Of his grandsons Isaak and Gumpert, who both were at the start of their careers, only the eldest Isaak, who had already started work in the 'Behrens firm' could help. Gumpert still needed to be supervised to avoid him making silly mistakes such as the reckless purchase of the gemstones and jewellery for which no takers were to be found at the moment.

The following year was as full of cares and sadness as the year 1709. On 23 September 1710 Bendix Goldschmidt's father-in-law, Israel Fürst, died in Altona. Even if the news of his death was sent post-haste, that is by a relay of fast horses between post-houses, to Hannover, it was impossible for any relatives from there to come to the burial. Certainly they would have been able to come together for the last days of the week of mourning in the Fürst house in Altona, to sit on low stools in a circle of countless reflective friends and comfort one-another. In the evening, a prayer for the dead. But sobbing lamentations were usually over by the end of the ceremony at the cemetery. Such days of mourning always gave the opportunity for the joy of seeing each other again after a long time. Exchanges of news and old memories. How many years had Israel Fürst worked together with Bendix Goldschmidt at the Court in Gottorf. How he had smoothed the path for him and his grandchildren to the Danish Royal Court.

Ten years before, when he was already an old man, he had travelled as the delegate of the Altona congregation to Copenhagen to have Frederick IV confirm and extend the Privileges of our family. Only through him did the sons of Bendix, Ruben and Aron, get the permit to live in the genteel 'Snarens Kvarter' in Copenhagen and to trade there. The farewells in Hamburg were hardly said before an event with which no-one had reckoned, occurred: on 2 November, Elkele, Leffmann's wife died in Hannover. She was buried on the following day, right next to his first wife Jente and his son Herz. Are the blows of fate in old age, when one is near the threshold of death oneself, easier to deal with? Or is it the vitality of spirit if there is no retreat into apparent sorrow?

Leffmann carried on managing his chores at work without allowing himself a break. His correspondence with truculent debtors increased as the payment morals of the time broke down. The Emperor needed another 100,000 Gulden in 1711, which Leffmann sent to Vienna to support his son-in-law, the Imperial Banker Wertheimer. How this was to be repaid was unclear. If it was not forthcoming from the Province of Moravia as agreed, then by a compulsory foreclosure to squeeze out the money. Promises veiled the risks that every Court Jew had learnt to live with in his profession.

There is nothing to learn about Isaaks Behren's activities. But Gumpert was now given the necessary polish by his grandfather so that he might possibly attain a position as factor at the court. At first he had just the normal Letter of Protection that guaranteed him the right to reside in Hannover but was insufficient for journeys beyond the frontiers of the land. Herz Behrens remained irreplaceable, not just as a reliable business partner but also as a member of the family. The only comfort for Leffmann was his daughter Genendel who was at last able to leave Prague with her husband David Oppenheimer and settle in Hannover. Her children had long grown-up and left home; only the youngest, Särle (Sarah) also lived here, newly married at seventeen to Chajim Jona Theomim Fränkel.

Besides his work in the counting house, Leffmann took care of uprooted Jews who were seeking accommodation or who needed a Letter of Escort; he let an inventory of the enormous Oppenheimer Library be made and he supported printers who were publishing Hebrew books. His activity seemed undiminished. The year of mourning for Elkele ended in November 1711 when Leffmann was 77 years old and then he married the much younger Veile (Veilchen..Violet?), the daughter of Jehuda Selke Dillman who is unknown to us. Nowhere is it mentioned where the wedding was celebrated. Probably in rather inconspicuous quiet with the grandchildren, both the widowed daughters-in-law, Genendel and her Oppenheimer partner, also the new Fränkels and of course all the Goldschmidt relations who lived nearby.

In the private arena everything seemed quite happy. In 1712 Leffmann received the honour of the privilege from Her Britannic Majesty Anne Stuart to travel unrestricted through her Kingdom. The Queen knew precisely who this Court Agent was; the transfers of money between London and Hannover passed through his hands. The connections from Court to Court were close: Parliament had selected Anne Stuart, or for the case that she died without heirs her aunt, Princess-Elector Sophie, a granddaughter of King James the First as Heir Apparent to the Throne; second in line was her son Georg Ludwig von Hannover. Nobody suspected that two years later fate would precipitously call Georg Ludwig to the succession of the throne.

While friendly messages came from London, in Vienna the business of money since the collapse of the Oppenheimer Bank became increasingly tense, so that in early 1712 Leffmann Behrens once again sought backup from his Prince-Elector, and Georg Ludwig immediately sent a Letter of Intercession for his Chamber Agent. Certainly it was also in his own interest. This is the appropriately wounded tone of the letter sent to the Imperial Secretary and Bohemian Colonel, Court Chancellor Count Wratislaw. (Here more easily read and abbreviated.)

*Especially dear Count.*

*Your good self no doubt remembers that the demands for money which our Court and Chamber Agent Leffmann Behrens has through the deceased Court Jew Oppenheimer, were for the major part settled by assignments on the Imperial Treasury in Bohemia and Silesia. One had until now, nothing other to expect than the rightful payments and such is primarily thanks to the Count's wealthy and benevolent co-operation. But because substantial arrears from the agreed payment schedule have arisen, not only Our above-mentioned Agent but also Ourselves are very anxious that the greatest full amount possible soon be paid, so that Our and also the Count's desire and inclination that everything be right and proper, and whose, as far as We are concerned, well-meaning disposition and willingness during loving tribulations, is known, so are We recommended, out of particular trust to the Count not to forebear to give our agent further protection and promotion to the best of our ability. We would therefore with much acknowledgement be very obliged...'*

What the Prince-Elector describes as 'substantial arrears' was about 100,000 Gulden, so not exactly a little sum. To emphasise the demand a Gentleman von Huldeberg was engaged at Leffmann's proposal, to try everything possible to extract something from the heirs of the Oppenheimers. Weeks and months went by without result. Leffmann Behrens supposed that sooner or later he would have to send his grandson to Vienna so that someone could seek justice personally. No-one knew whether Emmanuel Oppenheimer, the son and heir of the banker, had a secret deposit of money somewhere.

Wait. Patience. Make plans.

But then something happened that put all money worries into the shadows and made them unimportant: On 13 June 1712, Leffmann's daughter Genendel died at the age of 54. Genendel, there was an oil painting of her that captures her beauty and was even in 1913 still displayed at Frau Fanny Cohen's in Hannover, Genendel, the astonishing beauty left – perhaps the most valuable thing – her eighteen year old daughter, Särle (Sarah) who was expecting her first child shortly. If it were a girl, then her name would be Genendel. That was certain.

Only Särle's presence and the idea that the expected child might remind them of the lost Genendel, gave Leffmann new will to live. He knew that he could not neglect his work for the Hannovarian court. His lame money-lending business demanded decisions. In autumn he asked the Prince-Elector for a pass for his grandson Gumpert so that he could travel to Vienna and visit the Oppenheimer heirs who had still not repaid the loan.

In this autumn 1712, Särle's child came into the world and to her great-grandfather's joy it was a girl, a newborn Genendel. The precise date of birth has not been handed down and neither whether it was puerperal fever, childbed fever that Särle fell victim to – but she died on 22 October 1712.

Exhausted by the events of the last years, above all the deaths of three of his nearest and dearest, Leffmann wrote his will. And made Särle's baby girl, at just a few weeks old, his principal heir. All other important matters were handed over to his employee Michael David, with whom he had worked together for many years and whom he probably trusted more than his grandsons Isaak and Gumpert. That Michael David had already been very skilled in taking the reins from his master, doubtless in the hope of perhaps taking his position at the Court, seemed not to be noticed by Leffmann. Neither did he realise how Herz Behren's widow Särchen (Wertheimer) had started to involve herself in some affairs of his. In the months that still remained to him he seemed to have but one care – as is clear from his last letter of 14 August 1713 – helping his brothers in the faith who were in need. The Great Northern War, between Sweden and a coalition of Denmark-Norway, Saxony and Russia, and the events at Court could not move the almost eighty year old man.

The life of Leffmann Behrens, who for more than half a century accompanied our family with his cleverness and humanity ended on 30 January 1714. His tomb in the cemetery in Oberstrasse in Hannover is among the largest there, but the text engraved on the stone and in the Memorbuch is so objective and uncomplicated, just as Leffmann Behrens would have wanted.

> *Devout and gentle, a true son of Aron, chief and leader of his time, he gave generously to the poor, supported scholars, arranged marriages for orphans and gave them an appropriate endowment, studied before and after prayer-time, sent money everywhere to maintain schools and to support orphans and poor children, especially the associations and poor of the Holy Lands and he also built schools himself.*

# The Heirs

After Leffmann Behrens' death there is no trace in the family book of a baby by the name of Genendel Fränkel. We must presume that this child whose inheritance her grandfather Rabbi David Oppenheimer was to manage died soon after 1714. The testament made quite different default provisions: now the beneficiaries were David Oppenheimer, the widow of Herz Behrens, Serchen Wertheimer and his youngest grandson Gumpert who was still not able to stand on his own feet like his brother Isaak. Because neither Serchen nor Rabbi Oppenheimer were able to work in the Behrens Firm, they demanded that Gumpert should buy out their inheritance. The whole estate was valued at 200,000 Reichstaler, which of course was not lying around in sacks in the counting house but was rather circulating in various indebted Courts. Serchen, a true banker's daughter, seemed to accept this and did not press. However David Oppenheimer, who mostly busied himself with cataloguing the enormous library, demanded 9,000 Taler at once. Gumpert, who knew how little cash there was in the Behrens' till, prevaricated. It came to a disagreement. The impatient Oppenheimer could in no way go to a town court, less still to a Royal one with his demands. As a consequence he called on the rabbinate court that gave a Solomon's verdict on 31 July 1715: The Herr Rabbi David Oppenheimer could, by agreement with Gumpert and the widow Serchen, receive the 9,000 Taler, but could later make no further demands. Hardly was this trouble put to one side, than did Serchen take the initiative to vary the inheritance because she found it unjust that Gumpert's brother, Isaak seemed to be excluded from the inheritance: he should get the same share as she and Gumpert.

From now on there is not much news about life at Court. Only when certain landed rulers did not want to bring themselves to deal with long overdue repayments of their loans did Gumpert and Isaak Behrens confidently and 'humbly' seek help from the Prince-Elector Georg Ludwig who never let the grandsons of his unforgotten Chamber Agent down.

Meanwhile, soon after Leffmann Behrens, the old Dowager Princess-Elector Sophie died, whereby Georg Ludwig became the direct Heir Apparent to the English Queen. None of her thirteen children had survived. Indeed, on the other side of the English Channel, one knew that the Queen was suffering from gout and obesity, but that she, at the age of just 49, should succumb to her illnesses just a few weeks after the aged Princess-Elector Sophie was not expected so quickly. With the death of Anna Stuart on 1 August 1714 the Prince-Elector Georg Ludwig was acclaimed by Parliament in London as her successor as King George (the First) and on 24 October he was crowned as King of England and Scotland in Westminster Abbey.

The Hannovarian Court with a few chosen personalities removed to London. The administrative departments of the Principality remained behind, and as a refuge for the Prince-Elector King, the intimate Palace Herrenhausen, which he often visited. That he did not take his advisor, Leibniz, who had been with him for decades to London was an insuperable loss to the great old man. The recognition due him, that he had received under Georg Ludwig's father and grandfather, had not been given to Leibniz for a long time. His commission to write the History of the Welfen House was already wrecked in the chapter dealing with the eleventh century, all too many drafts had been tried and left aside. His longing to at last leave the limitations of Hannover, to settle in Berlin or now to spend his retiring years in London remained unfulfilled. The Princes of the Court knew not how to deal with his philosophy, his theological interests which included so much free-thinking, nor with his thoughts about a united peaceful Europe. None of them, none of the strict Protestant Court, was present when the outstanding universal scholar was carried to his grave in Hannover in November 1716. With the Court's move to London, a large part of the credit hungry clients of the Behrens brothers vanished too – after all there were also a great many money-lenders in London too. At first Gumpert and Isaak Behrens were able to please some German Princes with astonishing advances but the decline of their money-lending business was palpable and in the end irreversible.

At the Court in Schwerin, Bendix Goldschmidt also felt the change in the economy. Indeed after the death of his patron Duke Friedrich Wilhelm (1713), his successor Karl Leopold had renewed all his privileges and confirmed his release from paying the poll tax that other less important Jews had to pay, but when his debts had overwhelmed the Duke and Goldschmidt hesitated to give more loans, Karl Leopold turned to the Court Jew Gompert in Berlin for more credit. Luckily for Goldschmidt, a disagreement between the Duke and his baronetage in Mecklenburg came to his aid. The country gentry, who were not at all pleased that Karl Leopold, as the husband of the Russian Czar's niece, had made Mecklenburg available to Russian troops as an operations and provisions base against Sweden, now registered with Bendix Goldschmidt as new clients. When the Russians slowly withdrew after 1718, not just the fields but also the castles of the temporarily absent large landowners had been left ravaged, Bendix helped the gentlemen back to a better life with loans of in total 27,000 Reichstaler.

In the year 1719 there was talk of a general crisis in the economy which did not leave the Goldschmidt businessman unaffected: The repayment of his loans faltered, he did not dare to give new credit to the impecunious country gentry but recommended that they approach his grand-nephews Gumpert and Isaak Behrens who seemed to be still solid in business as Leffmann's heirs. But only 'seemed'. Of course the Behrens brothers did not refuse even the most risky business, unlike the careful Bendix Goldschmidt. Whether or not the two of them actually had massive amounts available or whether they were able to borrow themselves when necessary is not known. We only know (thanks to the State Archive in Hannover) that two years later they were still waiting for repayment from their clients in Mecklenburg whose indebtedness had by now grown to 109,000 Reichstaler.

Bendix Goldschmidt, who had been the Danish Imperial Chamber Agent since 1689, was now concentrating his business on the Court at Copenhagen, where he was more concerned with luxury articles than credit. Two of his eight children were already planning to settle permanently in Denmark: Zwi (Stag, the male deer) who would soon be better known by the pretty nordic Hartwig, was busy as a silk merchant and Aron was a jeweller and money-changer. We owe their Danish descendants our unending thanks, for without their mania to collect and keep Letters of Protection, pictures and memoirs we would not know the greater part of our family history.

When on 4 July 1717 Bendix Goldschmidt lost his wife Henrietta, called Jittche, after forty years of marriage, his house in Hamburg was empty. All his children were long married, three sons who had again found wives in the Fürst family, among them Ruben, the oldest, and his brother Aron who was a few years his junior were earning well in the tobacco monopoly which they had long been able to defend against covetous competitors. The last instance being a court case against two members of the Fürst family who lost after years of lawsuits. As so often, in this case the Danish King Frederick IV stood at the side of the Goldschmidts.

A year after Mother Henrietta's death, Aron, who had specialised in trading in colonial produce, mainly tea, cane sugar and coffee, decided to extend this business in Denmark for preference and in 1718 moved with his wife Freude (Fürst) and his growing swarm of children to Copenhagen. There were no difficulties because as a citizen of Altona, he already had a Danish Letter of Protection. Ruben, however, the first born, remained in Hamburg closely tied by the work of his father, that is he helped to procure fashion accessories and precious stones which the Danish Royal Court ordered from its Chamber Agent, Bendix Goldschmidt. Extravagant valuables were naturally not to be had in the Hamburg market, for them Ruben needed to journey to Amsterdam or Antwerp, a tribulation that the over sixty year old took on gladly.

George I by Godfrey Kneller (Courtesy of National Portrait Gallery London)

In the hope that his children would continue to be somewhat prosperous and so remain blameless and devout, as one demanded among the Goldschmidts, Bendix allowed himself to think of his own affairs, that is he found another wife after the year of mourning was over. A new marriage, a new wife, who presumably would not be much younger than himself: Dina Reizche of the wealthy Warburg family, which had arrived in Bologna after the expulsion from Spain and from there to Warburg in Westfalen and then had happily settled in Altona. Of course they all knew each other well from meeting in the Synagogue in Altona and on the Bourse in Hamburg.

The relationship with the very wealthy Warburg family enabled Bendix to finally bequeath a pretty nest-egg against hard-times. All Jewish fathers think of providing their children with financial security. One never knows how quickly the mood of the Christian world might veer. Centuries of persecution, expulsion and humiliation remain unforgotten, even if one never speaks of it. One realises first, how inferior and vulnerable to extortion one is in the eyes of those who can exploit one for their own benefit, every St Michael's Day, when one as a Jew must pay for one's Letter of Protection, the Residence Permit and double excise duty and taxes. At home one lives modestly in order to keep one's savings together against a possibly difficult future. Bendix Goldschmidt did not think about dying just three years after his wedding to Dina. Nothing is known of illness, old age or infirmity but on 5 January 1721 one would have seen a great stream of mourners to the cemetery in Altona where Bendix Goldschmidt had been laid in his grave next to his first wife Henrietta a day before. Exactly one year later as proscribed his gravestone was erected with the inscription:

> *The spirit turned away and a man of the tribe of Levi left us. This memorial is erected to remind us. Under here lies the most influential devout man who single-mindedly worked and showed love to strangers and locals. He is in peace in Eden with the righteous, because he always found the ways of justice with the best and wisest. He was chief and leader and fought like a lion in the face of Princes and Kings, and he was wise to every Prophet. It is just that he enjoy the reward of eternal life. He was the prince and the lord, the leader and chairman of the congregation, the well-born Herr Bendix of the clan of Levi, son of the well-born Herr Juda. He died and was buried on 6th Teves 5481.*

Now the Goldschmidt descendants had to show what they're made of. Their future would not be in Hamburg and Altona much longer. Our sights are targeted in Potsdam, the Residence.

# Last Chance

The example of their ancestors before then: the hunted, unwelcome everywhere, pedlars buckled with obsequiousness, dealing in only the few goods that the authorities permitted – odds and ends, old clothes and self-made things – and keeping their hard earned money together so that after years they would be able to afford a residency permit or even a Letter of Protection and who in the end climbed to diplomatic service. Respected but invisible, nothing was given them. At the time when they were the financial geniuses of their Rulers and also lived prosperous private lives, there were no sacks of gold sitting around in their counting houses. As soon as a debtor had repaid his credit together with interest the money flowed to the next client. The rate of interest payable was regulated by each small state by itself. The word 'usury' was only currency in the minds of the Christian world. The things that one could hide and carry away safely at any-time were diamonds and gems, a sort of provision for old-age. Who could know what might happen in the future.

What came first was a permit from the King of England and Prince-Elector of Hannover Georg Ludwig on 5 January 1717 for Leffmann Behrens' grandsons, Gumpert and Isaak, to continue to run the cloth manufacture in Lüneburg. A refusal would hardly have been worse because already in their grandfather's final years, the turnover had fallen away significantly, the wages, however, still needed to be paid, even if there was less work to be done. Leffmann had decided that none of the poor people who where employed there should be let go and probably forced on to the streets. The Lüneburg business, although a bottomless pit, must be upheld. Grandfather's wishes remained holy.

At first the credit business was apparently still profitable and there was hope that the debt repayments long awaited from England might at last be redeemed. The expected 149,997 English Pounds would re-invigorate their entrepreneurial courage. Of course Gumpert and Isaak had no idea of how dependent the English King was on his House of Commons. A Letter from King George dated 9 April 1717 to his Ministry in the Electorate of Hannover still exists. It is clear that the grandsons of Leffmann were by no means forgotten by the Prince-Elector:

'You shall give them our assurance that We, through the Parliament, will grant them the best possible help and support in order that they shall soon have their money paid back.'

In the next and the following years there was still no sign of the urgently needed money. Further letters from the King followed, further comforting words. Finally in February 1720 a document arrived that promised to give new support to Gumpert and Isaak who were by now were slithering on the thinnest of ice:

*Georg King and Prince-Elector*

*Certifies that We are moved by a sense of mercy towards their father and grandfather and for their own welfare, and engage the Brothers Gumpert and Isaak Behrens as Our Senior Court Factors. Hereby is this done with this effect, they are named and declared and engaged as Our Senior Court Factors, that they remain in the same quality under such predication in Our service, true to Us, propitious and obedient, that they should organise with all industry, unsullenly and correctly the commissions completely and especially as our Senior Court Factors as they are instructed on Our behalf, and also should show themselves and behave as honest, reasonable and busy servants and Senior Court Factors as is suitable and due. For this the Brothers Gumpert and Isaak Behrens are under Our special Protection beside the personal exemption from Our New City Debtors Courts jurisdiction, also sundry privileges and prerogatives in kind and in specie which Our Jewish Agents have enjoyed until now and will still enjoy and harmoniously gladden them.*

*St James 29 Jan/9 Feb of the 1720rd year of our Lord'*

Gentrified! At last not just 'Court Jews' but rather Senior Court Factors. The desirable title signed and sealed!

No later than this Andreas Scheits, the Hannovarian Court Portraitist was given the order to paint the Senior Court Factor Isaak Behrens: a reserved glance from an over thirty year old, extremely elegant gentleman whose posture and whose thin face under the chest-long curly 'allonge-perucke' cannot deny his Sephardic ancestry.

Relax. The clients have confidence once again. The rumours the House of Behrens might be at the brink of bankruptcy disperse. New borrowers contact them, among them several noble residents. Isaak and Gumpert could now believe in a rosy future, but their pockets were empty.

Isaak Behrens, oil by court painter Andreas Scheitz (Courtesy of the Fränkel family)

So, borrow money! From the family first. Not from the Goldschmidts, they are careful enough to hold themselves back from doubtful intentions. The connections with the Fürsts are not as close as once they were. But Isaak's father-in-law Behrend Lehmann in Halberstadt, banker to the Polish King and Prince-Elector of Saxony, August the Strong, would not refuse his son-in-law. He owned his own bank in Halberstadt and had the counting houses in Dessau and Dresden necessary for the Saxon Court. Naturally he had heard the dubious rumours. But this was a family matter, always only second to God in importance, and so he arranged for 200,000 Reichstaler to be sent to Langestrasse 8 in Hannover-Neustadt immediately. Whether the amount would be sufficient for the money-lending business of the brothers, he knew not. Neither did he know that Gumpert and Isaak had arranged other sources of money in order to get their ship underway in these becalmed times.

Unfortunately not a penny of the pounds awaited from England was in sight. The months passed, in the end the Behrens brothers once more humbly reminded their Prince-Elector of the long overdue repayment. whereupon they received the following answer on 14 February 1721: *"The payment does not depend on the King, but on Parliamentary appropriation. But the supplicants should not doubt that the payment will be taken care of – as far as possible next year."*

This news was devastating. But one may not let it be noticed. Even the wives should not get to hear anything unsettling, particularly not Isaak's Lea (Lehmann) who would shortly give birth to her third child and who belonged to those Jewish women who in dicey situations, who when the rudder threatens to slip out of their husband's hands, wrench it decisively into their own. She had her rich father behind her. They may have noticed that a bookkeeper was given notice by the Behrens brothers but perhaps in such times of business difficulties that is not unusual and did not have to signify anything bad. The tension that was palpable in the family in those days in March 1721 had several causes: Easter was very near, the Jewish Passover with its enormous preparations, the annual spring clean and the expectation of countless guests. And the forthcoming birth. If Lea's baby arrived on time and it were a boy again they could celebrate the circumcision in eight days time. As well as all this the Spring fair in Leipzig was upon them and Gumpert and Isaak were already packing their cases, the boxes with articles from their cloth and tobacco manufacture, and of course the wine caskets with the money that they would spend in Leipzig on purchases for the Court, or God forbid! have to pay out to their creditors who would probably be waiting for them there. The fact that a credit giver must on occasion borrow money was not unknown to Lea. She had certainly heard that her frivolous brother-in-law had debts of several thousand Reichstaler: what she however did not know was it was not thousands. It was almost half a million.

A report prepared by Isaak Behrens reads like a theatre play in which many characters appear. It was among his papers that he left us and was written in the days after the celebration of his third child's circumcision, Lehmann. Isaak wrote: the Departure for a Business Trip to Harzburg with my brother Gumpert. This report starts on 31 March 1721 and ends on 20 February 1726. Only the following few excerpts are quoted so as not to tire the reader with the circumlocution of his style and to start I must list the characters of the first Act that is headed by the title:

## The End. Flight.

Place: Roads and small villages between Hannover and Hildesheim
Date: 31 March to 7 April 1721
    Dramatis personae:
    Isaak Behrens, Senior Court Jew to the Prince-Elector of Hannover
    Gumpert Behrens, his brother, with the same position
    Nathan, Gumpert's servant
    Manes, cook to his father-in-law the banker Behrend Lehmann of Halberstadt
    A coachman

The Employees of the Behrens Firm
    Abraham Sturm, bookkeeper
    Samuel Altona, cashier
    Moses Danzig, his assistant
    Wolf Offenbach, clerk
    Hieronymus Stutzer, clerk for German
    Seckel Hildesheim, clerk for Hebrew
    Hemi, particular clerk
    Wolf Joseph, copyist
    Joseph Hamburger, copyist

Gentlemen of the Elector's Court and the City Authorities
    Privy Secretary Bacmeister
    Privy Court Advisor von Bernstorff

Sakan, his Adjutant
Erdmann, courier for von Bernstorff
An armed wagon-driver
Official from Nedling
40 farmers from the area around Nedling
Hutmann and Radier, two couriers from Hannover
22 soldiers and a sergeant from Peine
2 mounted guardsmen
Sentries

The people listed, who populate the first sheets of the report, hint at bad things. But we discover at least how many employees worked for the Behrens Firm. At any rate until the morning of 31 March 1721, when at about eight in the morning, two hours after the departure of the Behrens brothers the rumour with the name 'Bankrupt' spread through the town like a forest fire and soon afterwards the Privy Secretary Bacmeister appeared at Isaak Behrens' house to speak to his wife Lea.

At that moment the Behrens brothers were in their coach in the direction of Hildesheim. With them was Nathan, Gumpert's servant. Manes cook to his father-in-law Behrend Lehmann of Halberstadt who had come from there bringing distilled spirits for the circumcision celebration of Isaak and Lea's offspring was supposed to meet them on the route to Harzburg – just 4 miles distant from Halberstadt – but had, however, been sent ahead by the Post coach to Steierwald, a small place before Hildesheim, in order to organise rested horses there for the further journey together.

Exactly what Lea told or concealed from the Privy Secretary, of whom she knew only his name, is unknown. There were many suspicions.

What business trip was so important the that Senior Court Factors had to travel together? Why, just the day before, did they send their cashier Samuel, who was indispensable at the counting house, together with his assistant to Celle so as to deliver a bridal gift to the daughter of a friend? Anyway the court knew about this journey that was to take two days because the Privy Secretary Bacmeister had prepared a travel document for the cashier and had taken the opportunity to give a couple of commissions for the court at Celle. But why, on the last Post coach, so at about midnight, did Isaak send *'several chests with silver and gold ahead to Steierwald'* which lay outside the jurisdiction of the Principality of Hannover? The chests were to be waiting there with Manes and the nags for the change of horses when they expected to arrive there the next morning. What was the reason for Isaak and Gumpert to travel at first to their wax-bleaching works, which was part of their candle factory near Hannover, where they changed from their usual coach to a better travelling coach? Why did they stop once again in the small village of Klei (now called Gleidingen), one and a half 'meilen' (about 11 km) from Hannover, taking the new horses and the horses coachman from the local Posthouse and telling their own coachman to wait for them next morning so that they could travel back with their own horses? Also they had told the employees, when they left the counting house, that they would be back the next day. They had even told the commander at the Aegidien Gate in Hannover that one should keep the gate open *'in case they did not return before night-time'*. Did they not actually want to travel to Harzburg? What happened in Steierwald? According to Isaak's report there was a meal together after the horses were changed. No rush. No word about the chests.

Had the chests with their valuable contents that the Senior Court Factors of the Prince-Elector of Hannover had entrusted to the Post been left in Steierwald, north of Hildesheim, perhaps they had been collected by another Senior Court Factor? Who might be able to check the worth of the contents, to estimate and exchange them into the urgently needed cash? Who other than the Chamber Agent to the Saxon Prince-Elector who had his own bank in Halberstadt? Had he, the impeccable banker to August the Strong, using a commissioned intermediary, come to the rescue of his son-in-law who had got himself into such financial difficulties?

First a change of horses. And then onward, near to Nedling (today known as Nettlingen) where they were surprised at about two in the afternoon by a courier sent at a gallop by the Privy Court Advisor von Bernstorff. It was Erdmann, whom Isaak knew, together with his coachman.

Isaak Behrens' report:

> *The coachman jumped from his horse and stood in front of our coach with a pistol in his hand, while Erdmann ran into the village. I asked him where he came from, he retorted that we would very soon discover that. I asked what was going on. He said that in Hannover the word was that we were bankrupt and wanted to escape. God Forbid! we shouted, come, we want to turn about. Then he called Erdmann back, but he did not want to let himself be convinced. Then we said: if he believed that the two of them were unable to watch us, then they should fetch some farmers at our expense. Erdmann did not want to be responsible for doing that. He ran to the official in Nedling who had us come before him and talked to us sternly. We served him obediently and explained that we were honest people and wanted to remain so. Now 40 farmers came to watch over us, but we were able to stroll in the street.*

*In the evening the coachman rode back to Hannover. We gave him a written note for Privy Court Advisor von Bernstorff in which we beseeched him not to rush into anything that might destroy us; we had never thought of bankruptcy. One should not do anything in our house. We would soon be back. At the same time we wrote to our wives, openly and in German writing. The coachman took all these letters with him. The courier added a note.*

*In the night we slept on straw. Whenever we needed anything from our coach, we were accompanied by the courier and several farmers who were standing guard over it. At ten in the evening a secretary from Hildesheim appeared, he let us be searched and put a seal on our things.*

*Next morning the official let his servant bring us coffee and sugar and a live welsh cock which we killed and let it be prepared for breakfast.*

*In the meantime at our house in Hannover, 20 soldiers had moved in and shut off all the doors and windows and had put seals on all our things. Towards the evening our courier Samuel returned according to our instructions from Celle. As soon as he arrived they brought him before the President of the Chamber, von Goertz, who spoke with him. Then he was taken back to our house and held under guard, as were all our assistants; that is Stutzer, the clerk, Abraham Sturm, our bookkeeper and Wolf Joseph a copier. I will explain later what happened to them. But first I want to report what befell us.*

*Seckel (the clerk for Hebrew) came to us in Hildesheim, but the official called for the preacher to come, for he spoke and wrote very good Hebrew, which I had rarely heard that a Christian could. He would be present as long as Seckel was with us so that we could not make any secret agreements with him. Seckel prepared a letter for us to my father-in-law (Lehmann) in Halberstadt, the preacher had to read it first and then Wolf from Hildesheim, who was present at that moment, took it to Halberstadt. In it we described what had happened and besought him to send someone to Hannover or to go himself. Seckel drove home again afterwards.*

*At about seven in the evening two sergeants, Hutmann and Radier appeared from Hannover as escorts. They brought with them letters from our wives and had orders to accompany us back to Hannover. From them we learned what had occurred at home. Hutmann had stood guard* there. The sergeants had previously applied to Hildesheim to take us immediately but the authorities there refused and delayed till the next day. So we had to stay another night.

The next morning (2nd April) Hutmann drove to Hildesheim so as to put our extradition into effect. Towards 10 o'clock a posse of soldiers appeared from Peine, a sergeant and 22 men. These let us go to our room because we were hanging around on the street. They took over guarding us and the farmers went away. Around midday a lieutenant from Hildesheim came with the order that we should be taken to Steierwald, which then happened at about 3 o'clock. Before we left, we thanked the Official for his goodness, paid the bills and gave 40 Taler for the farmers. By evening we were in Steierwald, where each of us were given a small miserable room with a warden at the door. The lieutenant also stayed, the sergeant from Hannover was, however, not allowed to attend us but had to stay in the Posthouse.

On Thursday (3 April) two mounted guards came to us. The soldiers from Peine stood guard only over the coach in front of the official's house and many of them were sent away. The courier had already been sent to Hannover to report on Wednesday. We had given him orders to take to our house as well, Hillel and Salmon Gans [grandchildren of Grandmother Jente's first marriage and thus half-cousins of Isaak and Gumpert Behrens] *had asked permission at the town-hall to ride to us and brought us wine and food. Also Seckel from Hildesheim sent meals to us. The lieutenant was not allowed to go. We played boardgames together.*

*On this day in the morning we were individually interrogated by a chamber-director from Hildesheim and by a secretary; Gumpert's servant and the cook, Manes too. Until then each of us was held under arrest alone in his room; afterwards permission was given for the servants to attend to us and we brothers were together. The interrogation was unremarkable. It was suggested that we go to Hildesheim to seek protection but we refused with thanks and urgently asked to be allowed to go to Hannover and our families.*

\*\*\*\*

At this point in the report some thoughtfulness is necessary: If the brothers really had guilty consciences and had done anything completely criminal why did the turn down the protection offered at Hildesheim? And returned instead to Hannover as notorious bankrupts? Everyone in their counting house knew what was happening; everyone was, as the written record later proved, examined, put on oath and examined again, without any talk of a fraudulent bankruptcy. Everyone knew that perjury under oath from Jews would be punished significantly more severely than Christians would be. None of the employees would have dared to cover-up for their indebted bosses and thus endanger their own families. Perjury was not just punished by imprisonment but much worse, by exile. Without a Letter of Protection from the ruling Lords, the life of no Jew was safe at that time.

Did the brothers believe that their Prince-Elector would free them from an intransparent debt trap on the basis of the merits of grandfather Leffmann and uncle Herz Behrens? Anyone who forsook the Prince-Elector's financial house under such contradictory circumstances must be suspicious. Already in the morning, soon after Isaak and Gumpert's departure, a Colonel Wecht had appeared in the counting house and demanded the key to the debentures safe. However that had been locked up in the cashier's safe by the cashier Samuel before he went to Celle and of course he had the key to the cashier's safe with him. A locksmith was called for, who opened the safe. A law-court official looked through the papers of the interested parties, found them to be in order, made a written record, put a seal on the counting house and summonsed the employees, who had at first been sent home, to the Court advisor Bernstorf in his chancellery for the next day. Oath-taking and interrogation. In the end everyone was released except the bookkeeper, a clerk and a copyist who had to remain under house arrest at Herz Behrens' where the counting house was.

In the meantime the wives, Lea and Sprinze, shocked by events, were courageous enough to go to the Court on the third day to complain that they had no more money in the house and did not know how they were to manage with their children. Immediately the councillors ordered a Salman D. (the full name is not known) to advance the ladies some money.

In Steierwald it was starting to become boring. Because although the brothers had politely refused protection in Hildesheim, they were in no way released from there or allowed to go to Hannover. First, Best, the War Commissioner for Hannover, had to speak to the Government in Hildesheim before the delivery of the two accused, who had no Protection, could be put into effect. This took a few days.

Isaak Behrens' report:

*Monday 7 April, the War Commissioner best came to us and announced that we would be taken to Hannover that afternoon. We set off about 3 or 4 o'clock. Best had a coach, my brother and I had another with Nathan, my brother's servant and the cook, Manes on the box outside; the sergeants Hutman and Radier on the box. The lieutenant wanted to take us to the prison cells with his mounted guards but Best did not permit that. Thus we travelled to Klei. There we found our coachman with the horses, paid all the bills and sent him back to Hannover with the horses.*

*In Heide we paused because we did not want to arrive in daylight. In the evening we travelled on until at last we came in by the Aegidien Gate and to the door of our house in Neugasse and waited there until someone opened it. Hundreds of people had collected themselves around our coach which was under guard. The adjutant Jaken with a few soldiers received me and took me up to the first floor to the bedroom. Gumpert was likewise accompanied to his house. Each of us had a sergeant and a corporal in the room and a guard outside. They were not to let anyone in to us. When we demanded something to eat the servant had to place it before he door and the corporal brought it in.*

*As soon as we went into our rooms, the law-court official appeared with secretary Lidmann and he said to me, that here were some clothes, I should put them on and put those that I was wearing aside. As soon as that was done, those clothes were placed in a case that was then sealed and locked in a room. Manes and Nathan remained downstairs with the guard in Gumpert's house.*

*Tuesday 8 April, at 8 a.m. the Gentlemen, von Bernstorf and von Werner appeared to examine us. My interrogation lasted almost all morning; that of my brother the whole afternoon and into the night. After the interrogation, the sealed cases were opened and the clothes examined. A tailor and cobbler were fetched to cut open all the pieces of clothing and search through them. But nothing suspicious was found. The results of the interrogation are in the minutes.*

\*\*\*\*

The way they were being dealt with was still earnest but not impolite. Of course one had to obtain clarity, whether or not diamonds were hidden in turned-up cuffs or collars or braided seams and which might thus be smuggled out of the state. An obvious address was Isaak's father-in-law Behrend Lehmann whose wide reaching financial power was well known. In the Residence at Dresden, he was known to drive a coach with six horses and four liveried servants. The financing of the King's title for August the Strong had not made him poorer. In these economically lean times, he might have been the sole person who was able to purchase the diamonds and gemstones hoarded by the naive Gumpert Behrens. But Isaak, as the elder, would have to take responsibility for much that was not his fault.

Suppositions shot out of the ground like weeds without any crime being uncovered or even accusation being raised. An exhaustive search of the counting house had not until now been made and the measures taken so far seemed to remain in the realm of normality. Oddly enough the chests filled with silver and gold that were sent to Steierwald through the post were never mentioned in any minutes except in Isaak's report that he wrote later. Manes who had gone ahead to Steierwald was considered cluelessly unsuspicious and was allowed to return to Halberstadt after a few interrogations, *notabene* on a riding horse that Behrend Lehmann had provided for his cook for the journey to the circumcision ceremony.

Passover – Easter, came nearer and Herr von Bernstorff helped the Jewish Court Factors by allowing them to shave themselves at last and to receive their wives and children. Naturally it was not to a be proper Passover Feast, such as had been celebrated over the centuries in the same fashion by all Jewish families on earth, with tasty food and Hebrew anthems praising exodus of the children of Israel from Egypt and the escape of the people from imprisonment. Here the most important thing was a form of house arrest and a junior officer had to be present all the time to be sure that they all spoke to each other exclusively in German.

Only on 15 April, when the Jewish and Christian feast days which often coincided, were over, did individual interrogations commence once again, but with lengthy gaps between them, above all because the counting house was now being inspected in much greater detail. Especially the part that belonged to Gumpert where the cashier Samuel had laid all the cupboards and safes open to the inspectors with a zeal that was obvious and allowing a remark that was only understandable to family members: If everything here were not in order, and the commission were to unable find anything, the widow Särchen would follow the Behrens Brothers to the world's end.

Isaak gave no further explanation in his report. But we know who was leaning over his shoulder. Särchen, the widow of Leffmann's dearest son Herz Behrens, equally upright and veracious as her late husband. And as sister to the Imperial banker Wertheimer. She may well have foreseen the bankruptcy of her nephews and must have been outraged at Gumpert's mistaken speculation and at their holding on to the loss making manufacturing works. Särchen understood accounts and it may be assumed that she, together with the Oppenheimers and Lehmanns belonged to the family creditors who now had to contemplate how they might recover the lost money as soon as possible because it was likely that with time more and more creditors would appear. Without doubt there were considerable receivables but as yet they lacked an appropriate overview. Gumpert did not even have the last year's accounts ready. Now he was commanded to provide them and also a plan how he intended to satisfy his creditors. Unlike at his brother Isaak's house, things seemed palatial at his home. Plenty of silver and gold was visible. An inventory was prepared. Under supervision of three secretaries of the Justice Authority and an assessor. Mercy could no longer be expected.

Isaak Behrens' report:

> *On 7 May (1721) in the afternoon the Adjutant Vogt appeared and reported that he had orders to take us to the Cleves Gate that evening and he asked whether we would walk there or preferred a sedan. At any rate he did not want to take us till it was dark because of the people.*

> *We sent for the Lawyer Rickmann who had been appointed as our Defence a few days earlier. He explained that it could not be done in that way, we should first be accused before we could be taken to the gate. He immediately made a submission, went to the Privy Secretary himself and it was sent everywhere. Despite this, at about 10 pm. we were sent with an under-officer from the castle and the Adjutant accompanied by our guarding sergeant and 22 soldiers in two sedan chairs to the Cleves Gate. Before I left I was with my wife in the living room. One can imagine the crying and tumult in our house.*

> *When we arrived at the Cleves Gate, the Clerk of the Court Kehr was there. He let my brother walk on his right-hand side and me on his left. Then he had chains put on us. That took till midnight. Then we were shut in and no-one could come to us.*

# Arrested

The Cleves Gate was not a prison in the normal sense that one found in the Residence City of every Principality. It was a gatehouse inset in the medieval city wall that had originally been closed by a drawbridge and later by a solid gate and that had, since 1712, spanned in a wide arch the Langestrasse, which started here and led to the Calenberger Neustadt, where once Leffmann Behrens had lived in number 8 and his son in number 20. Now only the two widows, Feil and Särchen, shocked to the core by the catastrophe, and who hardly dared to cross the street, lived there. When on a May evening at 10 o'clock, 22 soldiers escorted two gentlemen hidden in two sedan chairs along the Langestrasse in the direction of the Cleves Gate, the residents in the street behind their curtains could guess who they were. Hannover was a gossip factory working overtime.

Of course no-one could know what went on in the upper chambers of the gatehouse. But everyone knew that simple thieves were not taken to the Cleves Gate. It was reserved for prominent sinners who belonged to the 'embarrassing' criminals, that is those who, if they did not voluntarily confess what was wanted from them, would be put through a painful interrogation. To speed the confessions there were a few torture instruments in the cellar. An axe and block, forerunner of the guillotine, was available for those who were sentenced to death. For the strong man responsible for torture was called the Tyrant here.

The first night in this place was not exactly luxurious for the Behrens brothers but at least they did not have to sleep on a heap of straw infested by fleas.

Isaak Behren's Report:

> I slept well in the night, which was a wonder but probably came about due to the worries and tribulations. At 6 or 7 in the morning the door was unlocked. We prayed, drank coffee and because in the night they had only given us a recliner, I was now given a good bed with curtains. By the way, an order had been given not to let anybody come to us and whenever the Clerk of the Court let the door be opened an under-officer

*of the Cleves Gate had to stay by us at all times, also a guard stood at the door. Whenever our people brought meals to us, they were inspected closely in case they had a slip of paper or something similar to pass to us. The door was unlocked only in the mornings, at lunchtime and in the evening when food was brought or the bed made up. Then we were locked in again.*

*On Friday the 30 May we were both interrogated in the Cleves Gate as the protocol or minutes prove, I in the morning and my brother in the afternoon. This time we were not asked for an exact state of accounts. We began that in the following week. Present were the Secretary Ewers, our clerk Stutzer and our bookkeeper Abraham Sturm. But he did not come very often because he was busy in the chancellery. Meanwhile two proctors or advocates were appointed by the chancellery, Schrader as 'procurator litis', (acting for the litigant or prosecutor) and Scharbrügge as 'curator bonorum', (the administrator of an insolvent debtor).*

*They had the order to be present while the statement of accounts was drawn up. Schrader came every morning at 7 o'clock.*

*We worked till evening because they were keen for us to finish as soon as possible. As long as we worked on the accounts we brothers were together. We worked on our justification calculations at the same time so as to put it in the accounts. It was made up of profit and loss statements as can be seen from the files. By the way I must remark, that all the while we sat in the Cleves Gate we received half a taler out of the insolvency estate each day. Later, however, when Schrader came to us, he thought that was too much and he decided to give us just 6 groschen (maybe a fifth of a taler). That was approved, as one can later read, until we were chained up.*

\*\*\*\*

During the first week in June 1721 they attempted to recreate the accounts out of their memories. An impossibility. The request by the brothers to be allowed to deal with this in the counting house was refused: One had brought the complete paperwork to the chancellery by then and would summons the delinquents there from time to time, of course on foot and accompanied by 12 soldiers. This run of the gauntlet through the staring passers-by was not to be spared the brothers. The only allowance given: on those days Isaak and Gumpert ate lunch in the officer's room so as not to need to make the journey along the street twice more.

At the chancellery the names of the creditors were at last listed and in case the rumours had not yet reached them, they were informed what should happen next. That was, wait patiently for the sacks of money that it was suspected would turn-up at some time, or in the worst case for a wait for not calculable insolvency estate. Only now was it clear just how many Court Officials and country gentlemen from the region and also from other Principalities had been prepared to willingly lend substantial sums after the law against usury for Christians had been lifted, in solid confidence in the hundred percent reliability of a bank that was connected with the name of Leffmann Behrens although it had been acting under the name of Gumpertz Brothers for some time.

There came no word from the Goldschmidt relatives who fortunately mostly lived in Hamburg and were not among the creditors. They of course knew all about the disaster. It was self-evident that the wives of those concerned and widows of Leffmann and Herz Behrens would be cared for in an emergency. There was already talk of an auction of all the assets to pay off the horrendous debts and Lea and Sprinze, Veile and Särchen could imagine just how long they would continue to live in Neustadt, Hannover. With whom could they discuss this. It was forbidden to make any contact with Isaak or Gumpert.

Only the cook who brought meals from Isaak's house to the Cleves Gate knew at least how things seemed in the upper chamber over the gateway arch, at least, as seen from the steps to the cell where the two were in chains. What went on besides seems only to be known to us because of Isaak's father-in-law Berend Lehmann.

Yes, the banker was worried. Less about Gumpert who in his opinion had been ill-advised and who had to be punished for his escapades, rather more about his son-in-law who was to suffer 'harsh procedures': and – this cannot go unremarked – about the 200,000 Reichstaler that he had advanced the last time. This he wanted back, if you please, and preferentially out of the insolvent estate. As financier to the King of Poland and Prince-Elector of Hannover he was able to exert some pressure on the Gentlemen of the Court of Hannover.

On 6 July 1721 Berend Lehmann wrote as follows to King George in London

*Most Humbly – most obedient Memoriale*
*Berendt Lehmann, Resident of Halberstadt in the King of Poland and Prince-Electorat of Saxony*

*Your Most Royal Majesty, All Powerful King, Most Merciful King and Lord.*

*Your Royal Majesty will no doubt have heard report from Your Ministry in Hannover of the credit status and loss of sustinence of the Brothers Gumperts and how severely at the instance of some but indeed not many creditors these two were imprisoned in the Cleves Gate. Now the highly enlightened Ministry of Your Royal Majesty will best know how to proceed to best gain their rights. Because however, these people who did not act well or sensibly, more out of ignorance and youthful carelessness, than out of maliciousness and fraud and thus came into this labyrinth, in similar insolvencies and also today in far too many procedures the Constitution of the Reich sets no special penalty but rather prefers that one be satisfied when the insolvents 'bonis cediren' and give all their assets to their creditors: besides with harsh treatment the creditors are little served in that they do not receive compensation for their losses: It is also known to me that if all the creditors come together, only the fewest can be satisfied. So I live in the most humble hope that Your Royal Majesty will treat me most mercifully when I plead at Your feet, for these unfortunate people who are close relatives of mine and one of them, Isaak Behrens, is my son-in-law, that Your Royal Majesty be moved, in most merciful consideration that their grandfather Leffmann Behrens and his sons Herz and Jacob were well-known in the Royal and Prince-Elector's House, to command Your Ministry in Hannover to end the harsh procedures against the Brothers Gumperts, release them from arrest and allow them to give their estates to their creditors. Because unfortunately I am also affected by this misfortune, because I advanced 200/m. Rtlr. in cash, whereby with such caution, because no-one had thought of such an insolvency then, that already two years ago I let quite a part of their effects be ceded to me, so that I have the freedom to help myself be paid: Nevertheless these assets are confiscated so that I must forego my damages. Nevertheless they cannot be used for the creditors, because one had not been aware of an insolvency, or thought to be vigilant or to prevail on them particularly at such time and so I beseech Your Royal Majesty as your most humble servant to command Your Ministry to relax the arrests and allow me the freedom to encash my rights to the ceded goods and serve myself. In this my justified attempt I trust to my Most Merciful Highness and Your Royal Majesty*

*Your most humble knave, Berendt Lehmen.*
   *(State Archive Hannover: Hannover 92 xvii, V No. 13 Vol. 1)*

Whether Lehmann's letter ever reached the hands of the King is not known. Perhaps in landed in the files of the Electoral Court in Hannover as an unimportant matter or it may have been withheld by Herr von Bernstorff who had but one aim: to make the Behrens brothers talk or to punish them. Bernstorff needed a result in this matter. For weeks the interrogations brought no success. Despite threats of dire consequences there was no confession. In the papers which have lain open now for a long time, there has been no valid evidence that the brothers still had any massive sums available to them or that they might have secretly salted away such a sum. In a report dated 18 November 1721 a conglomerate of dark suspicions: according to this an estimated eight tonnes of gold or a million Reichstaler is written about. Even the name of the Saxon resident Berend Lehmann and his son-in-law Isaak appears under the presumption that they were in conspiracy together, also the unusually Jewish-friendly Government of Hildesheim and the Prussian Court, whose finances were looked after by Jewish Court Factors that were loosely related to the Behrens clan.

Isaak's clerk, Nathan Seckel who lived in Hildesheim, gave a surprise of a special sort when he was summonsed for suspected dealing in stolen goods and outraged that he was suspected of a misdeed that could not be confirmed, turned for help to the highest Reich's Court. Everyone knew that there things were decided impartially, without bribes and correctly. If the Behrens brothers who had been merely arrested on suspicion also sought such a path to their rights, then Herr von Bernstorff must forestall them.

# Torture

Isaak Behrens reported:

*Thursday 21 August (1721) we were both taken to the chancellery by 12 soldiers in the morning, then again at about 3 o'clock although there was nothing special to do. We remained till 6 o'clock. When we were taken back to the Cleves Gate again the Adjutant Vogt went with us and at the same time the executioner Kahl was called for from the town-hall with his town assistants. They were there to lock us onto a thick iron bar with two leg irons round our feet so that it was between our legs, this was called a bulken. The feet could not be spread wider apart than the bulken was long. From the middle of the bulken was attached a thick chain which was also fixed to a hand with a handcuff, which was also locked. The order was given that they would unfetter us for meals and prayers but that otherwise we were to be fettered by night as well as by day.*

*Next morning came an order to release my hand at midday but never my legs, even at prayers they were not to be opened. Although we complained that we could not thus pray according to the law because for one prayer we must bring our feet together – this was disregarded. At the same time it was strictly ordered that our cell was to be locked at all times except in the mornings, midday and in the evening. Besides this our daily money was reduced to 3 groschen. When meals were brought the executioner as well as an under-officer had to inspect them in case a note or something was in them.*

*The night after there was a house sentry, the executioner had to open the gate and check the lock. This happened almost every night. Sometimes the sentry came into our room and looked about, sometimes the town assistant came and searched, sometimes the sentry was satisfied just to call from outside the room and one had to answer. Since Kahl (the executioner) was in charge, the Clerk of the Court was not allowed to be let in.*

*Early in the morning the executioner appeared with his town assistants and an under-officer to inspect. They looked around in the room and checked the dishes. At midday our hands were released for half an hour and again at dinnertime, after that we were inspected again and locked up. While we ate, an under-officer was by one of us and the executioner was by the other. We always let them eat with us, just as we had let the Clerk of the Court and the under-officer.*

*On 27 August Schrader came (the Court lawyer), took our clothes off our bodies so that we had nothing left except a pair of old hose and a sleeping gown, thus we could not even dress ourselves when we were called to the chancellery.*

*Friday 28 August there came an order that the doors of the prison should remain open and in front of each of them a guard with unsheathed sword should watch and an under-officer should pay attention that the guards were alert so that everything we did could be observed. Despite this we were still chained and the executioner was just as active. They both stayed while we ate, the under-officer mostly with me and the executioner with my brother.*

*One can imagine how much pain the bulken gave because it was very heavy and one was not able to walk, one could hardly get from the table to the bed. It was also difficult to lay down because if one lay on one's back, the iron pressed behind the feet, and it was impossible to lay on one's side, on the one side because of the lock and on the other because of the knob on the bulken. Also standing was hard, because of the weight. It was almost unbearable. Actually our legs swoll up. We complained very explicitly and the Over-lieutenant Quernheim came to inspect us. Kahl had to release us and he was persuaded how swollen we were and sent two regimental field surgeons, Frede and Thibeau, who reported that we could not endure it.*

*Then on 2 September came the order to chain us crossways, so the right foot to the left hand. Now we complained that we could not put on the Tefillin* [phylactery – one of two small, black leather, cube-shaped cases containing Torah texts written on parchment, which were strapped to the left arm], *whereupon it was ordered to chain the left foot to the right hand and to release us for dinner.*

*Every evening and morning the executioner with his assistants had to inspect us in the presence of the under-officer. Each time the strictest order was renewed that no note be allowed to us nor sent by us, also we were no allowed ink nor pens. We brothers were not allowed to be together and no-one could come to us except those who brought us our meals.*

*Wednesday 3 September there came a further special order: instead that the executioner should be with us at the midday and evening meal, a corporal from the Cleves Gate should come up and in the night an under-officer was by one of us and the corporal by the other in the room to sleep, and the executioner came up as often as he wanted to inspect us. As often as the miserable fellow wanted, we had to get out of bed and let ourselves be inspected. The Over-officers inspected diligently and indeed as often as they made a main sentry circuit. The first came at between 11 and 12, the other between 12 and 1 o'clock, the third in winter between 4 and 5 o'clock in the evenings, in summer during the day between 1 and 2 or 2 and 3 o'clock.*

*Wednesday 5 November, we were as usual escorted by soldiers to the chancellery. I was interrogated first as the minutes show. We objected to not having any clothes because Schrader had taken them all. We were told that we must come as we were, even if we were naked. But we received clothes from our homes.*

*On 11 November we were taken to the chancellery and for no particular reason other than that it was so commanded, by a way that passed our house, when we had otherwise always been taken by another route. We had meanwhile solicited that we be allowed to prepare our defence, and now demanded a clerk. That was at last permitted. The clerk Fischer was appointed after being put on oath at the chancellery. Lawyer Albert was to be on our side and he was given the books and other things necessary to look after. In this way we at last able to start on our defence papers on 17 February 1722. During the work we were unfettered; as soon as we were finished we were chained again.*

\*\*\*\*

After the torture of the bulken was at an end, apparently at the objections of the medical man, the gentlemen at the chancellery considered whether the chain between the right hand and left leg was sufficient torment to finally discover something about the hiding place where the supposed mass of money was. Actually the Principality's expert, who was busy with the case, must have been able to calculate from the accounts that it was just a sort of mirage. Even if the chests filled with silver and gold mentioned by Isaak when he was in Steierwald had been received by a helper's helper in Hildesheim, it could only have been an object wrapped in a cloth but not Gulden or Taler because cash, on account of its enormous weight, was always transported in wine barrels of inconspicuous size. It is conceivable that the contents of that chest came out of their own objects, carefully put aside, such as candlesticks, serving plates, wine goblets and diverse silver boxes which were kept in every rich Jewish household. One did not just use them on the Sabbath and other feast-days. They represented at the same time a sort of provision for old age, for the women who survived their husbands, a hoard which one could sell for cash in times of need. But could that which had been sent to Berend Lehmann's address have been sufficient to redeem all the debts?

The creditors began to lose patience. And the legal advisors of the Court considered whether they should ratchet up the torture or, if there really was nothing more to squeeze out of the Behrens brothers – rather to concern themselves with the insolvent estate. The legal position was anything but unambiguous, so that the Court sought advice at the law faculties of the universities at Halle and Jena. This now created a miserable delay in the writing of the defence papers because all the files, accounts and minutes had to be sent there for inspection and many weeks passed until the answers came. They seemed in no way unfavourable for the accused. At least the torture could not be intensified – but instead the real property of the Behrens family was to be auctioned off: the cloth and tobacco factories, the wax-bleaching works and their houses complete with furnishings and their own coaches.

The gentlemen at the Justice Chancellery had never worked so quickly as they did now. Large public placards announced the auction of all the houses in the Calenberger Neustadt that belonged to the Behrens family and immediately the Goldschmidts, Wertheimers and Lehmanns prepared, in steadfast unity, to take in the wives and children of the Behrens brothers and to save whatever was still salvageable. The precious library in Leffmann's house needed to be found a new home. Leffmann's grandson Joseph Oppenheimer (the son of his daughter Genendel) was determined to take it into his house. However, he only rented, and it was far too small; he had never managed to buy his own house, let alone build one. Now he was prepared to offer everything that he could scratch together and borrow from his cousins and brother-in-laws In fact he managed to buy the Leffmann house at Langestrasse 8 at auction, which met with little approval from the town councillors. Suddenly they announced that Jews were not permitted to buy houses at auction. So the auction was declared invalid and a new date set. This time, no other parties showed any interest to overbid Joseph Oppenheimer. Perplexity at the Town-hall.

Joseph Oppenheimer grasped a quill-pen with determination and wrote a letter overflowing with submissive pleading verbiage to his King in London on 18 September 1722:

> *Your Most Royal Majesty, All Powerful King, Most Merciful King and Lord.*
>
> *Your Royal Majesty has in regard to your humblest truest knave Lefman (sic) Behrens, my blessed grandfather, the special Royal mercy and most gently moved, has most mercifully promised to cherish me and in 1717 gave me a Privilege, the mercy to allow me to live in Neustadt, to reside near my own people and to follow my trade, in the same way the Lefman Behrens once enjoyed; as Your Royal Majesty mercifully allowed. Because I have no trade as a money-lender I have not been able to establish a permanent counting house or apartment until now, although I wished to, but now the possibility has arisen that the house of the Brothers Behrens should be sold 'sub hasta' (under the hammer) and this was made public by the local Justice Chancellery and the curator in public newspapers that it was to be put up for auction to Jews and Christians as a commodious house.*
>
> *All the while my grandfather served the land and the most merciful Gentlemen with his money changing business to his best ability, which now I with God's help will be able to carry on, and the houses which date back to him and were built for trade, I would most unhappily see in the hands of strangers, thus I, in consideration of the publicized invitation and with the authority and privileges granted me by Your Royal Majesty, found my place at the first auction of this house and bought it by giving the last and highest bid. I will also present myself as a buyer at the forthcoming and third auction in the most humble and undoubted confidence that the privileges granted me, the same as were allowed Lefman Behrens and other local protected Jews, to possess my own house and ground and besides because these were always Jewish houses as far back as my grandfather there will be few, other than Jewish buyers and the creditors of the Brothers Behrens will be well served by my purchase.*
>
> *And although I cannot understand the letters of the privileges grant to me any other way except that Your Royal Majesty's opinion is that I as*

*well as Lefman Behren had and other protected Jews still have their own possessions to my and mine essential requirements, as the Ruler of the Land in high mercy indulges. Your Royal Majesty's most merciful orders are that we may not buy houses and attached land without high consent, thus I ingratiate myself at the feet of Your Royal Majesty to most humbly plead for your most high declaration over my aforementioned privileges to let me flourish in the greatest mercy and mildness that the content of the same be allowed as for Lefman Behrens and other local protected Jews to possess real property that may be bequeathed. Whereby such exceeding worry and fretfulness could be removed from the purchase, and I should be so much more comforted at the forthcoming sale. Also the maintenance of the house for money-changing will be for the best for the land, the local Residence and the Commune, if God will, and continue to successfully find better opportunities. Trusting myself to the most merciful will I persist in deepest devotion with good and blood*

*Your Royal Majesty's most humble and truly obedient knave*
    *Joseph David Oppenheimer.*

Many days passed before Oppenheimer's letter was shipped over the Channel and at last arrived in London. But already on 2 October 1722 dictated by King George in Kensington Palace, came a highly remarkable answer – not to the pleader Oppenheimer but to the Privy Secretary in Hannover.

*Secretary and dear Servant*

*We have been made aware by the Protected Jew David Oppenheimer, the grandson of our former Court and Chamber Agent Leffmann Behrens, that after his grandfather's house in the Neustadt was put to auction for the highest bidder by the wishes of the creditors, he gave the highest bid for the same house at the first auction, in the second he was outbid, at the third 'subhastation' (Auction) that will take place on the 22 October he will appear again, but arraigned that if he bids the most he will not be permitted to buy the house because it has been ordered that local protected Jews may not acquire real property without express consent. Now indeed we let such orders stand for the time being but do not think that they should be applied in this case because the purchase of the Leffmann Behrens' house is not a house that previously belonging to Christians would now become a Jewish house, which is the purpose and intention of such a prohibition, but instead the house was built by Jews, has for all time been owned by Jews and is so equipped that a Jew*

> is better served by it than a Christian. Therefore the creditors of Behrens would be undoubtedly harmed and the house sold too cheaply if the local protected Jews were excluded from the sale. We therefore order that at the third auction on 22 October anyone who wishes to bid, be he Jew or Christian, be allowed to the auction and that the house be sold to the highest bidder be he Christian or Jew. You will inform our local Justice Chancellery as to their performance and disposition of the necessity.

From the letter it is shown that at the second auction, Joseph Oppenheimer was outbid by another unwanted buyer, thus another Jew, and we can be almost certain that it was one of the Goldschmidt cousins or sister Freudel's husband Simon Wolf Oppenheimer, who had a money changing business in Hannover, who jumped in to help. In the end the third auction achieved the hoped for success for all those involved. The library, for which the town had anyway not found a buyer, was rescued. And Leffmann's widow Veile could decide in peace how long she wished to stay in this house that now belonged to her great nephew Joseph Oppenheimer. Both Ruben Goldschmidt in Hamburg and his brother Aron in Copenhagen were prepared to have her stay with them until the end of her life. Because she died a few years later in Hamburg (17 August 1727) we know which her preference was.

Joseph had bought not only his grandfather Leffmann's house but also it seems the houses of Gumpert and Isaak for it is certain that their wives stayed in them. What they and their children lived on while their husbands were in *Knast* (a Yiddish word for prison that is common in German!) is not known. But as both Lea and Sprinze (Esperanza) came from wealthy families it may be presumed that they were supported by them. Of course they wished to remain in the same place so that they could quickly go to the Cleves Gate if permission were unexpectedly granted, and in case of need stand in for their husbands at the chancellery, naturally extremely devout as would be expected. They were brought up to display such an attitude and now had the opportunity to display it in the face of their Christian neighbours' malice every day. What a life.

Almost a paradise – if one compares the lives of their husbands who could only wait for the law professors out of Ingolstadt who had studied the files to pass sentence on them.

Only on 7 May 1723, two years after they were taken prisoner did that happen.

Isaak Behrens reported:

> .... and we heard the sentence together with the reasons for the decision, which was very favourable for us. However the creditors and their

*lawyer, Schrader, immediately appealed to Celle and that was accepted as the files show.*

\*\*\*\*

The answer to the objection took a long time. It was winter. On 11 January 1724 Isaak wanted to split a log of wood for the fire in his room and as the axe in his hand slipped it made a deep wound in his right ankle. Hours passed before one allowed it to be bandaged. The chain between his his hand and ankle was now transferred to the 'good' unhurt side. No mercy. Four weeks later, Isaak was stricken by a colic that frightened the guards, it might be something infectious, so that a doctor was called. He prescribed a period in bed and medicine. The chain, only temporarily removed, was again locked on.

At last on 12 February 1724 an answer came from Celle: If the accused did not voluntarily confess that they had put money and securities to one side, then *'severe questioning'* would be required. Torture grade 2. At once the defender raised objections and from Celle received the charge to prepare a written defence with the Behrens brothers in the presence of the secretary Knolle and hand it in. It was studied in Celle. The gentlemen took their time. On 24 May 1724 the answer was: the threat of torture remained unchanged.

The sentence created shock wave which reached even the Prussian Court in Berlin. Queen Sophie Dorothea, daughter of the Elector of Hannover, now the King of England, had not forgotten who had organised the longed for expensive robes from Paris for her marriage to the Crown-Prince Friedrich Wilhelm: Leffmann Behrens. How was it possible that his grandchildren could be threatened with torture for truly unknown crimes in order to clear up a matter in which other debtors must also be involved? Was there not a debt of 68,500 Reichstaler of the Mecklenburg Knighthood, so embarrassing for the Prussian Royal household, which after the insolvency of Isaak Behrens should have been paid to his father-in-law Berend Lehmann? As security for the loan in the case that they were unable to repay, the Mecklenburg gentlemen had given a charge on their manors. Did Sophie Dorothea need to talk to her spouse about the matter? Or had he already undertaken something towards rescuing the unlucky brothers? He had.

Already on 25 March 1724 an Intervention from Friedrich Wilhelm I had been sent to King George in England:

*Your Serene Highness Omnipotent Prince,*

*Friendly beloved Cousin, Father and Administrator. Your Majesty will without doubt be aware of the stiff sentence passed by the Senior Court of Appeal in Celle in the matter of the Jews Gumpert and Isaak Behrens published on the 12th of the ultimo month of February, which content, that were the said Jews not to acknowledge the preparation of fraudulent Letters of Exchange and simulated assignments, they were to be exerted to such a confession by strict painful questioning. Now I indeed allow that the Senior Court of Appeal must have been given the circumstances and reasons for such a favourable sentence which the interrogated received from the Justice Faculty in Ingolstadt and with which two responses from disinterested parties of Law professors completely agree, and as a consequence have a strong legal presumption for the sentence to be changed and intensified.*

*It is in no way my intention to inhibit or stop the flow of justice by my intervention, much less, Your Majesty to set the least objective or measure, however, it is easy to be of the opinion that by following the instructions of the Senior Court of Appeal against the interrogated, they out of fear of martyrdom not only for themselves but also against others, might damage the truth and that such types of suspicion of the reason for the ceding of known Mecklenburg Obligations by the interrogated to the Jew Behrend Lehmann, and indeed how one has very significant causes to believe, that in completely innocent ways, by these assignments the Halberstadt Principality's Laws and Powers have a marked interest in the matter of the intended accusation of the Jew Lehmann which may cause still greater and irreversible difficulties and complications.*

*Thus my friendly-brotherly appeal to Your Majesty that you will, in consideration of these significant circumstances, give the command that the Behren brothers be not over-hurriedly heard but rather contrary to more over-zealous sentence of the Senior Court of Appeal and that the files may be sent on for an outsider's legal acknowledgement. In my opinion it would be the best way to relieve the accusations against the accused and all others who are participants in the matter and nonetheless bring the truth to light.*

*I should therefore hold that if the matter is proceeded with in this way, the Senior Court of Appeal pleases itself and should calm itself because whether indeed all are persuaded of the legality and right of the Judiciary and all its members, many of the same are either creditors or debtors of the interrogated and if they continue in the matter and do not rather subject themselves to a disinterested outsider and distance themselves to gain in reputation it would be as if they were judges in their own matter but which is so unlikely to be believed of You, that Your Majesty would allow that there cannot be the least suspicion.*

*Much more I promise myself that Your Majesty's highly regarded zeal for Justice and Mildness that is known by all the world will in this manner give a just reflex to this well meant notion, and my above mentioned appeal which I now repeat will not be in vain and that I also hold You unchanged with the highest regard in all things.*

*Your Majesty*
*happily cousin, son and relative*
*Friedrich Wilhelm R.*
*to Your Royal Majesty of Great Britain.*
*(State Archive Hannover: Hannover 92 XVII, V No. 13 Vol.III)*

Friedrich Wilhelm's father-in-law, King George was distant from these happenings and when Rickmann, the brother's defence lawyer now stormed into the chancellery and pleaded the gentlemen to wait with the torture because the Behrens relations had sent an emissary on horseback to Halberstadt to the banker Behrend Lehmann and awaited at any moment suggestions as to a settlement but even this objection could not help. Because in Hannover neither the King nor Elector were in control, here apparently only Herr von Bernstorff had anything to say. He commanded, he signed the orders and he was in the City Hall, where Gumpert and Isaak were for interrogation, when a letter from Joseph Oppenheimer and Samuel Hamburger, two cousins of the delinquents, arrived with the request to speak to the councillors to offer a settlement before the torture began, he threw the letter to the ground in a rage.

Isaak Behrens reported:

*But then he picked it up again, read it and laid it in front of him. Meanwhile the executioner who had been expressly brought from Osterode was called in. Herr von Bernstorff spoke to me. 'I want to introduce you to another person, you will tell him the truth better than you do me.' And as the executioner stepped in he said to him: 'Master, here is someone who will not tell us the truth, you will be able to get it out of him' and the executioner commenced shouting at me with a terrifying voice and banging my head and tore out my side whiskers – I had no other hair on my head so that I shouted: is this the amicable settlement? I was taken out with the executioner and made to wait* outside the door, where he again shouted horribly at me while raising his stick and threatened me so that I thought he would crack open my head.

Shortly after the order came to bring me back into the chamber and Gumpert was fetched, he was also examined and introduced to the executioner who jumped about him in the same way as he had with me. during this I made my evening prayer – I had already performed the afternoon prayer – and this time I confessed to so many sins as if I were already one who was condemned to death.

About 5 o'clock the executioner appeared and said that I should be taken to the cellar. The sergeant stepped forward to the gentlemen and asked again. They explained that yes it should be so. The adjutant Vogt followed me down. As soon as I was in the cellar the executioner called: Off with the clothes! I took off my nightdress and the 'kantuschen' (an under-shirt, maybe) The executioner shouted: Everything! Then he ripped my shirt up – it was still buttoned – and struck me 40 or 50 times with all his strength even before the other gentlemen had come in. He whipped me in my face between the eyes. I bore the marks for a long time. Then he hung wooden wedges round my neck, that was 6 or 7 pieces fitted together so that as soon as I wanted to cry out they went into my mouth so that I could not shout. Then I had to sit at the lower end of the bench. Now the gentlemen came in. The assistant asked if he should free me and this was affirmed. About 12 candles were lit and my eyes were bound with a broad rope. A youth had to remove my stockings and trousers; these last he had to tear because he could not get them off quickly enough. In the same way he tore the shirt off completely and bound a hair-shirt as large as a handkerchief which was tied behind.

Now the actual torture began. The executioner and his knave placed my hands at my back and put thumbscrews on, tied a rope to my hands and pulled them backwards above my head. As I cried, they should rather cut off my head, I was whipped on my back. Between times they asked me whether I intended to be bankrupted and whether I had put something to one side. I had to answer every question. If I cried too loudly they pushed the wood into my mouth which I bit into in pain.

Afterwards they put a 'Spanish Boot' on each leg: they are as wide as a hand and are screwed together till the calves are quite flat. At the same time I was asked as before and answered the same. Now a screw on each foot was turned that was a little narrower and tightened them so much as possible. They alternated the larger one above and the smaller below and the other way about and indeed individually from ankle to knee and that very often.

Then they took a thin rope and tied it from the shoulders to the hands and tightened it so that it cut deep into the flesh. This pulled the shoulder-blades so close together that the head and chest sank down. Thus I hang in a line. It was pulled up high and as soon as I was stretched out so that my toes only just touched the ground I was pulled half an ell higher and that again and again. At the same time I was beaten with a whip.

Then they threw fire on my back. I don't know what it was but imagined it was sulphur and pitch. I was sick a couple of times, then they held the burning sulphur under my nose or hit my head until I was punch-drunk. This often happened. They dropped 18 fire-drops on my back so that I screamed, they were burning me to death. That was not enough for them. They made a plaster of the burning material and laid it burning between the shoulder-blades and let it burn. One can imagine how I screamed.

Then they undid everything and let me down so that I sat on the bench. That was just for a short time then then pulled me up with all their strength. The screws were once again tightened and fire was thrown at me again, mostly my right foot. After that they took a stout stick tied it to my left elbow, pulled it tight and then took it off again. The executioner said that I still didn't show the 'sign'. He looked me over from all sides, held up my head, observed something on my neck, so that I thought that death was near because of what he must mean with the 'signs' and I felt near to death.

This all lasted about two and a half hours after which they let me down and undid everything. I knew nothing about my life any more. The men commanded that I should remain sitting. Then they fetched my brother Gumpert down. They persuaded him that he should voluntarily confess and not let himself be treated in the way he could see I had been – because I was covered in blood as one can imagine. Then they took him upstairs again and threw my shirt over me but it was not possible to put it on. With much effort they covered me with the nightdress but my slippers would not pass over my big toe, not to mention my thickly swollen feet. While dressing me they put my hands over my head, I was *not aware that they were my arms. One of the executioners dragged me upstairs. At each step in the cellar and on the stairs to the courtyard I stumbled to the ground; everything in me seemed to be broken, body and soul had crumpled like a ball of yarn. Before I left the cellar, I asked Herr von Bernstorff not to chain me again. He answered No.*

*As I came up they brought me over the leaden ground behind a wooden screen in a proper hole where poor sinners were kept. I was thrown onto the straw like a dog and they left me uncovered as my shirt had been torn open and I had nothing to pull over me. I asked for water to drink or a glass of beer; I was given nothing and the hole was closed.*

*Now Gumpert was taken to the cellar and martyred as I had been.*

*At the same time I froze so much that one could hear my teeth chattering through the courtyard. After a while the adjutant Vogt opened up and covered me with straw which did not help much. Between 9 and 10 o'clock the executioner came and allowed medicinal spirits for a groschen be fetched; the money was taken out of my trouser pocket by the female guard; I drank it in one gulp. Also a couple of drops of water from a couple of litres in a flask. He also allowed red spirit wine be fetched and tearing a piece of my shirt, wet it with the spirit and bound my feet. Afterwards the cook came – but she was not allowed to give me the bottle of 'Broyhan' a dark beer, which was held to my mouth by hand of the female guard till I had drunk it. She also brought me a couple of pillows and a feather-bed. They covered me but I could not get warm. At last the cook came to my prison, I spoke to her through the spyhole in the door, complained about my condition, told her about the torture, asked after my dear wife and asked that she come to me early next morning.*

*In the night I could not sleep for pain and thirst. I whined until eventually the guard, named Engelmann from the company of Capitan Wackerbart, passed a pot with Broyhan beer in and with the help of a long stick held it to my mouth so that some went in, the rest ran over my bare body. The pain was so strong it was as if I was still being tortured and they were still tightening the screws. In the night the sentry appeared at my prison, called and I answered.*

*Early Friday the cook came and brought me coffee, I drank a couple of saucers full which she held to my mouth as I could not hold anything myself. The executioner came and ordered that camomile oil and brown wine with saffron be rubbed in and so that the wounds would close. That was done the whole day and until midday next day. On that Friday Dr Ebel was directed to me by the chancellery. He visited in the afternoon, prescribed medicine and something for the thirst. At night towards 10 o'clock the adjutant Vogt came with an order to take us back to the Cleves Gate. That was done at the request of our wives. Mine sent a chair with a back and two sedan poles to the City hall for the purpose. I was carried in a calico sheet out of the dungeon to the leaden ground. On the chair were feather-beds on which I was lain. At each side were four people and a carrier in front and at the back: thus was I carried past my house to the Cleves Gate. I saw many people who were standing in front of their doors and called to them 'Good Morning!'*

*Thus I gained my room, was carried up in the canvas sheet and laid in my bed. The room was heated; but I still was cold. I had not slept in the night but let cold compresses be made all the while. Both the under-officers had to go out, the door remained open so that the guard could see what was going on. On the Sabbath the order to allow the door to be closed was given.*

*The transport from the City hall to the Cleves Gate was done under close guard. Now everyone was allowed to come to us. On the Sabbath morning two assistants of the medical man Wrede appeared, bandaged us and cut open many burn blisters. My right foot was found to be very bad, it was quite black almost like a dry burn. The executioner Kale appeared quite often to check on us. In the afternoon the young Wrede came with several assistants and bandaged us.*

    *In the evening I let my wife come to me, but could not touch her, neither with my hands or feet could I move. When the bed was to be made up, ten people had to lift me in a sheet and lay me in a day bed. On Sunday the old Wrede came with his son, some journeymen and other chaps, also Dr Ebel in order to bandage us and prescribe medicine.*

*On Monday it was ordered not to let anyone visit us except the Doctor, the barber and the cook. But as it was impossible to help us because each of us needed two or three people and to get us out of bed as many as eight were required, the order was given at 3 o'clock to limit the number of the servants allowed to us to 14. One of the Wredes' assistants had arranged that by saying that it was dangerous and impossible to bandage the sufferers twice a day without help.*

*The burns between the shoulder-blades were so dangerous that they wanted to cut them open by a hand-width. Also the city surgeon Körber, who was often present, demanded this, It did not happen because I refused energetically as I had on the Sabbath when the field surgeon wanted to remove my right foot.*

*On Tuesday our wives went to the chancellery and forced Herr von Bernstorff to let them spend the day with us. Meanwhile I was so bad with fever that Wrede could not bandage me anew, but looked in on me every two hours. In the night he bled me after which I felt better. But I laid so ill for five weeks that I could not pray for weakness, nor speak a blessing and had to be fed like a small child.*

\*\*\*\*

It is not possible to find out what was happening in the chancellery at this time, what was decided there or rejected. But certainly the exchange of very contrary orders was by now obviously chaotic, the new orders regarding how the prisoners were to be guarded were different almost every day. The impression that Herr von Bernstorff was increasingly losing countenance became stronger. His plan to use torture to uncover a fraudulent insolvency had to be seen as a failure. The mangled bodies of those tortured could not make him reconsider, maybe in his eyes Jews were just very tough. The results could have nothing to do with bravery, belief in God or simply with the truth. Already the positive edicts from distinguished lawyers in Halle, Jena and Ingolstadt did not fit into his scheme, neither the offer of a fair settlement for the creditors, that was still open to discussion which a bundle of relations, all Court Jews against whom no reproach could be made even with the most vicious will. And again the wives of the delinquents came to the chancellery because they were unable to exist on the two and a half Taler per week that was allowed them out of the insolvency estate and because they were subserviently and persistently ready to do anything to obtain the freedom of their husbands or at least to be allowed to visit them in the Cleves Gate every day. There the executioner in his rage tried to beat Isaak in his bed without any reason or command so that the guard interposed himself. The angry executioner was then himself arrested for half a day and later was only allowed in the prisoner's cell while under observation of a guard. The only thing that Herr von Bernstoff could still do was to delay forwarding the files because of some statement that was lacking. The Justice Chancellery of the Electorate's Court, which was situated in Celle as before would be informed of the outcome of the 'painful questioning' at some time.

It was autumn. Winter came. No word about a final sentence. Not only did Celle have to decide. Also the High Court in Cologne was expected to inspect the files which no-one knew whether they had even arrived at Celle.

Therefore the wives, Lea and Sprinze, travelled determinedly to Celle. It was several days before they were let in to be heard and then they came back with the modest news that Gumpert's and Isaak's sister, Hanne from Halle, would also be allowed to visit and also Phöbus, a cousin. Shortly after Celle sent a confirmation and an edict whereby the wives were permitted to spend an hour with the husbands very morning and evening. The Senior Lieutenant attached it to the door and said 'Everything else remains unchanged.'

At this point a whole year is missing from Isaak's report. He wrote, without further comment: 'Everything else that happened is to be found in the files.'

A year of waiting and still no sentence. Just the news that on 17 December 1725, Gumpert's and Isaak's mother was buried in Frankfurt am Main: the 'sweet' Susanne, née Gomperz. Her father was once the Military Supplier to the great Prince-Elector; her brother Ruben Elias Gomperz was allowed to take care of the finances of the Prussian Rulers and under King Friedrich I was promoted to the Senior Receptor of the Brandenburg Mark and was thus the first Jew to attain the status of a Prussian State Official.

Only in January 1726 did the High Court in Cologne pass the decisive sentence that 'complete release must be recognised'. On 19 February 1726 the same sentence came from Celle.

Isaak Behrens reported:

> *On Wednesday 20 February we were released and travelled at once over the Harz (to sister Hanne) in Halle, God grant us further happiness and blessings!*
>
> *What occurred during our journey from Halle to Hamburg and Altona may be found in my other small notebook of memories, as a thankful reminder of the wonderful mercy of God. This book I leave to my children as a memento and they should celebrate a Purim Feast on every 19 February because on that day God released my from the tribulation and suffering. May the Lord keep us from destitution and save us in times of affliction and please us and fulfil our wishes in his Goodness and Mercy. Amen.*

****

# An Epilogue

In this tragedy dominated by men, there were two female secondary characters whose importance was first recognisable after the final act: Lea, Isaak's wife, and the nameless cook. She was the sole eye and ear witnesses who could tell her mistress what was happening in the Cleves Gate. Because she brought their daily meals, also fresh clothes and even if the guards present made sure that only German was spoken, one can imagine that a softly spoken Hebrew remark escaped them: otherwise Isaak could not have written his report which concurred with the files after his release. Here he must have had help from Lea with her clever Lehman's head, in that she carefully noted the cook's descriptions with the dates, because at least in the first year of imprisonment, Isaak had no access to pen and ink, so that secret notes were absolutely impossible. First in Halle, in the house of his wealthy sister Hanne, where the family first took refuge, could he start his transcript. The text, in German but with many Hebrew or Yiddish words, was written in Hebrew script. The original script, apparently written up in a delicate handwriting by a secretary in the congregation, was made in 1738 and was translated into high German in 1860 by historian Isaak Markus Jost (1793-1860) and published in the yearbook of the *History of the Jews and Jewishness*, Volume II in 1861.

Acquitted by all the highest German courts consulted, exonerated from the accusation of fraudulent bankruptcy, the brothers were validated as rehabilitated. But they had lost the Court titles. Their possessions had been auctioned off and their wealth completely gone. Relying on the generosity of their relations, Goldschmidt, Oppenheimer and Lehmann, who immediately created a safety net for them together, a new start was anything but easy. Because creditors who were still waiting for the final balance were plentiful. And there was the commitment on oath by the brothers that every Taler that they might earn in the future should be passed to the not yet completely satisfied creditors. On the other side they counted even more powerful debtors who saw the arrest of the brothers as a good reason not to repay their long overdue loans.

We know about Isaak's later life in Hamburg, Altona and at the end with his son, the medical man, Dr Lehmann Behrens in Rendsburg. But how

Gumpert overcame the results of his torture is unknown. His wife Sprinze died in the year after his release, his only child, daughter Jente, followed five years later. Both were buried in Hannover. There is no further news of Gumpert, no date of death, no grave and no epilogue in the Memorbuch of the congregation.

# The Danish Protectorate

In Altona it was not only the Goldschmidts who were watching the trial of their cousins in Hannover with great interest and who were surprised by Gumpert's hair-raising wheelings and dealings; Count Reventlow, who was Oberpresident in the Danish Government also knew the facts. And when Isaak Behrens travelled to Altona after a short stay with his sister in Halle in order to find out whether there were possibilities for him to re-establish himself in business there, he applied to the Danish town council, presumably supported by Ruben Goldschmidt, and immediately received a 'Protectorate' from the Danish King Frederik IV after the Oberpresident von Reventlow put in a word for him. This revealed the reasons and background of the trial more clearly than any other document because in it we read of not only of things that Gumpert kept secret from his brother; debt transferred into a separate book, a great fire in Frankfurt also mentioned elsewhere – in which Gumpert's office there was severely damaged, but also of incitement against the Behrens by ill-disposed persons in Hannover, who wished to foil a very advantageous settlement for the creditors proposed by the banker Behrend Lehmann. The name of the Secretary von Bernstorff is not mentioned in this document of 29 July 1726. The banker Lehmann twice. Because it was he who was prepared to give financial help to his son-in-law, who had been tortured though innocent and imprisoned for five years, to found a business in Altona if he could be assured that the Danish Authorities would guarantee the supplicant a residence permit.

But of course! After the four highest German courts had unanimously pronounced him not guilty at the behest of the Government of the Principality of Hannover there could be no doubt of the decency of the former Court Factor. Apparently the Town Fathers of Altona who were consulted about the residence permit were able to overlook the openly admitted fact that some creditors who had not yet been completely paid out were still chasing Isaak Behrens. Accordingly the last paragraphs of the royal Danish document abbreviated and here in modern language tell us:

> ...granted that we accept the humblest proposal by our Senior Chamberlain, Secretary, General, Senior Hunt-master and beloved

*faithful Herr Christian Detlef von Reventlow, Oberpresident of Altona, that the supplicant is not unworthy of our protection which he humbly applies for in Royal mercy, we hereby issue the so named Isaak Jakob (Behrens) our Royal Protection and safe passage and wish that if he, together with his dependents and goods and chattels, settles in our Town Altona and earns the citizen's rights, carries on his allowed trade and business there as well as in our other realms, principalities and countries and that he shall not be subjected to demands, neither in court nor out of court, by his foreign creditors for his previously incurred debts. However he shall in time satisfy the same and also our own subjects if they have a justified claim on him with the same law.*

*Our Oberpresident 'pro tempore' and the Councillors of Altona as well as other Senior and Junior Servants and sundry others shall humbly respect this.*

Without doubt the faithful Oberpresident supported the Royal Protectorate to his best ability because he could thus show his thanks and loyalty to the Goldschmidt relatives; he had not forgotten that the Court Jeweller of Gottorf, Bendix Goldschmidt, had once helped him out of a precarious situation with two advances of, in sum, 75,000 Reichtaler through the mediation of his brother-in-law, Freiherr von Görtz.

Once again the Danish Altona became a safe home for the family. Of course it was not a painless new start for Isaak Behrens, who had felt himself at home in the Residence City of Hannover but at least at first he did not want to be seen there. As an asylum-seeker in his own house with his cousin Joseph Oppenheimer perhaps? Oppenheimer had in the meantime risen to be Court Factor but after buying the Behrens' houses at auction was anything but wealthy. He possessed a very valuable library but was unable to do anything with it. He would have liked to use it as security for loans but for ethical reasons could only do that after the death of his father David Oppenheimer, who was the actual owner. And Prince Eugen who had collected the books and presented them to the Oppenheimers, would have been horrified to hear of them being used to raise loans. So they waited. During the fourth decade of the eighteenth century family members from two generations died in numbers. The first: the major financier of many Princes, Berend Lehmann (9 July 1730), next year Gumpert's daughter Jente (30 December 1731) and his brother-in-law, Jehuda Löb Oppenheimer, the husband of his sister Simielies and grandson of the famous banker (4 March 1732); then Jente, Gnendel's daughter (18 March 1736); and half a year later, just a few months after the death of the library patron Prince Eugen (21 April 1736), the inheritor of the books, the old David Oppenheimer, Chief Rabbi in Bohemia and Moravia was carried to his grave with worthy condolences on 13 September 1736 in Prague. And immediately Joseph Oppenheimer in Hannover swept aside all ethical scruples. The book treasure was shipped to Hamburg, used as security with someone who was able to appreciate this book-lover's delicacy and lend it out. Just how the transaction finished is not known to us but since 1829 it has been in the Bodelian Library in Oxford. But remarkably thinned out.

From the family trees of the criss-cross relationships of the relatives it is clear that none of them was untouched financially by the bankruptcy of the Behrens brothers. The most fortunate were the Goldschmidts with their connections to the Fürsts, who were clever enough businessmen to weigh every risk and in case of need, step back. They lived a less baronial lifestyle than Gumpert who had by now disappeared like a phantom, of whom the Hannovarian Justice Chancellery in 1721 wrote that he *'exhibited himself splendidly masterful and very expensively, without regard to all his debts'*. But the Goldschmidts were not doing at all badly. All of them were under Danish Royal protection: Aron with his wife Freude Fürst and ten children in Copenhagen; his brother Hirsch (but rather called Hartwig!) and Ruben the eldest in Altona.

He is our direct ancestor, but despite this, we know little of him and his wife Johanna Fürst. Apart from Ruben's activity with his brother Aron in the often mentioned tobacco monopoly, we know nothing personal. No special privileges. Because his date of marriage is lacking, we can only speculate whether he married unusually late in life or simply had to wait a long time before Johanna and he had the longed for children. He was 48 before he had three children, of whom the first, Bendix, puzzles us. According to several family-trees – in Hebrew it sounds prettier: 'Megillen' – he came into the world in 1726; after him, a daughter, Röschen and at the end of 1729 Philipp. After his birth on 21 December 1729, Johanna died. Her gravestone in Altona describes her death as one of an 'abrupt birthing', so it may have been a premature birth.

But did his heir Bendix remain alive at all long? Why does his name appear in all the documents, and their Prussian accuracy allow no doubts, showing his year of birth as 1734? Did Ruben Goldschmidt marry again after the death of Johanna because his first-born had maybe died as a baby and his last child, Philipp had only a small chance of survival? Would a younger and more robust wife have given him a new heir with the same name? It was not unusual. Traditions, of which given names are a part, are passed on in this way.

1730 was a year of mourning for the widower. But it was necessary for a father of two very small children to enter a new marriage. Happiness for an all too short a time.

For this decade of dying still had some spaces. Already on 7 September 1734 Ruben Goldschmidt was buried in Altona, in the same year in which all official lists show the birth of his son Bendix as his sole heir. As his gravestone records 'at harvest time'. Shortly thereafter on the 26 November 1734 his sister-in-law, Freude Fürst, Aron Goldschmidt's wife died; four years later, 1738, cousin Blümle Oppenheimer and at last in 1739 also their brother Joseph, heir to the famous Oppenheimer library which had in the meantime been sold.

Certainly Johanna Goldschmidt was no longer young at the time of her last delivery which ended so tragically. Questions arise, whether her late blessing of children had other less private reasons. Perhaps the official financial hurdles which one liked to put in front of Jewish couples before a permit to marry could be given. Had the 'Limitation of Jewish marriages' cooked up by the Prussians spread like a wicked infection to other countries? Was it possible that in humanitarian, freedom loving Danish Altona, something similar existed? There is no answer.

# The Recruits' Treasury

If the rulers were themselves not especially inventive, they had their industrious, cunning advisors who helped them in war and peace, and who gave them new ideas to find new money sources. Jews were in no way unwelcome to the authorities as long as they brought money, had good business connections abroad and so enhanced the prosperity of the state. For the exchequer they were in any case – and these cases could easily be increased – profitable. Because every citizen's right that was self-evident for a non-Jew, required a payment by the Jews: for the right to stay, to reside, to travel over a border, to trade, without a shop of course, for permission to engage servants or private tutors, to marry and have children. One called it 'sprouting' children as one says trees sprout twigs. Thus quite frightening. Each twig created a new family, new competitors. As bankers they were admittedly, ingenious; as military suppliers indispensable, inventive, punctual. Competition enlivened business. But Jewish competitors, who by their ambition alone, grew out of the unloved minority and were so often significantly quicker and in many areas more competent than their Christian fellow citizens, were regarded as threatening.

Earlier, where Jews were seen as rivals at the feeding trough, they were expelled without further reason or when the locals arose in their masses looking for a scapegoat after an epidemic or increase in taxation, beaten up and chased from their homes. In the meantime the Time of Enlightenment had arrived and one had to seek other methods to prevent Jewish children 'sprouting'. Prussia made a start in 1714 with the Regulation of Jews Order, Emperor Karl VI followed up in 1718 with his own more rigorous laws.

These laws were not exactly new. By 1682 the Counts of Schaumburg had thought about how the number of Jews in their small country could be reduced. Recorded in a document for Isaak Heine, who wanted to settle in Bückeburg and to whom a letter of protection was sold for an annual fee, all the prohibitions and commandments that a Jew should obey are listed. Trading was allowed but only in those wares that were not traded by the businessmen who belonged to a guild. Thus did many opportunities to earn disappear. Guilds were closed to Jews. Jews were permitted to let their adult, unmarried children live with them. But as soon as they should marry and go into trade for themselves, *'they shall, within the next six weeks – if they have not achieved Protection by the grace of the Count, which remains his to freely grant or deny in his mercy – leave the country and not let themselves be found in a house on pain of a fine of 5 Taler'.*

Even widows and widowers were regulated. If they should wish to remarry after the death of their partner: permitted! But only once! And only, after they had registered their wish to marry at the high count's chancellery and received permission from the high count's chamber. If the newly wed partner should then die, a further marriage was not allowed.

The Royal Prussian Regulations for the constraint of the increasing Jewish population were decidedly stricter than these really small-state methods. The Edict of 20 May 1714 by Friedrich-Wilhelm I determined that only those Jews who had their own Letter of Protection (for the appropriate fee) or at least were named as an *'accompanying'* person in their father's Letter of Protection and recorded in a list might be allowed to have children. And not more than three. And of these three, only the first-born might marry and have children. Three. The second child who wanted to marry had first to prove a fortune of 1,000 Reichstaler and pay a fee of 50 Reichstaler into the so-called Recruits' Treasury before approval to have children would be given. The hurdle was raised even higher for the third child. The wealth to be shown was doubled, thus 2,000 Reichstaler and the permit cost twice as much. Now one has to know that in 1700 the average family could live for a year on 1,000 Taler. So one can see that the state was assured that no poor beggars had to be tolerated and at the same time with the help of a few papers and stamps, revenue could be effortlessly raised.

Of course it occurred that some wealthy families capitulated in the face of such demands. For more important than the Recruits' Treasury was a decent dowry. Thus it was mostly the youngest daughter who was affected: she remained in waiting, until – God forbid – the elder daughter might die and then her widower, as was not unusual at the time, might take her home. Often, she was by then no longer able to bear children. That was fine for the state. Secret marriages, with the Rabbi's blessing in a back-room, were unthinkable. If that were to come out, the loss of protection privileges and thus the expulsion of the whole family, would have been the consequence. Besides the Rabbi was threatened by a monetary fine of 1,000 Taler. Neither was one allowed to marry in the neighbouring county and then to return with a marriage certificate and so evade the Recruits' Treasury. Even engagements between minors were suspicious and could be seen as secret marriages. Beware the young couple who had children while living under a parent's roof. That would not remain secret for long. The state had its eyes everywhere; the official apparatus was enormous. It was dependable. And if the Ruler in his palace were not to notice something, he had his whisperers who only wanted the 'best' for the Christians who were so disadvantaged by the Jews.

Thus the Very Secret State Councillor von Schlippenbach advised his King in 1722 to publish a new Regulation which gave him, Schlippenbach, the Royal command to take care of the question of limiting marriages under the Regulation of Jews Order… *'and those that contravene shall be denounced without further ado and the avoidance of His Royal Majesty's greatest disfavour and arbitary prosecution'.*

An appeal to those who felt disadvantaged by the Jews to spy on any suspicious neighbours who might long before have stopped wearing kaftans with a yellow recognition symbol such as rings and spots or even a pointed hat. In every case any obviously pregnant companions of pedlars were most obediently denounced. Those, who for lack of ready money had been unable afford to marry or have offspring and who had had to disappear in the darkness, to heaven know where outside the towns. Certainly the more prosperous were also deeply troubled. Should they emigrate? But where to? Other Germanic countries had also thought out the oddest measures to slow Jewish reproduction.

Could one imagine that our Ruben Goldschmidt who probably only married his Johanna Fürst in 1723 was affected by such regulation if it existed in Altona? Did he too, belong to those who could only afford three children? In the next Edict, of 29 September 1730 this sort of birth regulation was renewed and strengthened. Now only two children were allowed and already for the first one had to prove wealth of 1,000 Taler and 2,000 for the second and the extra fees had to be paid into the Recruits' Treasury. Ruben's younger brother Hirsch/Hartwig Goldschmidt, noticeably had no children with his wife Buna Bruck. Which later showed itself to be a blessing because when Johanna died unexpectedly young the baby Philipp and as we may assume the barely two year old Rosy were put into the care of their childless uncle, who later, when Ruben had died, adopted the youngest. In this way yet another Goldschmidt child could named in a Letter of Protection and thus his future made safe. There was never a word about an older son of Ruben who might have been included. But we cannot ignore the possibility that the uncle who traded as a silk merchant played a role as mentor to the boy Bendix, born in 1734. They lived in the same town and the growing lad must have picked up from his uncle how silk in all its varieties was manufactured and how one earned money by trading silk materials. Enough money to be able one day to leave Altona and set himself up as a silk merchant and money-lender in Potsdam at the court and to seek a bride in Potsdam.

Of course the idea of starting a family and a swarm of lively children was hopeless for the young ambitious Bendix. Because since 17 April 1750, Jews were only permitted to set one child in the world; that is, only this one child might be written into the Letter of Protection. Any children born later were excluded from their father's privileges and thus practically without any rights. A secret marriage would be punished with a fine, a tax on marriage in varying amounts; and also 14 Taler for the marriage lines and for registering the birth of a child up to 160 Taler.

Who helped Bendix in Potsdam? Had the King's mother Sophia Dorothea thankfully remembered the Chamber Agent of her father, Leffmann Behrens? Perhaps she also knew his Goldschmidt relations?

Bendix Goldschmidt had confidence, understanding and good fortune. In Potsdam he found not just a good place for his business but also his future bride, Ziporra, the daughter of Ari Löb. In the files he is usually named Leib Levin.

# Who is Leib Levin?

He appeared in Potsdam in 1733 without revealing from where. At first he was able to take shelter in his five-year-older brother's house, Salomon, who must have already achieved prosperity in the linen and woollen ware trade – otherwise he would not have been allowed to trade or live there. But his King, Friedrich Wilhelm I was well-disposed to him; he was one of those industrious Jews who paid taxes, whom the Monarch was not unhappy to let stay in his land. Salomon Levin received a letter of Protection on 8 January, personally signed by the King himself. It was of course not cheap. In the smaller Principalities, Jews generally had to pay about 10 or 25 Reichstaler per annum. Friedrich Wilhelm however demanded a one-off but awesome sum for the registration in the Prussian files, which sounds a little strange. Salomon Levin had *'to buy a house from Grenadier Knopel of the Royal Regiment for 1,000 rtl and pay in cash'*. Who was Grenadier Knopel? Did he want to, or did he have to get rid of a tumble-down house that the King regarded as a disgrace in his residence city, knowing that a Jew with a good income would make it an ornament soon after acquiring it? Or was there an agreement between Friedrich Wilhelm and his willing Jewish servants to treat certain Grenadiers preferentially, especially if they were very tall? We have the Resolution of the King to Jakob Gumperz, who was related by marriage to the Goldschmidts, dated 5 December 1732 regarding recruitment.

> *His Royal majesty grants the Jew Jakob Gumpert at his humblest application on 27th November the most merciful Resolution that, if he finds good-looking young recruits, 6 foot tall and more in their bare-feet, he will be gladly paid the following amount: For one 6 foot tall, 300 Rtlr, 6 foot 1 inch, 400 Rtlr, for one 74 inches tall, 500 Rtlr and for one 75 inches tall 1,000 rtl and for a seventy-six incher 2,000 Rtlr, but the people must be delivered free to Wesel, where His Royal Majesty will pay him the moneys through his General von Mosel.*

As one sees, Talers flowed through odd channels to please the Ruler. It was Leib Levin's good fortune that his brother Salomon counted as one of the few Ordinary Protected Jews, who contrary to the Extraordinary (or Supernumerary) was permitted to transfer his expensively acquired

Residence Permit to his eldest son or a brother. They were even allowed to bequeath their right to reside to their near relatives. The Letter of Protection for Extraordinary Jews was only a lifetime tolerance. And that was that.

As we know from the lists of citizens which the Prussians made so accurately, a third Levin brother had been living in Potsdam since 1730: Leibman Levin. Of course he had a Letter of Protection. However it did not allow him to have a guest to stay for more than a few days. Not even his own brother. Presumably Liebmann had a son who was included in his privilege. After that there was no allowance for a further member of the family and so no protection.

For Salomon who still apparently had no children, things looked different. He was able to let Leib Levin, who had arrived from some village or another – perhaps Schönflies? – live in his house, at least until the next Royal decree forbade it. Leib Levin, the last child of Arje Löb, was born shortly before his father died. This is recorded on his gravestone that is still visible in Potsdam. In 1733. When he knocked on his brother's door, full of sunny optimism he was 25 years old. Not a useless pauper wanting to have an easy life. He arrived with everything he possessed to hand so as to make a promising application for his own Letter of Protection at the Potsdam Authorities. And he got it at once. One was aware of the usual agonisingly long delay until the officials had checked everything and counted the savings that one brought in, weighed and scrutinised the bales of silk and wool that were taken to them and with which Leib Levin wanted to trade in the Residence city.

Perhaps the silk sample that he took to the Court appealed to the Queen because Sophie Dorothea, the spoiled daughter of the King of England who had grown up in Hannover knew about quality materials. Or perhaps he was just lucky. Because after an astonishingly short time on the 9 June 1733 he was handed the concession for trading in the Mark Brandenburg. And if he managed by living extremely modestly to save 1,000 Taler in the next years he might think about making a conquest of a wife and the Marriage permit that he would require.

Didn't the family of the well-respected Isaac have a daughter, Hanna? Was her father perhaps that David Isaac who belonged to the same congregation as Hirsch/Hartwig Goldschmidt, and who had by now moved from Hannover with the children of his deceased brother Ruben Goldschmidt and who was one of the congregation elders? How could they not know one-another if they prayed together every Sabbath? Anyone who chatted to Hirsch/Hartwig Goldschmidt after the service would talk about more than the manufacture of silk, a business that was not at that time prospering in Potsdam, they would also get to know the Isaac family better.

Hanna was still single at 25! Had the Recruits' Treasury swallowed too many of her father's Taler for her elder sibling's marriage permit, so that Hanna had had to wait?

For Leib Levin, who had no longer had a father to show wealth of 1,000 Reichstaler to the Recruits' Treasury it meant getting out and about, selling material and saving until the money necessary was gathered together. It took five years.

That the State of Prussia seemed particularly attractive to brave young social climbers was no accident. Friedrich Wilhelm I had cut-back the expenses on unnecessary luxury dramatically, dissipation at his Court was a thing of the past. Apart from a few regimental trumpeters the grand orchestra that had given concerts at the Court under Frederik I was let go. If Sophie Dorothea wanted to celebrate with a little chamber-music in her Palace Monbijou for her own pleasure that was down to her. Now the building of a frightening army was more important. A part of it were the 'long guys', and even Jews happily contributed to their hiring. For a long time now the descendants of our Goldschmidts, Oppenheimers and Wertheimers had not expected to achieve riches like their ancestors had and then maybe lose them in a noisily embarrassing bankruptcy again.

The King's troops required not just weapons and boots. They were dressed in blue uniforms and the wool, mostly imported from England cost a fortune which could be economised on. It would be profitable to offer cheaper materials made in Prussia to the Court. Mixed weaves of linen and local wool, tough drill or serge. The Long Guys (Lange Kerle) had better quality material, in red of course, and for the princesses occasionally some silk, embroidered for preference. But without pearls.

Within two generations the Jewish bankers' sons had moved from money-lending to trading in textiles. Imports from Spain and abroad, such as pepper and rare spices, with which one could earn so much, were forbidden. Prussian subjects had to make do with marjoram, parsley and other similar herbs that grew in their own gardens. The General Jewish Regulations of 1730 set out what Jews were allowed to trade in: among them were, besides jewels and silver, also silken, golden and silvery galloon, a decorative woven trim or braid, also nettle-cloth and white kattun or calico. Especially calico because the cotton-wool needed for its manufacture was on the Import-Index, but the King thought that it might be replaced by a thinner woollen weave, the one called simply 'stuff'. But first the necessary weaving looms were lacking and even more the women to spin the wool. The King had already years before remarked on this shortcoming and had passed the following Edict on 14 June 1723:

> ...that all the women squatting next to their wares and abandoned riff-raff should spin a pound of wool each week for the usual payment and deliver it to the warehouses in the Residence, also those at public stalls at the market or tradesmen's wives and citizen's daughters should apply the time that they have to spare with spinning, knitting and sewing rather than sitting lazily about in the lanes...

Now if one was unable to find women to spin among the female citizens of Potsdam then one had to look for them in the backward Mark Brandenburg as Leib Levin did. There in the villages, they were to be found. The situation for the future Court Factor was ripe with opportunity.

Jewish entrepreneurs were accepted! So long as they had a Letter of Protection, no more than three children and money to build a manufacturing business without state help, they were welcomed by the King. Of course only in limited numbers so as to avoid difficulties from the rest of the population who were quick to feel aggravated by the ambitious Jewish competition. For this reason only 120 Jewish families were allowed to live in Berlin in 1720, and in the thinly populated Mark they were forbidden to buy houses. In Potsdam however, they were able to acquire a house if they promised to set up a factory and had considerable wealth.

Developing the Residence City of Potsdam with new houses was an idea close to Friedrich Wilhelm's heart. A heart that principally beat lovingly for his soldiers. Heavy overheads were not wanted however. The King's thrift awoke the strangest ideas. For example: Presenting non-Jews such as retiring soldiers with privileges as recognition of their war-service. These documents, whose worth was hundreds of Taler but cost the King just a sheet of paper, could be sold to well-off Jews and in this way, as one can say in Yiddish 'einen Reibach machen', that is 'make a killing'. This was the experience of Simon Levin of Brandenburg in the year 1735 when a gentleman who was unknown to him, a Herr von der Groeben, a former lieutenant of the Crown Prince's Regiment, who after some haggling, 'mercifully gifted' one of four 'Jewish Privileges' that the old serviceman had received from the King 'to build a house in the Friedrichstadt'.

Nothing very worthwhile has been passed down about Leib Levin. The best that happened to him or that he 'conquered', was Hanna, the same age as he, of the Isaak family that had established themselves between Schönflies in the Neumark, Prenzlau and Potsdam. These should not be confused with the Itzig family who also lived in Brandenburg but alone by the different way of writing the same old-testament name could not deny their descent from Posen and Upper Silesia. There are no documents that reveal who Hanna's father was. It is certain that she brought plenty of money into the marriage because when she wed Leib Levin, most probably in 1738, the regulation that the bride, too, had to pay in a significant amount of money to the Recruits' Treasury, was in place. Perhaps a certain Moses Isaak of Schönflies who was already wealthy in Potsdam helped her. Moses Isaak was just a year older than Hanna. He may have been her brother. His father came from Schönflies, his mother, born in 1671, was called Ziporra, but in the official register the name has been Prussianised, Vogel, or bird, a masculine name because there is no feminine form in German.

The idea that Hanna might be the sister of Moses Isaak, who later became a highly respected banker, is a hypothesis. But with marked evidence which is neither to be overlooked nor purely co-incidental: Hanna named her first child, that she had in 1740, Isaak, her second daughter born on 12 December 1740, Ziporra; her third, Moses. If Hanna belonged to the Isaak family of Schönflies, all of these namesakes in their honoured sequence as is popular among Jews is almost proof.

Was Leib Levin able to offer his children, to whom a fourth was added, Israel, in 1749, a lavish adolescence and a promising future with what he earned as a linen dealer in modest Brandenburg? Who was supporting whom? From whom came the blessed Privileges? On his gravestone, Leib Levin is described as a well-disposed modest man who *'had joy with the share that God the creator gave him'*. Had the great Jewish God made him noticeable by a significant wedding present?

It cannot be denied that 1738 was a good year for the Levins and it is imaginable that there was a rising star called Moses Isaak who was also allowed to marry in 1738. He took the wealthy Bela Itzig, whereby, without needing a single Taler, on 21 September, he was put on his father-in-law's exceptional Letter of Privilege that held ready all possible advantages for him and his own.

What a father-in-law! Isaak Daniel Itzig, also called Itzig Jaffe (the 'beautiful') or Itzig, son of Daniel from Grätz, a village west of Posen was born in 1678 and was a horse-dealer. But not just any old one. It was he, who organised the horses for the whole Hussar Regiment of the Knight-general von Ziethen and was responsible for the bridles and saddles that they needed. Anyone who was allowed to serve General v. Ziethen was doing well for himself. Without the brisk Ziethen, who on 20 May 1745 broke through the Austrian position in Upper Silesia with his regiment, the 2nd Silesian War would not have ended so happily for Prussia. The Jew Itzig, who knew the difference between a field hack, a post-coach stallion and a riding horse for the light cavalry which Herr v. Ziethen turned into a battle-winning weapon that would gain victory for his King in the Seven Years War at Leuthen, Liegnitz and Torgau – the Jew Itzig had helped him: he remained unforgotten: Not least as the father-in-law of Moses Isaak who in the meantime had worked together with Itzig's son, Daniel, and Veitel Heine Ephraim at the Prussian court.

Three coin minters, who did not just obsequiously obey their King but supported him in dubious ways too. When Friedrich II, ruined by the horrendous expenses of war, commissioned them to melt down full-value coinage and then to mint them again with a reduced silver content in the Leipzig Mint – whose personnel rejected such cheating practices – and then emboss them with the Saxon Stamp – the one-third taler coins were back-dated 1753 – the gents did not say no.

Of course they wanted to keep their positions and privileges which secured the living of the whole family. Also their houses. Veitel Heine Ephraim was so powerful in 1766 that he was able to build himself a palace in Berlin, Poststrasse 16. Daniel afforded a house in the centre of Potsdam, in the Hohewegstrasse. Today it's the Friedrich-Ebert-Strasse. A few years later Bendix Goldschmidt bought it after he became the Senior Court Factor. He was of course not one of the Mint Magnates. Moses Isaak who lived in the Rosen Strasse in Berlin soon left the consortium which had dragged the best Jewish names into the mire. The name of the firm, Ephraim & Co, had long since become a byword for cheating and fraud and greed among the Christian population who had no suspicion of the Royal instigator.

Friedrich II who had skidded from one financial crisis to the next in the last years, had earned well on the coin falsification. It was said that it had brought him 25 million Taler, many times what he needed after the end of the Seven Years war to build a new palace next to his beloved Sanssouci, which was far too small for prestigious receptions. The foundation stone was laid just four months after the Peace of Hubertusburg, which had left five great powers exhausted and drained of blood, was signed on 20 July 1763. The inflation which was a consequence of the debasement of the coinage had without doubt been anticipated by the King and he knew a remedy.

With Prussian energy and the well-known Prussian pace or speed, the ruined local economy was once again made to flourish. The import of any article that could be produced in the state was throttled back. Silk from China? Silkworms were breed by experts in Brandenburg where the required mulberry bushes were already growing in their own gardens. But not in sufficient numbers. The Monarch immediately set a good example by having the new avenues below the Bornstein Vineyards lined with 388 mulberry bushes instead of the usual lime trees. Already in 1752, Friedrich II had demanded in his *'Politischen Testament'* that schools where *'the maids and country folk could learn how and when the worms should be exploited'* (they are boiled and unravelled) and that the caterpillars *'should get no leaves damp with dew because they then become addicted to water'.* Certainly the King had busied himself with this topic as he had with countless other small matters.

The Levins and Goldschmidts and, one by one, their sons, must have been more thorough in their researches into the manufacture of silk and the new 'stuff' that was going to replace the cotton calico. Potsdam was the best place possible for them to observe the promising future that the local material had. Especially the shining, embroidered sort because the King, lacking any Prussian silk at the time, was having his Neue Schloss, or palace, decorated with silk from Beijing.

Isaac Levin Joel of Halberstadt had already established himself in Potsdam with a silk manufacturing factory, in which thanks to Royal support, he was able employ children from the military orphanage in Lindenstrasse. Children of all ages whose fathers had fallen on the battlefields of Europe, were numbered in hundreds. They were given a basis in the three 'R's', reading, writing and arithmetic and taught a useful trade. While the youths were shown how to make weapons, the girls were busy on weaver's benches and with embroidery. During their four year apprenticeship the King paid for their food and lodgings, checked the material delivered and of course was satisfied that these growing youngsters were paid just pennies. The new factories cost him enough tax revenues, the purchase of more weavers looms by Christians would have to be subsidised by the state. Among Jewish investors these extra costs were unnecessary: the Jews had to show sufficient investment money at the moment they sought permission to set up a factory to be used for the further glory of Prussia.

Certainly, the Levins and Isaaks also benefited from the help of the orphanages. Leib Levin's eldest, Isaak, set himself up as a self-employed silk manufacturer at the age of seventeen, when he came of age. He already had a Letter of Protection. A celebration feast for the family! Because by it, a free place appeared on Leib Levin's privilege which allowed just one child at a time on it. An exercise in calculation: Should the father Levin favour his second son, eleven year old Moses? Or his daughter, Ziporra, who was five years older? Naturally, Ziporra! For her the whole family had long had a bridegroom called Bendix Goldschmidt in view. The son of Ruben Bendit Goldschmidt from Hamburg, now at home in Potsdam, worked for Leib Levin's brother Salomon in the linen and woollen material trade and had not only a worthy name, he certainly also had sufficient savings to soon entice the beloved Ziporra into a substantial home. Then the younger brother Moses would take her place on the Letter of Protection. Moses would become somebody quite exceptional.

We have all profited from him.

# Ziporra

The marriage was discussed in family circles. One haggled over a dowry, one laid the Letters of Protection and had the confirmation of the most recent tax payments ready. But a wedding day could not be decided. The state alone decided that, more particularly the Royal Prussian Electoral-Mark War and Domain Chamber. It was not the bridegroom's place to make an application for a marriage permit, that was the father's prerogative, in this case Leib Levin. Ziporra was by now 17 years old, it was time to bring her under the 'Chuppa'; the wedding baldachin. But first she had to be written into the vacant space on her father's Letter of Protection. Without such an 'escort' she would have to – under the revised Marriage Conditions of 1750 – leave the city fourteen days after her wedding, even if she appeared on her husband's Letter of Protection. Leib Levin could make his plea to have his daughter added to his at the same time as he sought permission for her to marry. It seems to have been a matter that was hurried. Perhaps he was feeling unwell in these March days of 1757. On the 23 March he sent in his request to the responsible authority, six days later he was dead.

Why the King personally busied himself with Levin's application cannot be explained. In the middle of war, on the 15 April 1757, three days before the Prussian troops marched into Bohemia in four armies, the King made time to put questions about Levin's application to the gentlemen of the War and Domain Chamber. It remains in the Brandenburg State Archive:

> *First our merciful greeting, highly respected Councillors, dear faithful ones! We order you hereby with grace to examine the regularity of the written application by the Protected Jew Leib Levin of 23 March wherein he personally and most humbly requests permission to have his daughter Ziepora written into his Letter of Protection as first child and at the same time that she may marry Bendix Goldschmidt, and then to report. Our mercy be with you!*
> *Given in Berlin 15 April 1757*

The family, in mourning for Leib Levin, received no quick answer. The war councillor Voss, who was busy with the matter, first had to check the wealth of the Levins and Goldschmidts and their reputation. That could, one knew, take as long as a year. Or longer, if the chamber were able to think up another lucrative way of raising the wedding fees, or another delaying harassment. The Prussian authorities knew how to stretch or compress time according to the circumstances. Ziporra and Bendix waited.

Because it is not sensible to send a dead man a letter, no answer was sent. Whether the daughter Ziporra could be written into a Letter of Protection post mortem is questionable. The Chamber had a problem. A second problem – and they hung together – was the permit to marry.

Bendix Goldschmidt had the necessary money ready. But how did things stand for Ziporra? How much had Leib Levin left? Was it enough to provide for the brothers, Moses and Israel who were still minors, and for his widow who was used to keeping a generous house as is shown in the Citizen's list; *'two maidservants and a knave from Glogau'*? Apparently not. At any rate the authorities decided that after *'Examination according to the Regulations'* that for a marriage to be allowed *'Bendix Ruben Goldschmidt's property of cash money and diverse woollen fabric-wares was more than 1000 rt.'* but that of his bride however did not match the required 500 Taler. Therefore the application had to be refused.

The negative decision which Ziporra received in August 1757 was no surprise, she could bear it. Because before the year of mourning had run its course any wedding was in any case out of the question. If 500 Taler were not to fall from Heaven into her lap by the middle of the next year then another way had to be found for her to achieve her goal. Thus she asked the Chamber to let the application rest for a while. And so the authority's document was given a note in its margin: *'replaced in the files at the supplicant's own request:'*

What encouraged Ziporra to dare a second attempt in the next year remains her secret. Her relations could not advance her the required money under any circumstances. Were it to become known, she would be seen as a debtor. But she organised something and indeed directly after the anniversary of her father's death as shown on his gravestone in the Potsdam cemetery. But she was refused yet again: no Permit to Marry without sufficient proof of property. Even for her own Letter of Protection, were she able to pay for one, the necessary conditions were lacking because she had no own income as an employee nor as self-employed.

Which of her relations was a money-lender or otherwise had an important position at the Court? Did one of the Isaaks, Itzigs or Ephraims help the eighteen-year old Ziporra? What was it that prompted Friedrich II on 16 November 1758 to pay attention to Ziporra's case again after she turned to him for help through an intermediary as advocate for her? In any case it seems her petition had already been refused in the ante-chamber of the Royal secretary for legal reasons, because the King left the decision to his advisors: *'If the Resolution of 20 April anno Christi can not be overlooked then you must inform the supplicant accordingly'.*

Yet again a delay. Again waiting and pleading. Only two years later did a fourth application achieve success. By then it was high time for a marriage. On 18 December 1760, Ziporra stood beside her Bendix under the wedding baldachin. She was very happy and in her eighth month.

Ziporra Goldschmidt was worth living with; she didn't lack the courage to face up to the powerful King and his doubtful laws. At first in a rented place with just one maidservant to help. On 24 January 1761 Ziporra gave birth to the son and heir who had been so obvious at her wedding and as was usual in the family, was named after his grandfather, Ruben. Everything now seemed quite different in the world for them. Since 1760 Ziporra had enjoyed the protection of her father's privileges that had been withheld from her for so long and about which Friedrich II had at last reconsidered. The

Frederick the Great by Anton Graff (Courtesy of Stiftung Preußische Schlösser und Gärten: Fotothek)

document of the 8 January 1733 was personally signed by his royal father which allows us to infer that the Levins were among the 10 Jewish families that were authorised in Potsdam. Already then, they seem to have been people of no little consequence. Even Leib Levin's widow, who lived in her husband's house with the two younger sons received a concession to continue to manage the trade in textiles which she understood so well. Neither could Bendix complain, as he was also allowed a *'Concession from the High General Directors'* which let him leave his position with Salomon Levin and run his own business. At first he dealt in silk, linen and wool, occasionally with money as well, although it was not his intention to found a bank.

Concessions belong to the wonderful class of paper that one as a Jew humbly applied for and then paid for. For the State they meant a source of revenue that may not be underestimated and which gushed from the most varied sources. Even to employ a maidservant, Bendix needed a concession. And of course for the 'Mohel' who circumcised the little Ruben eight days after his birth according to Jewish ritual. Exactly a year later the 'Mohel' would have been summonsed again because Ziporra had no wish to hold back on having more children. She had no problem with the Regulations to Restrict the Increase of the Jewish Population. She also had pleasure seeing her brother Moses, the most gifted of her siblings, growing up. Perhaps because he possessed the same energy that she enjoyed. Certainly her brother Isaak was also no failure; with his Potsdam embroidery factory he was held in high estimation by the King, who now declared his goodwill toward the Jewish community in that he at last fulfilled their wish to be permitted to build a Synagogue. If they planned a modest size and acquired a plot of land that was already owned by Jews, then right in the centre of Potsdam.

# Porcelain

After 1760, Potsdam had a rabbi for the first time. The Jewish congregation fetched him from Poland because there were insufficient trained young men in Prussia. And he concluded that the knowledge of the true Belief among the Jews of Potsdam who had only been taught by their parents was not the best. A 'Mikveh,' a plunge-bath, also was lacking. Obviously no-one in the congregation had troubled themselves. Now a Mikveh was installed in the house of the cobbler Schultze. But the life-style of his believers under the hot sun of Potsdam, where even grapes could grow, who were so industrious in business, set up one factory after another, had let themselves be given a hunting-lodge in Glienicke in which a wall-paper factory was installed – did not please him at all. Heaven would punish them.

And Friedrich II would assist him in that, he, who was quite unprejudiced against other religions, however recommended his descendants in his *'Political Testament'*, one must *'keep an eye on the Jews, prevent them from being involved in Wholesale Trade, prevent the growth of their numbers and take their Right to Asylum away for any dishonesty'*. But they should none-the-less involve themselves in the wholesale trade of porcelain in Berlin. Whereas the trade in silk and cloth production flourished, the turnover in porcelain was in difficulties. The Prussian farmers had no need for it and over the border it was hardly known. Not only abroad, also the neighbouring German Principalities should learn to value the pricey products the Royal Prussian Porcelain Works conjured up. And which at the moment were threatening to remain on the shelves. Jewish businessmen, known for their salesmanship, would sell it abroad. Voluntarily? These fragile goods, of which they understood nothing, in which they had never traded? That would not function voluntarily.

If there is a divine court of punishment for slovenly devotion, then now was the moment to believe it: on 31 March 1769, Friedrich II approved a law that obliged all Jews to buy porcelain from the Royal Prussian Porcelain Works, to bring it out of the State and sell it there. Every Letter of Protection and Escort, every house purchase and marriage Certificate, every application for a concession for another child or other benefit was immediately bound together with the purchase of a *'certain moderate quantity of porcelain'*. What did 'moderate' mean for a king who was used to calculate in millions of Taler and had no inkling that among the rich Jews there were also poor people who attempted to live on 60 taler a year?

For an application for normal Letter of Protection, a Jew had to take porcelain to the value of 300 Taler, packed in cases whose contents, on being opened, often proved to be chipped or faulty. Then the Jew had to hold on to it himself. The perfect wares could be profitably sold. Where and when he carried the wares over the border was his business. At the city gate he had to present his papers to the War and Domain Chamber to confirm that the porcelain had been paid for, that it was stamped, dated and signed; also a Jewish gate-keeper, flanked by two Prussian overseers was always there to check the comrade-believers and to see whether any forbidden goods or Hebrew writings which no Christian gate-keeper could read were concealed. Everything according to the rules. On the return journey too, the same examination, to see whether he was attempting to smuggle foreign silk, which was a forbidden import. But the most important was the certificate of the customs officer for the excise-duty and the receipt, that porcelain had in fact been sold abroad to enhance Prussia's glory. If one had sold the wares at a lesser price than that dictated by the King, as set by comparison with the famous Meissner Porcelain, then one had to make up the difference.

The consequence was a fatal impoverishment of the Jews, even the richest were affected and did not know how they would get by without incurring debts. Suddenly the scene had changed: from being the financiers of the rulers to being debtors who had to borrow from the country gentry – at six-and-half percent interest. The wailing, complaints, and pleadings to the authorities were no longer, as previously the case, just on their knees but rather in the very clear words of the despairing. The state gave way. At least it helped the Jews by allowing payment for the porcelain by instalments. Which was no help because the outstanding debts were multiplying quickly. Soon, the poorest of the poor, if they did not pay in the end, would be threatened in writing by the 'execution', or sequestration.

Meanwhile Ziporra had given her husband six children in eight years and was pregnant with the seventh. Bendix Goldschmidt had to consider if he could afford to put yet another child on his Letter of Protection. Not only was the double amount payable for the permit fee but he would have to buy porcelain too. To the value of 300 Taler, in the hope that he might get rid of it among his business friends in Hannover or Hamburg. At first he could not think about it, and in any case he preferred to wait to see how the children would develop. In the last year, 1768, his second son Levin died and the third, Isaak, was just months old. Fortunately he had three daughters who would marry at some time, he needed not to worry for them. But how should one care for the widow of Leib Levin, who was unable to live on her slowing textile business. She had sacrificed 600 Taler for a privilege as an 'Extraordinaria'. As with Leib Levin's brother Salomon, the files show that *'she had to buy a house for 600 Taler from the Grenadier Knopel of the former Royal Regiment'*. But we will never learn what strange role the Prussian Grenadier played at the command of Friedrich II.

Also Moses Levin had money problems, Ziporra's favourite brother, who actually, after working and saving enough, wanted to set up his own factory in Potsdam. The Prussian State was ready to give him a general privilege to found a silk manufacture. That was the fattest decoy bird that could be used as bait for ambitious Jewish entrepreneurs at the time. However the general privilege held in prospect, that was but rarely given, was the most expensive of those *'benefits'*, which were tied to the purchase of porcelain. Moses would have had to pay 100 Taler to the exchequer and buy porcelain to the value of 500 Taler, a financial burden that the twenty-five year old was unable to manage. Thus he had to continue to work as before, as a trader and money changer and on occasion, he would take the silk material that had been delicately embroidered at the works of his brother Isaak Levin, to the sadly bored Queen Elisabeth Christine and her Court dames in Schloss Schönhausen. Nothing was more important than contact with the court, to show oneself well brought up and make oneself indispensable.

Apart from that, not to lose hope that the king might at last realise that his porcelain manoeuvre had back-fired. Because the orders for his Berlin Porcelain factory were declining markedly. He had not imagined that people abroad might buy his porcelain – that was already derided as 'Jewish porcelain' – much more cheaply now from the travelling Jews who had been forced to drop their prices in order to get rid of it. At first Friedrich II was determined not to alter a single new quill mark in this law.

His nephew, Crown-Prince Friedrich Wilhelm had long seen the consequences: that the Jews, for lack of their own capital were no longer in a position to support the Prussian economy with their initiative. The Crown Prince valued Jewish entrepreneurship. There were not so many Jews living in Potsdam at the time, that their numbers were unreasonable: 70 adults and 100 children. But 19 of the 39 Potsdam factories were in Jewish hands! This percentage should make one think. As soon as the Crown Prince became the ruler, many things would change for the better in the State.

But until then...

# 1786

...by then Friedrich II would have sorrowed for the death of his friend Ziethen and known of the passing on of the philosopher Moses Mendelssohn; Ziporra Goldschmidt, as if no restrictive regulations had existed, had given birth to a further eight children, two daughters and six sons and did not seem to be disturbed by the fact that none of them could be added to their father's Letter of Protection and so had no chance to marry and have their own children. Apparently she trusted in a miracle, a change of heart among the law-makers, an end to the compulsory expenses or – no, surely not the King's death! Because Friedrich II had in the meantime understood how useful her husband could be. He did not just sell textiles from his shop.

The Jewish Congregation, where he had been cashier and leader since 1778, spoke of the 'rich banker' Bendix Goldschmidt. Had someone new followed in the wake of his ancestors? There is no record of a prominent bank such as the Goldschmidt's friend Isaac Daniel Itzig in Potsdam possessed. Certainly Bendix occasionally gave credit but his priority was delivering 'stuff' to the court, that cheap textile for uniforms that the army, after being terribly decimated in the war, needed to equip its new recruits.

For special demands the Court turned rather to Ziporra's brother Moses Levin who was no unknown person there. Friedrich II needed a new instrument for his concerts in Sansoucci, a pianoforte. If possible from Silbermann and cheap. Of course the instrument should be checked by an expert. Moses Levin was told to take care of the matter. The Silbermann establishment for hammer-pianos was in Freiburg in Saxony.

Who other than some nameless music teacher could be found to give an expert's opinion? If possible he should be a Court musician and maybe even better a demanding composer. Johann Adam Hiller (1728-1804) lived in Leipzig; he was the man they needed even if he were busy with a composition. We suppose that Moses Levin had met him the year before when Hiller had stayed in Berlin and Moses, acting as Court Factor, had taken orders for him. That made contact by letter easier. If Silbermann had no pianoforte available – they were only made to order – then Hiller would know where one was to be had.

Pianoforte at Sansoucci (Courtesy of the author's collection)

On 15 June 1785 Hiller answered Levin in a letter from which we might have at last discovered Moses' exact Potsdam address, had it not been sufficient for the composer to address the folded and sealed sheet of paper with just *'Monsieur Moses Levin à Potsdam'*. Even this simple address sounds like a distinction for a Jew who still enjoyed no citizen's rights. Even more respectfully the final words of the letter *'have the honour with perfect and deepest respect to be your high nobility's*

*Humblest Joh. Adam Hiller'.*

Whether with or without Hiller's help: the purchase of the piano and its tricky transport from Saxony to Potsdam was happily completed. For the last years of his life, the King had pleasure at his house-concerts from this instrument that Moses Levin organised for him and which still stands in Sansoucci.

In summer 1786, as the roses were in full bloom and the grapes had started to ripen on the terraces at the Palace, Friedrich the Great died on 17 August, taciturn and isolated. The mourning of the Jews of Potsdam, expressed in many speeches, was not hypocritical, they corresponded to their estimation and their true feelings for the dead man, even if he regarded them as his *'little tenants'* and if they had suffered unbearably under his measures. They were not thinking at that moment about their debts which they had incurred at the porcelain factories.

# A New Home

Gradually the Goldschmidt's house was becoming overcrowded. One cot after another. Jews were forbidden to have two maidservants. Buying a house, which sometimes was possible with a special permit, especially if one worked as the Court Factor, meant, in every case, paying 300 Taler into the War and Domain Treasury for a few nailed up boxes of who-knew-how smashed porcelain. Where would Bendix be able to get rid of it? He might have to take it as far as Hamburg. Not only distant relatives but also some very rich and important businessman lived there. They imported cotton which was not allowed in Prussia – what an opportunity to make some business contacts! But what if the Hanseatic people did not like Prussian porcelain; they were spoiled by imports from China, Sèvres and Chelsea. Bendix Goldschmidt would have to forget his dream of a new house. Save and wait. Things might be easier under the King's successor.

They were. Already on 6 December 1786, Friedrich II had sworn to his cabinet that he would re-think this law that compelled the purchase of porcelain; up to this point the law had been neither profitable nor had it created respect for the Berlin porcelain. The overdrawn accounts of all the Prussian Jews who had '*benefited*' was a total of 78,865 Taler. Worried about the situation, the King added a paragraph to the *'Jewish matter'* in his own hand, *'This so terribly struggling Nation shall be relieved as much as possible and not bashed so much by the General Taxman'*. (Perfect German and error-free French were often lacking in the Hohenzollern Princes.)

Months passed before the heavyweight official apparatus finished its thinking and calculating. But it was clear that the Jews would never repay their debts to the manufacturing commission. With help from the richest of them and under the greatest sacrifices they found 35,000 Taler. But that was not sufficient for the Cabinet. The repeal of the law would only be possible if the Jews paid at least 40,000 Taler, and at once. 'At once' took some time. At last on the 12 February 1788 the sum was gathered together. On 21 April 1788 the Declaration of the repeal of the Compulsory Purchase of Porcelain by the Jewish Community – and it is kept in their Archive in Potsdam.

The oldest Goldschmidt daughters, Hanna and Dela, had married. The next who would need a dowry would be Jette. Bella Betty, our great-great-

great grandmother, and the baby of the family Gütel would have to wait a long while yet.

Among the sons, Ruben was already self-employed as a silk merchant in Berlin and he was able to take care of the apprenticeships of his younger brothers, Aron, Isaak and Liepmann: the hunger of the upper classes of Berlin for silks was insatiable. Splendid prospects for the workaholic sons of a family in which the mother tended to fire her somewhat slower children with the terrible battlefield cry: To the battering ram!

Were it not for the Cabinet watching the new King, regarded as a '*lightweight*', with their strictly moralistic eye and slowing his efforts to accommodate his ' protected Jews' – he had in fact forgiven almost half their debts at the Porcelain Factory! – were it not for these Prussian drill supervisors, then the reforms which now began to be announced would have long been complete. The first thing that Friedrich Wilhelm II did was to repeal the inhumane poll-tax on Jews. A Ruler who lived contentedly in a morganatic marriage and had two other mistresses besides and uncounted offspring wanted to make life easier for those others who were doing so much to boost the Prussian economy. He made things easier for himself as well, and Ziporra's brother Moses Levin, who with just a common Letter of Protection for a Court Jew, seemed to have discreetly helped the King. What it was about and why the King owed him thanks has not come to light.

But in a letter the Queen wrote

*To the State Minister von Mauschwitz*

*It is a pleasure dear State Minister Mauschwitz that the Jew Moses Levin of Potsdam has been granted a General Privilege for him and his brothers, sisters and their children by the King my Majesty and Husband, and I plead that you take care that the necessary copies are advantageously prepared for the family and distributed to all the Provinces according to the King's Command, for which I shall be very grateful.*

*Berlin 24 February 1789*
*Your affectionate friend*
*Frederique Queen of Prussia.*

On the 6 April 1789 the letter was confirmed by the King:

*To the State Minister von Mauschwitz*

*His Royal Majesty of Prussia and our most Gracious Ruler wishes that the Letter of Protection for the local Jew Moses Levin shall be formulated in such a way as that, which was prepared for the Jew Kohen of Berlin because the same has been true and served well. For this, the General Directorate Privilege for Levin of 4th this month is enclosed so as to it may be expedited with the same privileges that Kohen has and then to be returned.*

*Potsdam 6 April 1789*
*Friedrich Wilhelm*

On the 12 April 1789 the document which gave a Jew together with his family unimaginable freedom was in Moses Levin's hands.

*General Protection and Trading Privileges for Moses Lewin of Potsdam and his brothers Isaac Lewin and Israel Lewin and also his sister Ziporra, married to Bendix Goldschmidt of Potsdam and also her children and descendants.*

*We, Friedrich Wilhelm by God's Grace King of Prussia etc.*

*Give notice and declare that because of his loyalty and good service Moses Lewin of Potsdam be rewarded with a General Protection and Trading Privilege and also his brothers Isaac Lewin and Israel Lewin and also his sister Ziporra, married to Bendix Goldschmidt of Potsdam and also her children and descendants in all our lands and provinces without any exceptions. By our mercy and with freedom from any Stamp charges and other fees this is granted and issued so that Moses Lewin and his afore-mentioned brothers and sister and their children and descendants shall be given the same rights as Christian bankers and businessmen of all kinds to trade and exchange without any differences, and also to enjoy the same freedom as Christian bankers and businessmen to trade and exchange have in the Courts and out of them.*

*In particular the 'impetranten', and their heirs shall*

1. *with the same rights as Christian citizens have, may possess houses and plots of land in the places and streets and areas where they may*

trade most profitably in the whole of our Residence, also in the towns of all our lands and provinces.
2. not come before any Jewish court and be in no way mixed with the Jews but rather as other citizens turn to the State Dicasteria for their legal matters and be answerable to the same.
3. If the possessions of Moses Lewin and his brothers and sister and also their children and descendants remain at the normal estimation of the Jewish community and the expenses that are appropriate, it is left up to them how much they pay as voluntary gratification to the Jewish community.
4. The impetranten *when they trade in this land must, like the Christian Businessmen pay a paraphen-jura, or 'initials tax' each year then without the already repealed Jewish Poll-tax and Compulsory Purchase of Porcelain and its export shall nevermore be expected of them.*
5. Finally their Oath and Witness, whether for or against a Christian, as well as from a Christian shall be valid and not exceptionally in Exchange Business shall the value of currency need to be proven where in similar cases a Christian would not be necessitated to do so.'

We therefore command that also all Our War and Domain chambers, State Justice Colleges and Lower Courts as well as the State and Tax councils shall by the grace of the content of this General Protection and Trading Privileges respect accordingly all the rights and freedoms granted therein to Moses Lewin and his brothers and sister and all their children and descendants without the least hindrance and thoroughly protect them and maintain them so that their religion and Jewish customs shall not be considered relevant at any time or in any way.

We have certified and signed this Privileges with Our own hand and stamped it with Our own Royal Seal.

*This occurred and given in Berlin 12 April 1789*
*signed Friedrich Wilhelm.*

Praise be God and the King! Purchasing a house is permitted at the same price that a Christian had to pay – when had that happened before! For Ziporra and Bendix Goldschmidt their future domicile would be in the main street of Potsdam, exactly where the privileged banker Isaac Daniel Itzig had lived for many years but now was removing because he had just built a palace in Berlin to be nearer to his diverse factories there. His house at Hoheweg

Strasse 9 was now vacant and Ziporra bought it on 31 July 1789 in her name for 2,500 Taler. Without the General Privilege of her brother it would have been encumbered with the usual compulsory expenses which were always payable by less favoured Jews and would have been too expensive.

At last enough space for the eight children who were still living at home and more than that a splendid hall in which socialising along the pattern of Court councillors could be done – only a little smaller. What a life! Two years later, in May 1791, Friedrich Wilhelm also repealed the marriage fees for Jews. At last her son, just turned twenty, Aron Bendix, who would soon change his name to the less biblical sounding Adolph Benedikt, could marry his cousin Henrietta Goldschmidt.

It would not happen completely without Christian opposition, which Jews nick-named 'the love of the neighbour's neighbour'. (In German, 'Uebernaechstenliebe', and a pun on 'Naechstenliebe', the German word for the concept presented in the New Testament as 'love thy neighbour as thyself'.)

In the official's bureaux they were too professionally accustomed to placing hurdles in the way of Jews to change their ways quickly despite the King's command.

On Friday 17 May 1789 the *Altoner Mercurius* printed

> *A while ago the King commanded by an order to the Cabinet that the Jewish Banker Levi of Potsdam, just as Cohen of Berlin should enjoy all the rights and freedoms that Christian Businessmen enjoy. The Senior Finance College thereafter reported on the difficulties that must occur, this alone displeased the King so much that he sent an instruction to the College to follow Royal Commands without any repost.*

> *We don't want to gossip about the love affairs and passions of the Prussian King. The fact that he took part in a war against France and that his troops re-conquered Frankfurt from the French occupation on 2 December 1792 is almost forgotten. Rather we are amused by the celebrations and balls that took place directly afterwards in Frankfurt where the Ruler inflamed the passion of a nineteen year old banker's daughter, a short flare of love, not a conquest, no victory. Perhaps it would be more reasonable, now that both his sons, Crown Prince Friedrich Wilhelm and Ludwig have returned from the battlefield, to consider their marriages. How persuasively George von Hessen-Darmstadt, his brother-in-law, has described the charms of Princesses Luise and Friederike von Mecklenburg-Strelitz who both lived in Darmstadt! They could be the ideal daughters-in-law!*

*A discreet meeting was arranged in February 1793 at a theatre evening in Frankfurt, easily reached from Darmstadt. Both the Prussian Princes were informed: they should get to know the family in Mecklenburg-Strelitz better, there were two unusually enchanting daughters. Luise and Friederike, just 17 and 15 years old, had no idea yet of the good fortune that Friedrich Wilhelm had laid before them.*

This small story of an arrangement actually deserves no place in our family book, except that the two princesses spent the evening before both their weddings a few months later in the house of Bendix Goldschmidt in Potsdam – the dancing went on till four in the morning.

On 21 December 1793, both the brides, Luise and Friederike arriving from Darmstadt together with their father, grandmother and a governess in Potsdam, stayed overnight in a city palace on the Havel and the next morning were received by the whole Court in Berlin. They were admired and the evening was celebrated with music and dancing until late. While the preparations for the wedding of the Crown Prince with Luise on 24 December and for Friederike and Prince Ludwig on 26 December were going ahead in Berlin, the brides were to recuperate from the excitement in Potsdam. But at this age, young people cannot have too much fun. Some form of amusement would hopefully be arranged in Potsdam! In the city palace, which was not comfortable in winter, Luise's room was soon improved with some better furniture from the Neue Schloss and the bed, in the form of a ship, exchanged for another in red damask, but in the marble coolness of the great hall no exciting hen-night had been planned for the exuberant brides, who just wanted to dance, other than a short reception by the town of Potsdam. That should be organised by the Goldschmidts at the King's request in the Hohenweg Strasse. There the sons had already hung garlands over the house entrance and Ziporra made the final plans for the maidens and her as yet unmarried daughter Bella Betty, while the youngest, the eleven year old Gütel, memorised the greeting speech that she should recite at the reception of the Princesses.

The *Vossische Zeitung* of 26 December 1793 gives us more detail:

*Potsdam 23 December 1793*

*Yesterday's report on the arrival of the Serene Highnesses the Princesses in our city must be expanded with the following: The parade from the Baumgarten Bridge was accompanied by 12 bugling postillions from the local Royal Post Office. The commendable Slaughterhouse Union led by Master Mister Peter; the Citizens' Company in Green Uniforms by Master Mister Böldicke; the other Citizens' Company in Blue Uniforms by the Court Master Carpenter Mister Brendel and the young Citizens' Sons wearing Green Riding Jackets by the Conductor Mister Krüger.*

*The celebratory arch like the Brandenburger Gate was erected under the direction of Mister Oberbaurath Schulze and the Building Inspector Mister Schadow. The Princess Brides' carriage and their High Princely relations were given cover by a commando of 2 officers, 4 under-officers and 24 men.*

*The Jewish Community organised a celebration under the instruction of two deputies, Mister Samuel Jonas and Aron (Adolf) Goldschmidt that also deserves to be more completely described than was done in our first report.*

*Ten young people of the Jewish Nation, in green uniforms, white shirts and stockings, hats with cockades and feathers carried a baldachin of embroidered golden cloth under the leadership of Misters Mendel and Joel from the first house and were accompanied by 8 chosen young girls in white dresses with green garlands.*

*The parade went through the Royal Pleasure gardens and the Palace Courtyard to the green steps and then into the Marble Hall. Here they let the baldachin rest until the Serene highnesses the Princesses arrived. Then the Misses Pessel Hirsch, Gütel Goldschmidt, Fromet Moses and Malchen Mendel after a short address, recited the Princess Brides a poem which the Princely Serene Highnesses heard with their usual favour and friendly manner and thanked them most graciously.*

*All the participants present at this celebration then went into the house of Mister Bendix Goldschmidt where a ball was given in the beautifully lighted Hall. The dancing was opened by the four demselles mentioned and only ended at 4 a.m. with trumpets and drums and the thrice happy shout: Long Live the Royal House!*

When one considers the number of participants at the reception in the Marble Hall of the Palace, one can imagine how large the Hall in the Goldschmidt's house must have been. Also the uncomplicated joviality between the citizens of Potsdam and the so-called 'Jewish Nation'.

The sisters Luise and Friederike von Mecklenburg as seen by Johann Schadow in the home of Bendix Ruben Goldschmidt in Potsdam in 1793. It was the evening before Luise's wedding to the Prussian Crown Prince Friedrich Wilhelm II (Courtesy of Berlin State Museum)

# A Gentleman called Bauer

While in Prussia, Friedrich Wilhelm II gradually relaxed the worst restrictions and compulsion that his Jewish subjects suffered under, in Hamburg these and similar harassments had long been done away with. The trade in goods from abroad had enriched Christians and Jews alike and here the import of cotton was not forbidden as it was under Friedrich II. In Prussia a significant number of 'stuff' weaving and stuff printing machines driven by water-power or ox-powered machines were already clattering. In place of the traditional monotone blue apron material, now highly coloured textiles were increasingly popular. Flowered muslin for clothes, also printed nettle cloth, cretonne, etamin (a very light net like textile) percale (very close-woven fabric) calicot fustian (heavy cloth often used in padded clothes) and zitz (a finer sort of calico). The Goldschmidts in Potsdam who had capriciously manufactured silk wares thought the example was worth copying. An area of business that one could expand in Prussia, particularly because the King was keen to welcome every new business as long as it helped the economy and that the founders provided a decent capital base.

The contact to the Goldschmidts in Hamburg needed to be intensified according to Bendix. Most of them were active in the wholesale business, only a few in handling 'stuff'. However of the 53 stuff printers registered in Hamburg in 1797, five were led by Jews. The largest of them, with 500 male and female workers, belonged to Hirsch Wolf Bauer. A name that had never appeared in the annals of the family, not to speak of the Court Jews. But the Bauers, we can see from the gravestones in Ottensen near Hamburg, had lived in Altona for many generations. They immigrated from Holland, so probably from Sephardic Jews driven out of Spain. Nothing is known of their business connections but one day in autumn 1798, Bendix Goldschmidt discovered, possibly from his Hamburg relatives, that Herr Wolf Bauer, a cousin to the manufacturers, was very interested to visit Potsdam.

He would be received as a guest by Ziporra in her house!

Whether Bauer really was interested in the cotton trade that was now allowed in Prussia again may be questioned. Wolf Bauer's wife Dina, née Stern, with whom he had been married for thirteen years and who had given him four sons, died in childbirth at the fifth child, a daughter, on 28 August

1798. Bauer, an important entrepreneur, widowed at thirty, with five small children at home, had very personal reasons for waiting on the Goldschmidts: that there was in Potsdam an as yet unmarried daughter of marriageable age was well known in Hamburg even though it was not publicized by the *Altona Mercurius*! Bella Betty was by now a twenty-six year old beauty and as gay and energetic as apparently all of Ziporra's Levin line. The first meeting with her was important for Wolf Hirsch Bauer: no reservations, no delay and no long mourning period, she must become his wife. And Bella Betty had nothing against it. Five children? The youngest, Henrietta, still baby? No problem at all. In the matter of bringing up children, Bella had long been trained by her mother. Move to Hamburg? Why not. There were sufficient relatives living there already.

No! Decided Bauer. Not to the foggy north with a woman like Bella Betty, who was used to the sunny views of Potsdam gardens. He wanted to go to Berlin. Completely different opportunities were on offer there. His cousin and companion could carry on managing the stuff printing works in Hamburg without him. He, Wolf Bauer, would on occasion go and inspect but in Berlin he wanted to start something quite new: small fashionable objects, costume jewellery, buckles and buttons, tapestries, velvet, vases of Royal Prussian porcelain, ceramics in short: the most noble accessories for the so called upper classes. Otherwise than in Hamburg, he would find a market among the public in Berlin.

But before he could think about a wedding with Bella Betty or moving house, he had to try to buy one in Berlin. Without a General Privilege? Hopeless. the number of houses available for Jews to buy, even with a royal permit was strictly regulated. They could set up a factory at any time if they could show the capital required – and not just on paper but in bare coins! A house of his own, a stranger to the town as well, was just not possible.

That prompted Bauer to go to extremes. Certainly not without scruples and probably not without internal wrangling, he let himself and his five under-age children be baptised into the Protestant faith – a step that would upset some Jewish branches of our family tree. Wolf became Wolfrath (Wolfgang in some documents), his second name Hirsch changed to Hieronymus and the newly baptised Christian added a third, Wilhelm. After all one wanted to remain true to the King. Now he could look round for a building plot, a Certificate of Baptism had made it possible.

How Bauer would have loved to honour his bride Bella Betty with a small palace as a wedding gift. But the house that he found in the middle of Berlin was not bad at all. Between the Lustgarten and Spree River. Unfortunately we cannot identify it any more: its foundations have been buried beneath those of the museum designed by Schinkel.

Already Bauer was considering acquiring more building land. But in the first place was the wedding with Bella Betty 'in that lovely lit up hall' where the two Princesses from Mecklenburg-Strelitz had celebrated their last evening as unmarried women. Because Wolf Bauer had been especially content with his first wife, whom he had married on the 6 June, he asked his future in-laws to let him begin his second marriage on the same date. That may have sounded a bit curious to Ziporra and Bendix who were among those Jews who refuted the mystical meanings of numbers as superstitious but they said nothing against it. Thus on 6 June 1799 the Chuppa, or wedding baldachin, was erected in the house of the Goldschmidts and the wedding ceremony performed – according to Jewish ritual of course. Because a Jew does not lose his Jewishness by baptism. The children that Bella Betty would give him would also be brought up in the Jewish faith.

Off to Berlin! The new house on the Spree was ready. Bauer's children, with a carer from Hamburg, were to come and be wrapped in the arms of the new family. No remaining as strangers. Suddenly taking on the role of a mother or getting used to the pulsating big city was no problem at all for Bella Betty. Six of her married brothers and sisters already lived here, Isaak as cloth factory owner, Ruben and Aron were making calico, textiles for decorating, flags and book bindings. None of them wrote books. But the fact that brother Abraham suddenly became known as Albert and Aron, Adolphus Benedictus, spoke volumes. Everybody in this family allowed the others freedom to be what they wanted, no religious objections. Because Bella Betty understood little of the evangelical faith the baptised children grew up with the Jewish feast days. Later they may have thought about their choice of religion. Later still we know they gave it no thought at all when they enlisted as patriots in the Prussian Army. That the devout relatives in Hamburg thought somewhat grimly about that, had been noticed at the Wolf Bauer's wedding. The Bauers as well as the Sterns had stayed away: they would have grudged the bridegroom his baptismal escapade.

If Wolf Bauer had not been baptised just so that he could enjoy the citizen's rights of a Christian and be able to present his beloved bride with a house in Berlin, then such a measure would hardly have been necessary after the wedding because Bella Betty, exactly like her siblings, enjoyed the same advantages that were unimaginable for other Jews by being included on her mother's General Privilege and could pass them on : free to do as she wished, live where she wanted and to trade wherever she thought best, free of all extra costs and fees such as the very obscure Fire Tax that was demanded from Jews if any house in the neighbourhood should be burned down because of an accident with a candle or lightning striking the roof.

Now Bella Betty could employ a second maidservant without needing to beg for a concession or paying dearly for the permit. She needed one because on 7 July 1800 she brought her own first child to the world, a son, who was given the name Abraham at his circumcision ceremony but was always called Albert. Their happiness seemed to be perfect. Wolf Bauer's businesses were prospering so well that he could afford his own carriage to ride with his children and occasionally make a visit with Bella Betty in Potsdam. The family's home remained a magnet. Love. And the knowledge of being secure.

# Following the Trail

But the news from Potsdam in winter 1804 sounded worrying. Bendix Goldschmidt, the patriarch, was ill and died on 16 May 1805 at the age of 71 of consumption (that is, tuberculosis). His death brought to an end the era of Court Jews and financiers in our family history.

There was nothing to hold Ziporra in Potsdam now. After her children had mostly moved to Berlin, the house in Potsdam was too big for just her and the two youngest. She knew the worth of the house, as a good business woman she had already sold the house in Hoheweg Strasse 9 for 4,100 Taler to one of her Levin nephews just three months after her husband's demise.

Of course all of her daughters in Berlin were prepared to give her a home. But Ziporra had decided that Bella Betty needed her most urgently and there she could influence the upbringing of her six children. Maybe there would soon be more, who knew what surprises lay in store for them. Wolf Bauer had plans.

He felt that it was time to invest his money and considered land, preferably far from the capital city, where his children could grow up more healthily under Bella Betty's care. The deadly consumption of his father-in-law strengthened his resolve. Recently he had heard of run-down manors that were cheap on the market. In Elster a gentleman called von Zedtwitz had announced his bankruptcy. Bella Betty and her mother Ziporra must have been shocked. What did Wolf Bauer, who managed an expensive accessories business in Berlin in the Werdischen Market, know about agriculture? Nothing!

He was not interested in buying the rotten Manor, but rather the supposedly curative water that was bubbling from a source beside it and in which some farmer's families paddled during the summer. One knew that in Elster there was a spring in the fields beside the Weisse Elster River and that the health-giving waters were recommended for drinking but there were other springs of mineral water that nobody was bothering about. How the idea took flight in Wolf Bauer's imagination: turning a mineral source into a source of gold! A bathing resort such as Marienbad or Karlsbad! He informed himself about the village of Elster. He would buy the source that was just bubbling into a farmer's pond in 1806, that much was sure.

We need to investigate this story that Bella Betty's granddaughter Lina Morgenstern recorded in her memoirs. At that time there were no registers of land and house for the village of Elster. From the available official files we see that after the bankruptcy of Herr von Zedtwitz, the manor passed into the hands of a Herr Wolfram in 1807. Perhaps he was really called Wolfrath, like Bauer after his baptism? From 1810 to 1817 the owner was called Vögele, in Hebrew that would be, Ziporra! Were there no other traces to be found in this place that Wolf might have left behind? We have found them!

In the middle of the centre, under the foundations of the assembly rooms 'Sachsenhof' there stood a 'Haus Bauer' a family name the was rarely found in the whole region – a house, built in a prominent position next to the two springs, the 'Elstersäuerling' later called Marien-Quelle and the Albert Quelle.

Albert was the first-born of Wolf and Bella Betty Bauer.

Who other than our Albert Bauer might have given his name to the spring?

King Albert of Saxony first appears in 1873 and so, even if, looking back from today it seems he must have been the patron name for for the Alberthöhe, Albertpark, Albert-bad, the Albert-Halle and the Albert theatre, he was not. No, this spring was called thus six decades earlier, at a time when no-one other than Wolf Bauer in Elster had dared to dream of turning this village into a spa. Only in 1818, after a disasterous harvest failure led to famine did the villagers decide to make money out of bathing cures. They erected tents under which people wanting a health cure could enjoy sitting in the warm spring water. But by then Bauer had made quite different plans, at any rate he was no longer interested in building up a spa business such as Marienbad or Karlsbad but rather more in the income from the spring and the house that he rented out.

The idea that his children should grow up in the wooded countryside had perished. The air in Berlin seemed invigourating enough, there Bella Betty had a second child on 9 May 1807: Bendit. His birth may have been the last great celebratory feast in the house of Bauer. Because after the Emancipations Edict of 11 March 1812 which granted Prussian citizenship on the Jews, which was certainly worth a celebration, there was no holding Wolf Bauer's oldest son from of his first marriage: he enlisted to protect Prussia from Napoleon and fell on an unknown day in October 1813. Probably at the Battle of the Nations in Leipzig.

They did not mourn only for him that year, on 20 December of the same year, Ziporra, Bella Betty's mother died. And two years later, Wolf's second son from his marriage to Dina drowned as a sailor in a shipping accident on the Norwegian coast.

After the loss of this second son, whose name we do not know, Wolf Bauer exercised his authority, before the next two could follow the flag he put them both into apprenticeships; Jacob would learn to brew beer; Isaac would take over the business management of Bauer's interests. The fifteen year old Albert would follow his footsteps.

In the year 1816, new plans were hatched: the foundation of a branch in Breslau and perhaps the acquisition of a similar source of money to the spring in Bad Elster. There was supposed to be a manor for sale in Altwasser in Silesia that the family of von Mutius could no longer hold on to and there, too, was a more or less unexploited health spring draining to nowhere.

The offer seemed tempting. A spot in the Waldenburg mountains, easy to reach from both Berlin and Breslau. It would be nice to live there. Not, of course in the ruinous manor house, Bauer had no need of that. He would find a suitable little house to use as a second home for the family that had become ever smaller. Henrietta, Bauer's daughter from his first marriage, was about to marry and so only the young Bendit was left at home. What interested Bauer about Altwasser was alone the source. The future of the spring. It is certain that he acquired it in 1816. Whether he modernised the very modest bathing facility in any way is no longer ascertainable in what is now Poland. Unfortunately we are lacking exactly those documents that appertain to the decade after 1816, also the family papers of von Mutius are missing. Here the trail goes cold.

Before the removal to Altwasser could begin, there was a wedding to be celebrated in Berlin. At last eighteen, Henrietta could marry the man that she had worshipped and loved since she was a child: Wolf Goldschmidt. That he was 26 years older than her, nor that he was her stepmother Bella Betty's younger brother, was no difficulty for anyone. One was not related by blood but the connection between the Goldschmidts and Bauers was now even tighter. The couple would live in Breslau where Wolf Goldschmidt had a business, and if you please, he preferred to be called Wilhelm and not Wolf. That was his name as officially recorded when he received a Citizens Letter in Breslau in 1813. We have the document and think the its remarkable form of oath should be included here.

*Citizen's letter for the Citizen Wilhelm Goldschmidt*

*The Magistrate of the Royal Prussian Capital and Residence City of BRESLAU gives notice and acknowledges that the Citizen*
*Wilhelm Goldschmidt born in Potsdam has been accepted as a citizen of this city after his application and proof of the necessary demands*

*And because the same has sworn the following oath*

*'I, Wilhelm Goldschmidt*
*pledge and swear: that I having been accepted by the honourable Magistrate as a citizen, will be a faithful and true subject of His Royal Majesty of Prussia, my all merciful King and Lord and will also obey and wait upon to him an honourable Magistrate of this City.*
    *Furthermore I swear that I will do my best for this City and Citizens to the best of my ability and fulfil all my duties and obligations as a citizen conscientiously, and especially hold myself without dereliction subject the Conditions and Bye-laws of the City dated 19 November 1808 and uphold them and in all my relationships show myself a true, worthy and deserving citizen.*
*So help me God to eternal blessing Amen!'*

*and praised the true fulfilment of all citizens duties, thus the magistrate declares to Wilhelm Goldschmidt all rights and welfare which a citizen of Breslau may possess and be blessed with and enjoy with the promise that so long as he does no prove himself to be unworthy thereof to protect him against everyman.*

*The possessor of this Citizen's Letter Wilhelm Goldschmidt has been registered in the Rolls of the Canton-free Citizens of this City.*
*Certified and published with the seal of the City*
*Breslau 22 March 1813*
*(Seal)*

Wolf Bauer's ambition to conquer new areas did not let up. He was continuously underway in his carriage between Altwasser, Breslau, Bad Elster and Berlin where just at that time the preparations were beginning for a business fair that he absolutely had to be part of. Often Bella Betty asked to accompany her husband to Berlin so as to see her son Albert who worked there. But on 26 May 1822 as Bauer was organising his wares for the exhibition she was alone with Bendix in Altwasser – when suddenly a courier appeared with the news: Wolf Bauer had had a serious accident in Berlin. Perhaps the news was formulated to sound less serious so as to prepare her, as she hurried to Berlin with Bendix in the next Post Coach, for the worst that awaited her there.

    Indeed when Bella Betty arrived she found that her husband was already dead. Shortly after a mugging and robbery, in which a *'money kitten'* which he carried round his belly was ripped from him he died from a stroke.

After his burial in the cemetery *'am Prenzlauer Tor'* (naturally following the Protestant ritual) Bella Betty had to depart from Berlin forever. Still in shock, without a Taler in cash she stood there determined to survive by diverse handiwork and the manufacture of night-lights. Her brothers of course forbade such brave nonsense and she was taken to her step-daughter Henrietta in Breslau. In the meantime her grandchild, Eduard Goldschmidt, had been born there. Yes, there was an end to the biblical given names.

For Bella Betty there was a final visit to Altwasser to clear up the things that she loved. Then the property in Bad Elster was auctioned, and the house in Altwasser and the spring-water source there too. A couple of decades later it had dried up, leaving no trace.

# Albert Bauer

Now we move into the present with Albert Bauer. Even if events at this point still belong to the past and seem to us to have sunk into a century that has vanished: but they still live in us now.

Albert Bauer fell in love at the age of 23. For the first time. Passionately and of all people with a Christian. Bella Betty had nothing against this. At her husband's Protestant funeral she had realised how the rituals of the Jews and Christians and even the prayers and blessings are as similar as twins. Let him marry a Christian. But fate decided otherwise. The beloved girl – Lina Morgenstern describes her in her memoirs – died tragically before the engagement. Albert fell into a depression which was apparent to those he met. Then one day an old customer visited him in the Bauer's Breslau branch where Albert worked. Graf M. asked if he were ill and suggested that Albert recuperate on his country estate in Upper Silesia, near to the Polish border.

We do not know which Count it was nor where the country estate was located on the map of Upper Silesia. We only know that Albert stayed there for a time while the country gentleman went about his own business in Breslau and that Albert on a stroll in the Count's garden saw a carriage roll up in which a good acquaintance from Breslau sat, speechless with surprise at finding Albert there 'I'm enjoying the hospitality of Count M' said Albert whereupon his friend answered 'If he knew that you were a Jew he would have you chased off his land by his dogs!'

Immediately after this conversation, Albert wrote in a letter to the Count, that maybe he was unaware to which religious confession he belonged and so as not to embarrass him not to abuse his hospitality for which he was very thankful, Albert would leave the estate and travel to Cracow.

Albert's departure took place as soon as possible. He took a horse at the nearby village and rode to Cracow, the nearest city in which he would find a post coach to take him back to Breslau. But as he entered the city, things took a dramatic turn. Albert's horse, whose moods were unknown to him, shied, threw him and dragged him some meters over the stony path and galloped away – while Albert lay unconscious. At once a passer-by rushed to his aid and carried him to the new hospital in Skawinska Street, where he came to. Because no-one knew the seriously injured young man, the matter was reported to Senator Jakob Adler, who came to the clinic immediately and learned from the doctors there that the stranger would need to convalesce for a long time.

The Senator agreed to care for him.

Not a day went by without the Senator appearing at Albert's sickbed. They understood one another. Speaking German of course. For Adler was a Jew, his wife Anna, born a Heimann – a name that had been Germanised from the Hebrew 'Chajim' or 'Life'. At each conversation the men grew more friendly. Adler undertook to send reports on the healing process to mother, Bella Betty in Breslau for the unfortunate who was probably still unable to write for himself.

Senator Adler was almost like a father. And as Albert was let out of the clinic, he definitely wanted to look up Jakob Adler to thank him once again for everything before he reserved a place in a post coach to Breslau. He did not need to find his way through the Cracow ghetto: Adler because of his position belonged to those privileged Jews who were allowed to live outside of the ghetto.

The visit was a surprise for the Senator and as is common in such cases the unexpected guest was asked to wait in a small reception room until the maidservant had announced him to the master of the house and had been told to admit him. Time enough for Albert to eavesdrop on a soprano voice that was singing behind a door. Certainly Mozart. As the door was opened, Albert espied a girl accompanying herself on the piano who now stood and curtseyed. The daughter of the house. Fanny. Eighteen, grey-blue eyes and dark corkscrew curls down to her shoulders. That this was the start of a love story must be clear to everyone. Whether Fanny wore her summer dress that left her shoulders mostly uncovered except for a light blue scarf as described for us by Lina Morgenstern, is doubtful. But at the latest, two years after this, Fanny would be painted in this very dress: a pastel that no-one who saw it could forget. (Until 1942 it hung in the Olga Stern Home, a Jewish Old-peoples home in Koenigsallee 11a, Berlin, in the gloomy basement room of Fanny's granddaughter, Clara Roth. Who might have inherited it? Or was it destroyed in the clearance after the old residents were transported to the extermination camp by the Nazis?)

For two years love letters passed between Cracow and Breslau. Then at last it was time. A day after her twentieth birthday on 16 October 1825, Fanny could marry her Albert in the great Synagogue in the Free Imperial City of Cracow, among the countless Adler family who spoke German as fluently as Polish.

The lengthy wedding certificate is written in Polish, signed by the witnesses Bella Betty Bauer and the bride's parents. And by the groom, not

Fanny Bauer and Albert Bauer (Courtesy of Muzeum Miejskie Wroclaw/Breslau)

with 'Abraham', the name given him at his circumcision and written on his certificate of birth and as may have seemed proper to the Rabbis but in his strong exact Prussian script: Albert Bauer.

# Breslau

Naturally Albert Bauer had located a house in Breslau's best area before the wedding in which he wanted to live with his Fanny: Blücherplatz, formerly Salz Markt, right next to the Ring with its splendid gothic townhall. There was no difficulty in furnishing the house completely for everything was available in the business of the 'Gebrüder Bauer' that Albert managed with his half-brother Isaac-Wilhelm and continually expanded. They had recently they taken possession of a small furniture factory but they also sold antiques and oil-paintings. Fanny, who came from a highly cultured home, should do without nothing, neither a comprehensive library nor a music room.

Eleven months after they moved into Blücherplatz, their joy was complete. On 3 September 1826, Fanny had her first child: Wilhelm. Two years later on 2 August 1828 a daughter followed who naturally took the name of her unforgettable grandmother Ziporra – but would always be called Cäcilie. As it seemed likely that Fanny would soon have a third child, Albert needed to look about for a more spacious home with enough room for more staff and also for his mother Bella Betty. That was not so easy because one wanted to remain in the city centre and preferably directly on the Ring. But there the patrician houses had been closely held by families who neither wanted to rent nor sell.

Perhaps it was Albert's prestige, or that the necessary money was available or simply a stroke of luck that quite by surprise in the very centre of Breslau, in Elisabeth Strasse, that runs behind the townhall to the Ring, the 'house with the golden double patriarchal cross' above the entrance was offered for sale. A finer domicile could hardly be found, here the Bauers could give their social receptions that were well-known in the town, here the third child would come to this world on 25 November behind the high bright windows, Lina.

Elisabeth Strasse had its own history. Today it is called ul. Sukiennice. Until 1821 the so-called Cloth Hall, a long roofed over part of a dark vault in which the cloth merchants of Breslau, also known as Chamber gentlemen, stored their goods which by old guild laws they were not permitted to sell elsewhere. Indeed the old brick-building was regarded as secure against fire and weather which was important for their wares but the facility with its narrow gloom had been outdated for many years so that there was a sigh of relief when in 1810, the 'Freedom to Trade' rules were introduced. At last the cloth merchants were allowed to present their wares in well lit showrooms, even in houses on the Ring which until then had only been used as dwellings. The 40 vaulted chambers fell into disuse, a centuries old tradition had had its day, the 'Cloth-merchants College' of just fifteen chamber gentlemen soon dissolved itself and decided that the old Cloth hall should be torn down and to build residential houses where once sinister sales caves had nestled together. The name Cloth Hall was changed to Elisabeth Strasse and the houses, all twelve metres high, were given a fashionable classical façade. Exactly to Albert Bauer's taste.

Of course there were more than three Bauer children; three more: Jenny on 18 July 1832, Anna on 4 June 1835 and Clara on 21 August 1838.

For a family of six children the house in Elisabeth Strasse was also not big enough any more. Sometime in the early forties the next, last move of the Bauers took place. Beyond the City Moat, opposite the royal palace, magnificent villas were being erected with prestigious rooms, a view of the chestnut avenues and the Exerzier Platz and above all with a comfort that no old city house at that time could offer. Here, on the Schweidnitzer Stadtgraben 11, the family could spread themselves over more than just two spacious storeys, Albert Bauer could use the upper-ground floor for his business showrooms.

Here his children could unfold their inherited temperaments in complete freedom. Modesty, tolerance, and obedience remained prerequisite. But Albert Bauer dispensed with some of his ancestor's customs: The old practice of parents deciding on marriage partners over the heads of their children belonged to the past. Also religious connections should no longer play such a role. The family background? One was German. And one was a patriot.

When in the year of the revolution 1848 on 21 September more than 12,000 people gathered on the Exerzier Platz in Breslau opposite the Bauer's house across the moat, with the intention of storming the royal palace, the Bauer daughters, Lina and Jenny stood at the open windows, fascinated by a voice which suddenly boomed over the crowd and called for calm. It was the voice of the young physician, Dr Sigismund Asch, member of the board of the Breslau Workers Association and candidate for the first Prussian Peoples Representation, a democrat of the best sort. The *Berliner Tagesblatt* described the scene:

> *There in the decisive moment, Dr Asch pushed through the crowd calling 'Fellow Citizens, don't be rash, don't be unjust!'. Quiet, quiet! Dr Asch wants to speak! was the clamour all around. 'Fellow Citizens, I repeat, don't be rash, don't be unjust! Yes I emphasise this, don't be unjust!*

> *Because that would be the worst injustice if you harmed a single hair by this weak-willed black reaction! They are sons even as we are. These unfortunates are bound by oath which they have given the flag and they cannot give in to your wishes without injuring their vows. They cannot resist and would rather give their lives than go against their oath. Therefore let us respect the involuntary mercenaries' reaction and loyalty to their duty!*

With this appeal, which one heard clearly over the City Moat as far as the row of houses on Schweidnitzer Stadtgraben, Sigismund Asch had prevented the destruction of the palace and probably saved the lives of the soldiers on watch. And Jenny Bauer, just sixteen at the time, fascinated by the ideas of the young democrat said to her sister: 'That is the man that I will marry!'

However until she could actually marry him – and so become our great grandmother – she had to be patient for a few years. Could the furniture manufacturer who supplied the Prussian nobility, accept the social ideas of a son-in-law who as a member of the Democratic Association had stood before the national Assembly in the St Paul's Church in Frankfurt, and had given a speech as Vice-president of the Second Democratic Congress in Berlin?

But from Father Bauer came no veto. He knew the women in our family history not just from hearsay but personally, he knew how they would get their way when it was a matter of justice and he would hardly have been surprised at the apodictic declaration of his daughter Jenny. He had himself taken care to clarify to his children, the exploitation and under-payment of the weavers in the Eulengebirge and the unmerciful poverty which was now driving people onto the streets. He had built a small housing estate for his factory workers. And mother Fanny showed how one must engage oneself by her activity in two charitable associations for the *'rescue of abandoned children'* and *'education of young girls'*. And not just now: for generations this family had given assistance to the underprivileged and oppressed. One thought and acted socially and dealt with Jewish understanding, whereby not belief alone made one blessed but good deeds.

Nobody had imagined that Sigismund Asch's good deed, his call for calm and no violence, might have less good consequences and put his character to the test. But when, at the end of November 1848, in Breslau, it came to bloody confrontation between those country associations that struggled under the banner of 'For God and Fatherland' and those as Asch formulated it 'crazy Reds', he resigned from the moderate *'Democratic Association' 'disappointed by the failure of his fellow democratic comrades and revolted by their intolerance and radicalism'* On the 18 December he was informed that legal action was being taken against him for his speech on the Exerzier Platz. It dragged on without any more information until the 4 May of the following year. The the result was given. The sentence was a year in the dungeon of Glatz in Silesia.

How and with which democratic friends Sigismund Asch served his sentence in this dank block of a fortress, once built by Frederick the Great as a bulwark against the Habsburgs, has not been passed down to us. We only know that Asch did not pass from young Jenny Bauer's mind, and that Father Bauer asked some questions. A son-in-law with a record?

But when Asch, free again in May 1850, settled on Klosterstr in Breslau as physician, and an application to be doctor for the indigent was denied by the city council – because of his political past – Asch instituted free office hours from 5 a.m. to 7 a.m. for patients with few means, the Bauers opened their doors: This unbendable man was one of them! He would be invited to the next family occasion. How fortunate that July 1850 already offered a good opportunity to get to know Asch better, because Albert Bauer would celebrate his 50th birthday then. It had to be that day, when Asch and Jenny first faced each other, and we actually know that on this encounter love struck them both like a lightning bolt.

Of course, marriage was not to be thought of as long as Jenny hadn't finished the last class of the school for girls (Hoehere Toechterschule, the private school for girls from affluent families), and had been trained in all aspects of the arts and home economics. But even after that, mother hen Fanny thought up the most unusual delaying actions in order to prevent her daughter entering into a relationship prematurely. Possibly Albert Bauer saw things a bit differently: at any rate, Asch's practice flourished. Even when on 7 January 1851, Asch was indicted on a long-delayed complaint of *lese majeste and attempted incitement to riot* because someone alleged to have seen him at a placard action – *The economy of Prussia, or how the people's money is spent* – it could only be a passing irritant to his future the father-in-law. On 22 May 1851 the complaint was dismissed by the jury of the Appellations Court as having passed the statute of limitations. Now there were no hindrances to marriage with Jenny.

With Sigismund Asch we end that era in which our family was closely tied to the political events in Germany. But Asch's essence, which united such wisdom, generosity and active humanity, lived on in his children, and he also formed and accompanied their descendants. All of us. To today.

# Epilogue

It was not my plan to extend this family history that covers ten connected generations from 1550 to 1850 into the twentieth century. But if I want to take to heart the quote from Job, then I must at least emphasise some of the later generations in the tale. The lives and efforts of the great grandfather's generations are, thanks to uncountable letters, diaries, newspaper articles and their own publications documented and manageable. With their grandchildren, however, the imagination cannot cope with such a variety of fates, alone those fates dictated by the Nazi era, so that one cannot do them justice by merely mentioning them.

We have more than 120 letters written by Sigismund Asch that give us an uncommonly colourful picture of his time, his position as doctor and city councillor, of his role as great alms-giver to occasionally bankrupt relations, and above all his great patience with the demanding Jenny Bauer who brought up three children with him, kept a hospitable home under her control, worked in many charitable associations and even as a fifty-year old hurried to art-history lectures and in no way sat at her easel as a portrait painter as just a hobby. She was a pupil of Albrecht Bräuer, a professor of the Breslau Art Academy who was left a memorial in Gehardt Hauptmann's drama *Michael Kramer*.

It is beyond the framework of this epilogue if I were to list the names of all the writers and scientists that were guests in the Asch house. But one of them must be mentioned because he was Asch's dearest friend: the theatre manager and director Adolphe L'Arronge.

Both men knew each other from 1874 when L'Arronge, who was actually called Aronsohn, became Director and Kappellmeister of the Lobetheatre in Breslau. (My father, Edmund Nick, stood at the same conductors podium in the season of 1921/22.) Adolphe L'Arronge swept not only the gayest theatre-life into the family but at the same time the family-life of the Aschs onto the stages of Germany. On a whim L'Arronge tried his hand as a comedy writer. After his popular play *Hasemann's Daughters* had such knock-out success, he decided to carry on in this genre. The next piece appeared as *Dr Klaus*, behind this title was hidden none other than Dr Sigismund Asch. Both comedies were translated into many languages and reached over ten thousand productions in his lifetime as his bookkeeping records. Horrified, Theodor Fontane wrote in the Kreuz-Zeitung: '*The public runs after this fun maker as if they were chained to him. The whole province is infected by this odd L'Arronge fever.*"

Another sort of L'Arronge fever caught Sigismund Asch's son Robert a few years later. He was at the time a leading doctor in the Women's Clinic when he fell in love with L'Arronge's daughter Käthe and married her. But by then a part of the blended together families lived in Berlin after Adolphe L'Arronge had become rich from his farces and bought the run-down Friedrich-Wilhelm City Theatre there in order to create the Deutsche Theatre. Four actor colleagues supported him, two of them, the famous Ludwig Barnay was one, were also Jews. The Deutsche Theatre – founded by more than one Jew? Who noticed at all? Five decades later Barnay's son Paul Barnay was considered unbearable in his position as Intendant of the Breslau United Theatres and was driven into emigration by the Nazis. He was a close friend of my father and accompanied my first lyrical footsteps after he, ill and lost, returned from England in 1945 to a land in which he could no longer find happiness. The fate of many.

The Deutsche Theatre remained a magnet in Berlin for my mother as a young actress, at the time under Max Reinhardt who sent her together with Hans Brahm and a troupe of actors to the front-theatre in Flanders in 1915.

Of course our great-grandmother Jenny Asch attended every premier in Berlin after Adolphe L'Arronge took sole control of the Deutsche Theatre in 1884.

It was a wonderful opportunity for her to meet her sister Lina, married to Morgenstern: Lina Morgenstern, the second name that must have more space.

Lina, like her sisters, Cäcilie, Anna and Jenny was brought up in the spirit of Jewish neighbourly love and truly driven by the need to stand by all the poor and helpless had already when she was eighteen excited comment when she, of course with the full support of her mother Fanny Bauer founded her first charitable Association in 1848, the

> *Penny association for the support of poor schoolchildren'*. She explained: *'If each of us gave a penny every day, many needy children would be helped. That the help does not go to those unworthy but only to truly needy children, is determined by the way the choice of children is made. Teachers who are also members of our association and who know the home conditions of their school pupils, chose those to be given support <u>without any reference to their religious beliefs</u>.'*

She wanted the last seven words to be underlined.

For the descendants of Albert Bauer, belief became a private matter. One lived in a land where a Jew could go to University and found charitable associations and if one had such a runaway temperament in matters such as good citizenship as did Lina Morgenstern, then one was outraged at the neglect of the state that ought to take better care of its subjects – and if nothing happened then one took things into one's own hands.

Why had Kindergarten been forbidden in Prussia since 1851 as being *'atheist and demagogic'*? For Lina Morgenstern, already mother of three children, an initiative to found the Berlin Fröbel Institute in 1859, so as to set up Kindergardens with the subscriptions. It worked. But soon she noticed that there was still something lacking: and so she offered seminars led by herself, for the training of child carers.

The war year 1866 was another challenge. The care and nutrition was catastrophic, the inflation rate so high that many were unable to afford even their daily bread. The government did indeed operate emergency kitchens but Lina thought it unworthy to make small officials and underpaid teachers stand in line for alms together with the very poorest of the poor on the open street for a dish of soup – and so she designed 'a Call to Found a Peoples Kitchen' in which meals would be sold at cost price, more cheaply and nutritional than any housewife could manage. With it Lina stormed to the Vossichen Zeitung where it was explained to her that such an appeal would only meet with success if famous men were signatories to it. Four days later she had the required signatures, the most important from Dr Rudolf Virchow. The appeal which now appeared immediately in the press, harvested an unexpected positive echo: the starting gun for Lina's foundation of the 'People's Kitchen Association', which guaranteed the financial security of her planned kitchen. In a rush she organised together with her husband and a friend the necessary cookers and ovens, kettles, plates tables and benches, and storerooms for the food and heating supplies purchased wholesale and of course the space needed – large cellars or time-served factory halls – where the food could be given out. Voluntary helpers, members of Lina's Association and women who knew about cooking in large quantities, came as well. Within four weeks three People's kitchens had opened their doors in Berlin. A few months later it was fourteen and in each of them up to 900 meals were served daily. For 25 pence, there was different dish every day, made from a litre of cooked vegetables and three pieces of meat to a weight of 75 grams. Lina was knowledgeable about nutrition. Recognition from the state was not long in coming, sometimes Queen Augusta appeared at Lina's side to give her a few bank notes in a little purse that travelled between the ladies for months until Lina was finally presented it by her patron. (It is today kept by the Morgenstern family in Strassburg.)

When the 1870 war against France began, the Prussian court understood what was needed and who should be given the responsibility to give a warm meal and provisions to thousands of soldiers before they departed for the front: Lina Morgenstern. In just three days she organised the required kitchens, canteens, food stores and the personnel to run it on two Berlin stations. A short time later when the first wounded started to return she set up a bandaging station which the State had neglected to arrange. The fact that she also allowed French wounded prisoners of war to be dealt with caused an outcry in the press. And Lina countered immediately: *'in the name of the rights of man and humanity it is essential to deal with prisoners of war just as we would wish that those of ours who are prisoners of war would be dealt with!'*

During the twelve months that Lina slaved at the stations, she slept at home on only twenty nights. At the end she received the Iron Cross for women and the Golden Augusta medal with a red cross *'in recognition of her service to the fatherland'*. Her husband Theodore Morgenstern also honoured for *'his service to the care of the troops'*: in 1871 Kaiser Wilhelm gave him the Order of the Crown.

Lina maintained her contact with the Prussian court until her death. It was the same Court – just with other personnel – to whom her forefathers were indispensable as Court Jews, as credit givers, just without being decorated with medals, instead they had been thankful to be granted a Letter of Protection, to be allowed to live and work in the country.

The list of Lina Morgenstern's achievements, foundations and books she wrote is long, too long for an obituary but the short form is readable. Her name, usually with the nickname 'Suppenlina' appears in lexicons, even during the Nazi time Lina's cooking recipes were used for the field kitchens. The fact that Lina was Jewish, seemed not to be known. In 1942 one could of course have realised it when the Nazis fetched Lina's daughter, Clara, who had outlived all her siblings who had died young, out of an old peoples' home in Berlin to a factory the was being misused as a collection camp, from where she telephoned us and asked us to send her a pillow. My parents seemed not to dither for a moment which of us should take it to her. Me of course, I, a schoolchild, who hardly seemed older than thirteen, would be allowed through the gate, into the murder-pit and then out again. I had no extra worry that I might be held in the collection camp; the quite usual daily fear was enough, it was in me like a second skin, it almost felt that it was an extra protection. Were children taken to work camps? I did not know. I knew only that the eleven-year old son of a cousin of my mother who had fled to

Holland had been gassed there in a 'bus' by the Nazis: one of the first attempts to see if it worked. But Holland was beyond the frontier.

In fact I passed through the broad gap in the fence to the street, went across the yard – whose square paving stones I can still see before my eyes today – and pressed the pillow with the name of the receiver attached into the arms of the SS man posted to the right of the entrance without looking him in the eye. As I ran away my feet had wings. We only heard after the end of the war that Clara had died a few days later.

None of Sigismund Asch, Lina Morgenstern nor their siblings suffered anti-Semitism personally, so far as we can read in their letters. Naturally they knew that anti-Semitism could be found in all classes of the population. But that a Jewish persecution ordered by the State as it had been in centuries long ago might repeat itself, must have been unthinkable for any of them or their children, our grandparents.

How could Lina Morgenstern imagine that the son of her daughter Olga who already in 1893, with her husband, Dr Otto Arendt, Member of Prussian Parliament had converted to Christianity, that her grandchild Reinhold Arendt would one day be murdered for his Jewish ancestry. Neither baptism of his parents nor his own was able to protect him from Hitler's racist delusions. In the First World War, Reinhold was expected to fight as a standard-bearer for Germany. In 1942, by now married and father of a son, Christian, he was arrested by the Nazis and taken to Moabit Prison and from there to Auschwitz, where he was murdered on 13 February 1943.

Baptism was no protection. The Spanish Jews who at the time of the Spanish inquisition preferred to be compelled to convert rather than be burned at the stake had not always been saved. Marked out as '*Marranos*', as swine, they stood before the pillory, always suspected of being secretly faithful to the old belief and thus often enough damned to death in the flames afterwards.

Lina's son Alfred was baptised too, Lina was not. In her obituary, Ludwig Geiger (1848-1919), son of Abraham Geiger, pioneer of Reform Judaism) wrote:

> *She observed no rules of ritual, she was effective exclusively in general, not in Jewish associations, thus she showed herself to be true daughter of the faith of her ancestors. She was one of those rare women who was able to harmoniously combine being German with being Jewish.'*

Not a subject of discussion between Jenny and Sigismund Asch. All three of the Asch children were baptised. First was Betty, my grandmother. At the time she was still at school and of course asked her father whether he had anything against her converting. He said: *'no, but you must understand that baptism does not change character: you remain the Mensch that you are'*.

Robert Asch was the next to convert. Then the youngest, Toni. Both married baptised Jews who knew nothing more of their Jewishness than did Käthe L'Arronge, and Toni's husband the doctor Richard Stern, leader of the Breslau polyclinic. Only Betty was different and fell in love with the blond blue-eyed Karl Jaenicke who was my grandfather.

Of that generation nobody except the already mentioned Aunt Clara and Käthe Asch lived until that year of fate 1933. The year in which in our home an unusual background conversation was to be heard for the first time, thus half whispered, ever repeated *'has been fetched'* or that word that at six years old I could not understand *Affidavit*, that seemed to have a lifesaving nimbus about it, *'if one got it in time'*. What did in time mean? And the question…*'but where to?'* This continual tenseness. No explanations. Not even what it meant if one day two tall men in civilian clothes appeared, opened draws and pulled books out of the shelves and did not put them back again but just casually threw them onto the blue carpet. Later the words *'house search'*. The words *'has been let go'*. Why did my parents suddenly want to travel? Without my brother and me? Just temporarily, they said. And we were taken to friends who lived nearer to our primary school. Emil Kaim, wood wholesaler, Patron of the Arts, Jew, possessed a villa, there we were *'in safety'*. For the first time the feeling of being under threat. Without our parents. Only five months later did my mother collect us to Berlin, to a tiny flat. When we parted, Emil Kaim said *'If they come for me, I'll rip open my shirt, so –* he ripped it open *– and show them my Iron cross, First class! I was an officer in the war! Then they can't take me away!*

They took him away. *'They'* by now I understood the word as law or a whip – they deported him and his wife to Theresienstadt in 1941, when they confiscated his wealth, withdrew his passport and the last chance *'to get out'* was finally gone. The Star of David, Jewish compulsion.

In Berlin one apparently lived seemingly safer. As safe as on a tightrope over a chasm. One just had to be careful. Keep your mouth shut. I became used to keeping to the edge of the pavement, keeping out of everybody's way. Not to be obvious. Never sit on a park bench: the green ones were for Aryans, the yellow for Jews. My father could have sat on a green bench. There were no striped ones for *'Mischling'*, those half-breeds. Making jokes was forbidden. At home everything was allowed. There it was lively as soon as the door of the flat was closed, a life as before, healing jollity, humour, music: the weapons of survival against everything that perhaps was still to come: The ring of the doorbell early in the morning. Because *'they fetched you'* before eight in the morning.

Being fetched was not the same as being taken away. Those who were previously informed, the old who could no longer emigrate because perhaps they had given their Affidavit, if they had one, to their children so that they at least might be saved; the old, who with a small case and a winter overcoat over their arm now clambered up to the two benches in the furniture lorry that was waiting in front of their house. To be transported to the collection place. The words Final Solution were still unknown. Only the words work camp and place names like Lodz and Lublin because from there postcards sometimes arrived. The name Auschwitz? Never heard of it. The instruction *'keep yourself ready'* offered a last cynically thought out pause for thought for those who suspected something far worse behind the *'work camp'* and possessed sufficient 'Veronal' for their suicide behind their own doors. That occurred quite often. Twenty pills sufficed.

Being fetched in Berlin meant: *'off to the Alex'*, the Gestapo Headquarters for interrogation or direct into the 'cudgel-chamber'. For that there was no warning. When the doorbell really rang for us one morning, I was already on my way to school. And when I came home at midday, no-one opened the door. Fetched. Two hours of ice cold panic on the uppermost stairs to the fourth floor – until my parents came up with completely grey serious faces. Others came back from Alex missing front teeth. Among them a friend who told us that he had to sign at the police station that he had been treated properly. Talking about it at home was of course self-evident but remained behind locked doors.

Also the occasional mention of us emigrating. But the plan was thwarted. In which country did we have any friends who were rich enough to give us an affidavit? A guarantee for a family of four? Unthinkable.

Conversations about the war to come. Those who could find no other way to leave the country, knew that soon it would be too late. But even those who were lucky enough to have relatives abroad to send an invitation complete with a visitor's visa, if only valid for a time, could fail at the exit if the frontier guards noticing the 'J' stamped in the passport, decided to send them back. Then the flat would perhaps be sealed, the edge of the door stuck with a pale David star made of paper and then the ony possibility was creeping in with friends who were still waiting to be fetched.

The waiting every day. And almost every month still more new Jewish laws. The prohibition to visit theatres, concerts, cinemas and bathing facilities. The compulsory forfeit of precious metals and jewellery. The Order to take the extra given name of Israel or Sara. Work prohibition for lawyers. And finally the revocation of a doctor's licence.

Now the terror came for those to whom we are nearest and had not left Breslau: Rudolf Stern, who had lost his professorship at the University and then saw the end of his Surgery, from then on he was degraded to '*Krankenbehandler*'. As the position never existed outside the Nazi world it cannot be translated, maybe 'a person who deals with Jewish ill people'. A job for Jews.

Most of Sigismund Asch's grandchildren had escaped abroad while the immigration quotas were still not severely restricted, to Paris, Copenhagen, Stockholm, London and Cambridge. (The difficulties emigrants faced has not been written here yet; neither the adventurous flight of Käthe Asch-L'Arronge to Denmark during the war). Cousins and distant cousins, the Casparis, Hamburgers, Goldschmidts and Honigmanns escaped to Kenya, Johannesburg and the Dominican Republic. Only Rudolf Stern and his family and his sister Lotte with her husband Dr Richard Kobrak in Berlin awaited a miracle. The 'Breslau Sterns' waited for gruelling weeks, daily hoping that the consent of the Immigration Authority of United States would at last arrive, Rudolf Stern had three Affidavits, one from his uncle Otto Stern, who later won the Nobel Prize, another from Hermann Haber, his sister's husband and son of the Nobel Prize winner Fritz Haber. But only in autumn 1938 was the Immigration Visa forthcoming. A whole month passed before all their possessions could be packed into a 'Lift' (today we say container) and the tax demanded by the Nazis for deserting the Empire had been paid and before his family – Rudolf, his wife Käthe Brieger, daughter Toni and the twelve year old Fritz – could leave Germany to the threatening sound of goose-stepping marchers, another month. Just four weeks after they, standing on the bow of the emigration ship, were greeted by the Statue of Liberty, it was the 9 November 1938 in Germany.

The incendiary devices were already in place for the most perfect scene setting that the Nazis had thought out till then. The supposed people's anger, mostly in SA Uniform, sent every Synagogue in Germany up in flames in the same hour. The shop windows of every Jewish business were smashed and the shops plundered and destroyed. The streets were littered with broken glass and remain unforgotten in the phrase 'The Kristallnacht'. It is good to know that the fire brigades were informed before the event so that they could prevent fire damaging neighbouring houses if they did not belong to Jews. The cost of the repairs of all the damage that occurred was demanded from the Jews; and a further special tax of a total of a billion marks was collected.

More Rules for Jews followed: now it was forbidden for dentists, veterinarians, dispensing chemists to work; tenant protection laws were repealed and punctually for the start of the war on 1 September 1939 a curfew from eight p.m., the confiscation of all radios and a prohibition of the use of the Air raid shelters when the alarms went off. Finally the deepest humiliation, the Star of David to be worn at all times. Shortly afterwards all emigration was forbidden. The trap now finally snapped shut. Only Elisabeth Goldschmidt was brave enough to swim over the Rhine near Lustenau to the rescuing Swiss riverbank. We stayed in continual contact with Lotte Stern and her husband Richard Kobrak, who had sent their children to England in time but had not managed to find a way to flee themselves. We shared all our rationed food that we had to buy with coupons – Jews did not receive them for milk, meat or eggs – and we shared with them the uncertainty, the fear and the waiting for the message *'be prepared to be evacuated'*. The most favourable version was: *'you are permitted to take a case (maximum 50 kg), complete set of clothes, good shoes, bed linen and duvet, a plate or pot with a spoon, a bucket and a little soap. Knives, forks and razors are forbidden'*.

That the shorter version *'just one piece of luggage'* was a ciphered death sentence, was still not known to us. But being allowed to take bedding with them sounded as if the destination might be Theresienstadt, the so-called *'show camp'*. So, hoping for the most favourable case, we organised bedding for the Kobraks on our clothing ration cards (Jews did not get any); a greenish material that would not show the dirt so quickly and I sewed pillow covers out of it. Lotte watched us: it was her last visit to us. Because after April 1942, Jews were no longer allowed to use public transport anymore. Only in March 1943 did the news of the imminent deportation come through. Then a postcard to us from Theresienstadt: Factory work. When Lotte became ill and was no longer capable of working in the armaments factory – and we only learned of this after the war from a fellow prisoner – she was transported with her husband in October 1944 to an alleged new work place. Eighteen such transports were sent within five weeks, in each a group of a thousand people directly from Theresienstadt to Auschwitz.

*Ask the former generation* said Job so as to learn from their experience. Who or what is responsible for the continual recurrence of persecution, pogroms and wars? Fritz Stern who had to leave Germany as a twelve year old and became an important historian in the United States may have an answer. I do not.

D.N.

*Appendix*

# Acknowledgements

I am very grateful to all those who have helped me with my research: the first of these is my niece; Dr Irene Newhouse, USA who shared her ancestors drawer with me and who has extended our family tree to over seven hundred people, also my uncle Helmut Goldschmidt, Copenhagen, from whom I received the manuscript by Joseph Fischer 'Mein Goldschmidts Vorfahren', my Goldschmidt Ancestors, and also many documents from the Prussian Secret State Archive Berlin; my cousin Eckart Nick, whom I thank for countless historic clues and documents from the State Archive in Hannover; my nephew Carl Studt, who was able to locate a letter in the Leipzig Archive from our Moses Levin written in 1785; finally the book dealer Mira Maase who by her untiring efforts to find lost works has stood by me for many years in my work on this family history.

Unforgotten is also the help, through which I discovered, from Professor Norbert Conrads' edition of the diary of Karl Friedrich Hempel 'The Breslau Revolution' in the collected 'Remarkable Years 1848-1851' (Cologne 1978), a view of the historic events in which our family were involved there both actively and passively. Felix Berul, the guardian of the Jewish Cemetery in Potsdam, I thank for accompanying me to the wonderfully preserved gravestone of our ancestral grandfather Leib Levin (died 1757). I am especially thankful to Professor Alexander Fried who helped me with all Hebrew and theological questions and last but not least the Museum Director of Wrocław, my friend Dr Maciej Łagiewski, without whom I could never have found the places in Breslau where our ancestors were active.

# Curriculum Vitae: Sigismund Asch

| | |
|---|---|
| 5.1.1825 | Born in Schweidnitz, the son of Josef Asch from Gleiwitz and Julie Prinz from Schweidnitz. Father Asch started as a merchant's assistant and later owned a ceramics and antiques business. |
| After 1843 | Studied medicine at the University of Breslau |
| 24.11.1847 | Doctorate |
| 1847 | Membership of the Democratic Association |
| 1848 | Member of the Board, Breslau Worker's Association |
| 1848 | Candidate for the First Prussian House of Representatives |
| 6.8.1848 | Famous first speech in the Scheitniger Park in Breslau |
| 21.9.1848 | Second major speech at a demonstration on the Exerzier Platz in front of the Royal Palace of Breslau, which prevented the storming of the Palace by the mob: Prosecuted for Lèse-majesté and sentenced to one years imprisonment; the trial dragged on till 1849 |
| October 1848 | Vice-President of the Second Democratic Congress in Berlin |
| 1848 | Withdrawal from Democratic Association |
| May 1849– May 1850 | Served sentence in the Dungeon of Glatz |
| June 1850 | Registration as doctor in Klosterstrasse in Breslau. Asch's attempt to be a 'doctor to the poor' refused because of his political past. Therefore he gave free surgeries between 5 and 7 a.m. for the poor and workers. |
| Summer 1850 | Meets Jenny Bauer |
| 22.5.1851 | Accused of 'Lèse-majesté and attempted incitement to disturb' because of a poster campaign. The jury of the Court of Appeal decided that the case was invalid under the Statute of Limitations and Asch was acquitted. |
| 1851 | Membership of the German Progress Party, Breslau |
| 17.11.1854 | Official Engagement with Jenny Bauer |
| 28.2.1855 | Marriage with Jenny Bauer |

| | |
|---|---|
| 20.2.1857 | Birth of daughter: Julie Bettina |
| 10.12.1859 | Birth of son: Robert |
| 1863 | Town Councillor in Breslau (until 1879) |
| 1864 | Asch pushes through Sewage and Clean Water regulations: The Ohle, which until then carried away all waste water was filled in. He also set up obligatory meat inspections. He demanded larger, brighter classrooms in schools. |
| 1864 | Co-founder of an asylum for homeless people, house doctor of the Catholic Orphanage, member of the staff of the municipal hospital |
| 25.8.1866 | Birth of daughter: Toni |
| 1866 | Director of the 'Medical Section of the Siliesian Society for patriotic Culture'; appointment as Chief Physician of a Lazarett with 600 beds and 30 doctors in the Kürassier Barracks in Breslau |
| 1874-1901 | Inspector-Doctor of a life assurance company (in 27 years he gave 81,000 expert opinions) |
| 1876 | Non-executive Director of the Silesian Banking Association; Chairman of the Medical aid insurance for invalid colleagues and doctor' widows in the Breslau District |
| 1888 | Board member of the Chamber of Doctors in the Province of Siliesia |
| 17.3.1901 | Asch died after a short illness: pneumonia |
| 20.3.1901 | Burial in the Jewish Cemetery in Lohestrasse, Breslau |

# Curriculum Vitae: Lina Morgenstern

Born on 25 November 1830 in Breslau, daughter of the furniture manufacturer Albert Bauer, married to the businessman Theodor Morgenstern, Berlin

She founded:
1848    The Penny association to Support poor Schoolchildren
1859    Fröbel Association, which set up the first Kindergartens under her chairwoman-ship

Lina Morgenstern (Courtesy of the family album)

| | |
|---|---|
| 1862 | A school for child carers |
| 1865 | The general German Women's Association |
| 1866 | Peoples' Kitchens |
| 1868 | The Child protection Association (against 'angel makers') |
| 1869 | The Academy for the Scientific Education for Ladies |
| 1869 | Female workers training association |
| 1870 | Commissioned by the Prussian Queen Augusta to set up Station Kitchens for troops being mobilised; later she set up the first bandaging station for war-wounded |
| 1873 | The Berlin Housewives association (for self-help against the rising post-war prices |
| 1873 | A laboratory for nutritional chemistry |
| 1873 | A free placement service for servants |
| 1873 | An insurance for house servants |
| 1874 | The German Housewives Newspaper |
| 1878 | A cookery school to train cooking teachers and house-keepers |
| 1880 | The association to Rescue minor girls after release from prison |
| 1880 | An agricultural house industry school |
| 1887 | The association to educate poor female school-leavers in household work |
| 1874-1904 | She is the editor of 'The German House-wives' Newspaper' |
| 1893 | Member of the Board of the German Peace Society |
| 1896 | Vice-President of the Paris Central Council for the World Association of Women for Peace through Education |
| 1896 | Vice-President of the Women's League for International Disarmament; and she is to be thanked that the International Women's Congress met for the first time in Germany (Berlin) |

She wrote ten books of fairy-tales, narratives and short stories; nineteen textbooks (cookery, nutrition, education etc.); three volumes of biographies.

She died on 16 December 1909 in Berlin.

# Family Trees

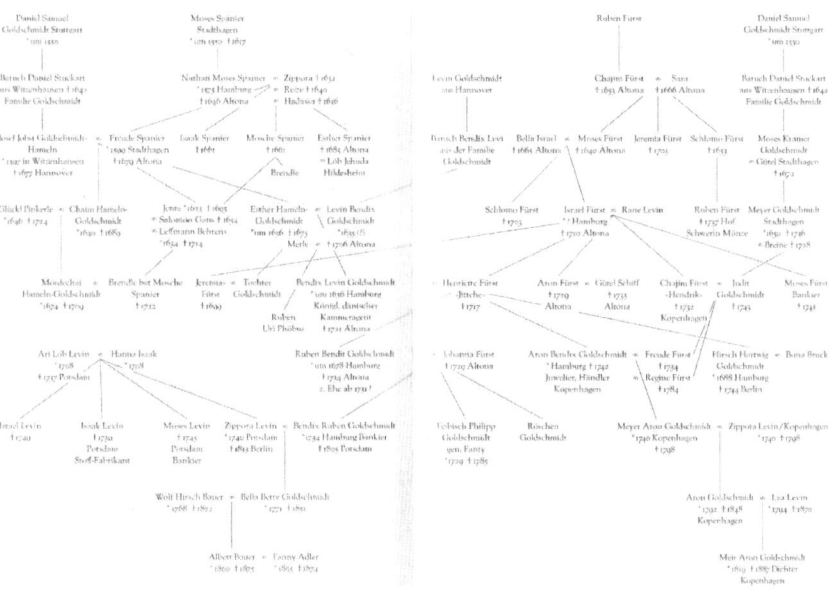

## Kinder und Enkel von Jente Hameln-Goldschmidt und Leffmann Behrens

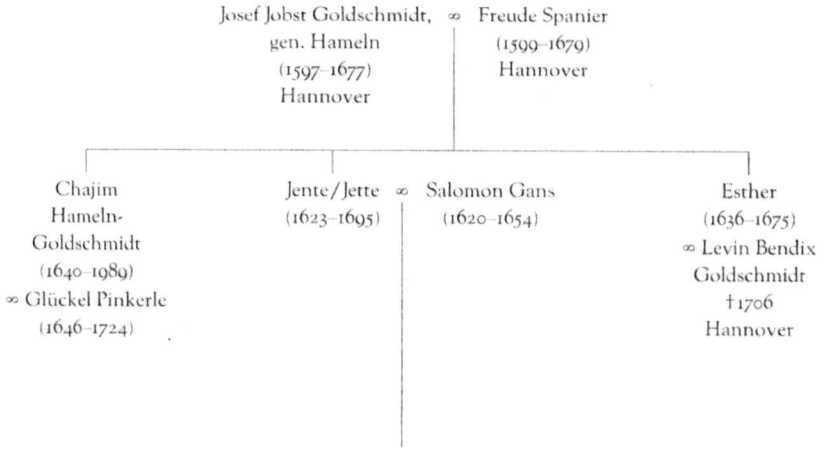

Aus Jente Hameln-Goldschmidts Ehe mit Salomon Gans stammen sechs Kinder. Unter ihren Nachfahren finden wir folgende bekannte Namen: Heinrich Heine, Fanny und Felix Mendelssohn-Bartholdy, Karl Wolfskehl, Theodor Lessing, Carl Sternheim, Albrecht Haushofer, Günther Anders (Stern).

Nach dem Tod ihres ersten Mannes heiratete Jente 1656 den elf Jahre jüngeren Leffmann Behrens (korrekt: Elieser Liepmann Behrens Cohen).

# Family Trees

**Jente/Jette** ∞ **Leffmann Behrens**
(1623–1695)   (1634–1714)
    └─ 2. Ehe

├─ **Naphtali Herz** Behrens
│  (1657–1709)
│  ∞
│  Serchen Wertheimer
│  († 1730), Schwester des
│  Bankiers Samson
│  Wertheimer
│    ├─ Lea          ∞ Seligmann Cohen,
│    │  (1676–?)       Pflegesohn von Bankier
│    │                 Behrend Lehmann
│    ├─ Tochter N.   ∞ Salomon Philipp,
│    │                 Kammeragent in
│    │                 Mecklenburg-Strelitz
│    └─ Seligmann
│       († 1744)
│
├─ **Genendel** Behrens
│  (1658–1712)
│  ∞
│  David Oppenheimer
│  (1664–1736), Neffe des
│  Bankiers Samuel
│  Oppenheimer
│    ├─ Särle/Sara   ∞ Chajim Jona Theomim Fränkel
│    │  (1694–1712)
│    ├─ Blümle       ∞ Michael Beer Oppenheim
│    │  († 1738)
│    ├─ Tolza        ∞ Berend Levi Gumperz
│    │  († 1761)
│    ├─ Josef        ∞ Tolze Wertheimer, Tochter des
│    │  (1686–1730)    Bankiers Samson Wertheimer
│    └─ Jente        ∞ Phöbus Cohen, Hamburg
│       (1696–1736)
│
└─ **Moses Jakob** Behrens
   (1663–1697)
   ∞
   Susanne/Sieße Gomperz
   (1658–1725), Tochter von
   Elias Gomperz, Cleve,
   Heereslieferant des
   Großen Kurfürsten
     ├─ **Isaak**      ∞ Lea Lehmann († 1741), Tochter
     │  (1683–1765)      des Bankiers Behrend Lehmann
     ├─ Freudel       ∞ Simon Wolf Oppenheimer,
     │  (1683–1717)     Sohn von Bankier Samuel
     │                  Oppenheimer / 2.Ehe
     ├─ **Gumpert**   ∞ Sprinze/Esperanza Kann
     │  (1686–?)        († 1726), Frankfurt
     ├─ Simelie       ∞ Löb Oppenheimer,
     │  († 1730)        Preßburg († 1732)
     ├─ Hanna         ∞ Mordechai Gumpel Beer
     │  († 1740)        Nachfahr: Komponist
     │                  Giacomo Meyerbeer
     └─ Jakob
        (1697–1716)

## Nachfahren von Wolf Hirsch Bauer und Bella Betty Goldschmidt

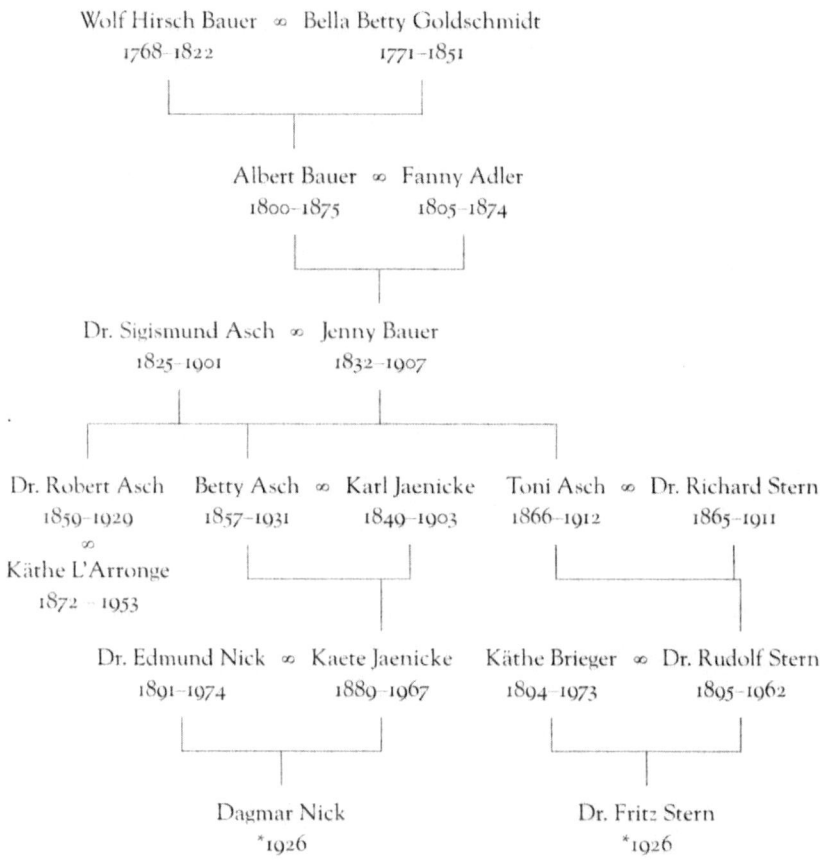

# Supporting Literature

Ackermann. A.: *Juden in Brandenburg,* Berlin 1905
Berliner, Abraham (Editor) *Religionsgespräch gehalten am Kurfürstlichen Höfe zu Hannover,* Berlin 1914
Breuer, Mordechai / Michael Graetz: *Deutsch-Jüdische Geschichte in der Neuzeit Band I.* Munich 1996
Brocke, Michael (Editor): *Verborgene Pracht. Der jüdische Friedhof Hamburg-Altona,* Dresden 2009
Diekmann, Irene / Julius H. Schoeps (Editor)): *Wegweiser durch das jüdische Brandenburg,* Berlin 1995
Dukesz, Eduard: *Zur Geschichte und Genealogie der ältesten Familien Altonas und Hamburgs,* 1914
Fraenkel, Louis and Henry: *Genelogical Tables of Jewish Families 14th-20th Centuries,* Munich 1999
Friedrich der Größe: *Das Politische Testament von 1752*
Glückel von Hameln: *Denkwürdigkeiten.* Edited by Alfred Feilchenfeld, Berlin 1923
Gronemann, Selig: *genealogischen Studien über die alten jüdischen Familien Hannovers,* Berlin 1913
Jacbson, Jacob (Editor): *Jüdische Trauungen in Berlin 1759-1813,* Berlin 1968
Jost, Isaak Markus (Editor): *Eine Familien-Megillah aus der ersten Hälfte des 18. Jahrhunderts; im Jahrbuch für die Geschichte der Juden und des Judenthums, zweiter band 1861*
Kaelter, Robert: *Geschichte der jüdische Gemeinde zu Potsdam.* Edited by von Julius H. Schoeps, Moses Mendelssohn Zentrum für europäisch-jüdische Studien Universität Potsdam, 1993
Kellenbenz, Hermann: *Sephardim an der unteren Elbe,* Wiesbaden 1958
Kopisch, August: *Die Königlichen Schlösser und Gärten zu Potsdam.* Berlin 1854
Leibniz, Gottfried Wilhelm: *Funeralien des Herzogs* Johann Friedrich, 1685
Marwedel, Günter (Editor): *Die Privilegien der Juden in Altona,* Hamburg 1976
Mittenzwei, Ingrid / Erika Herzfeld: *Brandenburg-Preußen 1648-1789,* Berlin 1987

Schedlitz, Bernd: *Leffmann Behrens, Untersuchungen zum Hofjudentum im Zeitalter des Absolutismus*, Hildesheim 1984 (Standardwerk)

Schnath, Georg: *Geschichte Hannovers im Zeitalter der neunten Kur und der englischen Sukzession 1674-1714, Band III.* Hildesheim 1978

Schnee, Heinrich: *Die Hoffinanz und der moderne Staat*, Berlin 1965

Steiner, Gerhard: *Drei preußische Könige und ein Jude*, Berlin 1994

Stern, Selma: *Der preußischen Staat und die Juden,* Tübingen 1962

Studemund-Halévi, Michael: *Die Sefarden in Hamburg,* Hamburg 1994

Vierhundert Jahre Juden in Hamburg, Katalog zur Ausstellung des Museums für Hamburgische Geschichte, 1991

Wahl, Magaret: *Der alte jüdische Friedhof in Hannover,* Hannover 1961

Zukermann, Mendel: *Dokumente zur Geschichte der Juden in Hannover,* Hannover 1908